THE HISTORY OF THE JEWISH KHAZARS

THE HISTORY OF THE JEWISH KHAZARS

BY D. M. DUNLOP

SCHOCKEN BOOKS · NEW YORK

First SCHOCKEN edition 1967

Library of Congress Catalog Card No. 67–26985

This edition published by arrangement with Princeton University Press

Manufactured in the United States of America

CONTENTS

INTRODUCTION

Readers of Gibbon are familiar with the name of Leo the Khazar, Emperor of the Greeks in the 8th century of our era, whose mother, a Khazar princess, had married Constantine V. The Khazars are repeatedly mentioned by the Byzantine writers, and evidently their power bulked large on the political horizon of those days. A simple example: in the 10th century, letters from the imperial chancellery on the Bosporus to the Khazar Khaqan, as their ruler was called, bore a more handsome gold seal than that judged necessary for correspondence with the Pope of Rome or the successor of Charlemagne.[1]

The Khazars have another and special claim on our interest. Their territory was situated between the lower course of the Volga and the northern slopes of the Caucasus, extending as far as the lands round the Sea of Azov, and, at least in the 9th century, even farther west to Kiev and the middle Dnieper, while eastward they exercised control over the tribesmen as far as the Oxus. The Khazar country thus lay across the natural line of advance of the Arabs. Within a few years of the death of Muḥammad (A.D. 632) the armies of the Caliphate, sweeping northward through the wreckage of two empires and carrying all before them, reached the great mountain barrier of the Caucasus. This barrier once passed, the road lay open to the lands of eastern Europe. As it was, on the line of the Caucasus the Arabs met the forces of an organized military power which effectively prevented them from extending their conquests in this direction. The wars of the Arabs and the Khazars, which lasted more than a hundred years, though little known, have thus considerable historical importance.[2] The Franks of Charles Martel on the field of Tours turned the tide of Arab invasion. At about the same time the threat to Europe in the east was

[1] Constantine Porphyrogenitus, *De Caerimoniis Aulae Byzantinae*, ed. Bonn, I, 690.

[2] Underestimated by Cavaignac, *Histoire du Monde*, t. vii (Paris 1931), 169.

hardly less acute. It is clear that the victorious Muslims were met and held by the forces of the Khazar kingdom. Though like the Franks the Khazars were thus in a sense the champions of Christendom, they belonged racially to the nomadic or semi-nomadic type of central Asia and at this time were still shamanists. Later as we shall see—and this is not the least remarkable thing about them—they converted to Judaism. It can, however, scarcely be doubted that but for the existence of the Khazars in the region north of the Caucasus, Byzantium, the bulwark of European civilization in the east, would have found itself outflanked by the Arabs, and the history of Christendom and Islam might well have been very different from what we know.

The question may be asked, Why has no attempt so far been made to write the Khazar history, if it is worth recording and a substantial amount of material is available? A continuous account of the Khazars was in fact given by the Cambridge historian J. B. Bury, in a chapter of his *History of the Eastern Roman Empire*.[3] This may be taken as the best account available, though there are others, besides a great number of monographs on various aspects of the subject and incidental references in modern books. The chief reason why we are not more familiar with the Khazars appears to be neither the lack of intrinsic interest presented by their story nor the absence of material, but rather the difficulty of dealing with the existing sources—partly because they are written in a variety of languages, Greek, Arabic, Hebrew, Syriac, Armenian, Georgian, Russian, Persian, Turkish, and even Chinese, with which no one can be expected to be conversant at first hand; and partly because of the contradiction and obscurity of the data thus afforded. The sources for the Khazars have steadily accumulated as our knowledge of Oriental history has grown. Last century saw the publication of Arabic geographers and historians who have much to tell us about them. In the present century, valuable new material in Hebrew has come to light.[4]

[3] C. xiii (London 1912).

[4] The opening up of the "geniza" (storeroom) of a synagogue in Old

The bibliography has increased to very considerable proportions, and critics have expressed their views on the Khazars in another range of languages, almost as formidable as that of the original sources. Certainly the position is very different from the days when Buxtorf connected the name of the Khazars, on whom he could get no information, with the Persian Chosroes (Khusraw). But in spite of the great additions to our knowledge, an attempt to trace their history is by no means plain sailing, as will be seen in the following pages.

Some time before the war Professor Paul Kahle, then Director of the Oriental Seminar in the University of Bonn, and Professor Henri Grégoire of Brussels intended to collaborate on a work on the Khazars. It was generally expected that an important and definitive book would be the result. Unfortunately, however, the outbreak of war and attendant circumstances interfered with their plans. Some years ago Professor Kahle proposed that I should take up the Khazar investigation, and I was very glad to fall in with his suggestion. In the course of the work I have had the great advantage of being able to consult Professor Kahle at need and am much indebted to him for his generous help in innumerable ways. Without him the book would not have been written. He has left me a free hand in the selection, arrangement, and presentation of the material, and while I have no doubt been influenced by his opinions on general questions, he is not responsible for the views expressed and particularly the misapprehensions and errors which, I take it, are unavoidable in a work like this.

My task has been to go over the available material and construct therefrom as coherent an account as possible of the fortunes of the Khazar nation and state. There is little new in the way of sources in the present work. Exceptions are some variant readings from manuscripts of al-Iṣṭakhri and al-Mas'ūdi sent me from Oxford by Professor Kahle—the texts have long been in print; a short account of the Khazars, probably by the

Cairo has contributed to this as to other historical questions. See Paul E. Kahle's Schweich Lectures: *The Cairo Geniza* (London 1947), 14ff.

Spanish geographer ibn-Saʿīd, which I also owe to Professor Kahle; a hitherto unnoticed passage in al-Yaʿqūbi bearing on the Khazar double kingship; and an interesting account of incidents purporting to have taken place at the Khazar court at an unspecified date, from a Persian manuscript in the Leyden University library, to the authorities of which I should like here to express my thanks. But I have taken notice of the Chinese references to the Khazars, which has not been done until now, so far as I know, even by the most recent writers on the subject. Professor Haloun, whose recent death is a great loss to many Orientalists personally as well as to Oriental studies, kindly helped me in this part of the work. Some of the Greek passages quoted will probably not be found elsewhere.

In the course of the work such subjects as the Khazar beginnings, their possible relations with the Persians before Islam, contacts of the Khazars and Greeks at different times, the wars with the Arabs, the conversion of the Khazars to Judaism, the alleged correspondence between Spain and Khazaria in the 10th century, relations of Khazars and Russians, and, finally, the collapse and disappearance of the Khazar state will be discussed. Some of these are highly controversial questions, and the reader need not feel alarm if on cardinal issues, such as the date of the conversion to Judaism or of the final eclipse, widely differing estimates have to be examined. He will be invited in the development of the argument to look for traces of the Khazars as far west as Denmark and as far east as China, and to consider that—apart from the conversion to Judaism, which is an undoubted fact—they are said to have adopted at different times Islam and Christianity as well. The evidence, obscure and contradictory as it frequently is, will be set down as clearly as is in the writer's power. Complete and, it is hoped, accurate translations of some of the most important Arabic texts are given in the course of the work.

Of a host of books and articles which have been consulted, one or two stand out as specially stimulating. The first of these is comparatively old and differs essentially in its conclusions from what is said here, J. Marquart's *Osteuropäische und ostasiatische Streifzüge.*[5] Another is Kokovtsov's *Evreisko-khazarskaya perepiska v X veke.*[6] The two books are poles apart in method and scope. The German's is diffuse and difficult to read, yet it contains a great many valuable suggestions about the period which concerns us. The Russian professor deals with a limited subject, the documents in Hebrew, half a dozen in number, bearing on the Khazar correspondence with Spain, around which, of all questions involved in Khazar history, controversy has been fiercest. This is discussed with admirable clarity and economy of words. To these must be added Professor A. Zeki Validi Togan's edition of ibn-Faḍlān's narrative of a journey to the Volga Bulgars, the notes and appendices to which contain material on the Khazars which has never before been published.[7] I have been able to use the book through the kindness of Professor Minorsky. Professor Minorsky's own translation and commentary of the 10th century Persian geography *Ḥudūd al-ʿĀlam* contains important new information.[8] I cannot omit one other work, the excellent bibliography of the Khazars compiled by the Slavonic division of the New York Public Library and published with a notice by A. Yarmolinsky in their *Bulletin* for 1938. My attention was first drawn to this by Dr. Cecil Roth of Oxford.

I must also mention briefly the extensive works of Artamonov, Poliak, and Zajączkowski, all of comparatively recent date, in which the problem of the Khazars is approached from very various points of view. Artamonov's *Ocherki drevneishei istorii Khazar* appeared in 1937.[9] Consonantly with its title, this book

[5] Leipzig 1903.

[6] The Hebrew-Khazar Correspondence in the 10th Century, published by the Russian Academy, Leningrad 1932.

[7] Ibn-Faḍlān's Reisebericht, A.K.M., xxiv, 3 (Leipzig 1939). A useful summary of Zeki Validi's material with an English translation of ibn-Faḍlān's narrative is given by Robert P. Blake and Richard N. Frye in "Notes on the Risala of ibn-Faḍlān," *Byzantina Metabyzantina*, i, ii (1949), 7-37.

[8] E. J. W. Gibb Memorial, New Series xi (1937).

[9] Subtitled *Études d'histoire ancienne des Khazares.* Leningrad 1936.

deals only with the early history of the Khazars, the last date given being A.D. 738. In his preface the author disclaims knowledge of Oriental languages and says that he writes as an archaeologist. Artamonov is specially interested in the Khazars as connected with the history of his own country. Within its limits his work seems to be an objective treatment of the subject. A. N. Poliak published his book entitled *Khazaria* (in Hebrew) at Tel Aviv in 1944. (I first saw Dr. Cecil Roth's copy, and later received another through the good offices of Dr. S. Morag of Jerusalem.) The book, which is conceived as the first, historical part of a larger work on the Khazars, develops theories earlier expressed by the author in his article "The Khazar Conversion to Judaism" in the Hebrew periodical *Zion* (1941), but offers a much richer documentation, especially in Jewish sources. Some of these theories are discussed below. The work has been the subject of a good deal of criticism.[10] Zajączkowski's *Ze studiów nad zagadnieniem chazarskim* (1947) is written from the standpoint of Turkish linguistics.[11] Both in this book and in a number of articles, the author, who is a well-known Turcologist, has thrown considerable light on the surviving Khazar nomenclature, which he proposes to illustrate from the dialects still spoken by the Karaite Jews in Poland and the Crimea.[12] These Karaites he regards as the principal present-day representatives of the ancient Khazars. He tends to minimize rather than exaggerate the importance of the Hebrew documents. Dr. S. Seliga of St. Andrews University has greatly facilitated my study of these Polish works.

[10] Cf. the review of M. Landau in *Qiryath Sepher*, XXI (1944), 19-24, in Hebrew. I have not seen A. Eshkolli in *Moznaim*, XVIII, 298-304, 375-383, with Poliak's reply, *op.cit.*, XIX, 288-291, 348-352. (These references to Hebrew periodicals are due to Dr. Morag.)

[11] Studies on the Khazar Problem, published by the Polish Academy, Cracow. There is a detailed review in *Der Islam*, B. 29 (1949), 96-103, by O. Pritsak.

[12] Recent articles of Zajączkowski include "Problem językowy Chazarów" (The Problem of the Language of the Khazars), *Proceedings of the Breslau Society of Sciences*, 1946, and "O kulturze chazarskiej i jej spadkobiercach" (The Khazar Culture and Its Heirs), *Myśl Karaimska*, Breslau 1946.

Finally, I should like to thank Professor H. W. Bailey of Queens' College, Cambridge, Professor V. Minorsky, and Professor C. J. Mullo Weir of Glasgow University, who read through the present work in manuscript and from whose advice and suggestions I have profited in various ways. I should also like to express my grateful thanks to Professor Philip K. Hitti and the Trustees of Princeton University Press.

D.M.D.

THE HISTORY OF
THE JEWISH KHAZARS

CHAPTER I

THE EMERGENCE OF THE KHAZARS

IF the commonly accepted derivation of one or two familiar words in European languages is correct, the name of the Khazars has a wider currency than we should at first suppose. The word "hussar" seems originally[1] to have been applied to irregular Hungarian cavalry, and as we shall see, the connection between the Khazars and the Magyars, the founders of the Hungarian state, is historical and certain. The German *Ketzer*, "heretic," has also been derived from the name of the Khazars, presumably as Jews. On the other hand, the derivation and meaning of the name are quite obscure. It is usually said that it is a participial form from the Turkish verbal stem *qaz*, "to wander" or "nomadize," so that Khazar="nomad,"[2] and this may be provisionally accepted. In the Slav languages there are various words for the Khazars with an "o" vowel in the first syllable, and this has led to other derivations, from *kosa*, Russian "pigtail" (Weltmann, 1858) and from the stem *koz* in many Slav words for "goat" (Tzenoff, 1935).[3] Such attempts may be discounted, as the original name is not Slav. There is not the slightest reason to suppose that the Khazars are "the wearers of pigtails" or "the goat-herds." It is note-

[1] I.e., as a military term. Dr. Alan S. C. Ross of Birmingham University writes that in the Magyar Dictionary of Bárczi *huszár* is said to be a loan-word from Serbo-Croat *husar*, which is itself a loan-word from Greek *chosarios*. This word *chosarios* is presumably the same as *Khosiarioi*, given by Reiske as doubtfully from the name Khazar (Constant. Por., ed. Bonn, II, 675), with the meaning *latrones et sicarii*. The word appears with the form and meaning indicated by Reiske in Harmenopulos (14th century), I, tit. 4, §9.

[2] So Zajączkowski, "Problem," §2, citing Gombocz, Németh and Rásonyi, and again in his *Studies*. Zeki Validi passes over the definition in silence (*Ibn-Faḍlān*, 225), and O. Pritsak in his review of the *Studies* (Der Islam, B. 29, 101) proposes as an alternative that *qazar* (Khazar) is "ein Kollektiv zu *qazan*," promising an etymology of *qazan* elsewhere.

[3] Cited Zajączkowski, *ibid.*

worthy that in Hebrew also the name is commonly written with an "o/u" vowel and pronounced Kūzāri (hence Buxtorf's Cosri), plural Kūzārīm. On the other hand, we have Arabic *Khazar* (with an impossible derivation from *akhzar*, an adjective denoting some affection of the eyes, "small-eyed" or "slanting-eyed"), Greek *Khazaroi* (*Khazareis*), occasionally *Khotzēr-* (*Khotzir-*), Latin *Chazari* and *Gazari*, and in the Hebrew of the document known as the Khazar Correspondence an unvocalized form, no doubt to be pronounced Kazar (Khazar).

As already said, the explanation Khazar=nomad is perhaps to be accepted. Yet Pelliot has pointed to the difficulties involved[4] (the Turkish verb *qazmak* always in the sense of "to hollow out," not "to wander," etc.) and refers to the suggestion of J. Deny[5] that the name Khazar might be explainable by *Quz-er, *Quz-är, *Quzar or *Qozar, from *quz* "side of a mountain exposed to the north" plus *eri*, *er*, in the sense of "People of the North." In favor of Deny's suggestion, it may be said (a) that no satisfactory explanation of the "o/u" vowel in some forms of the name has yet been given, and (b) that in ancient Armenian and Georgian the Khazar Khaqan is repeatedly referred to as the "King of the North" and Khazaria as the "Land of the North," which could be a rendering of the native name. But the forms in the Khazar Correspondence, presumably Kazar, Kazari, are on this view difficult to account for, and the Cambridge Document, also written in Hebrew, offers Qazar (hardly Quzar).

Our first question here is, When did the Khazars and the Khazar name appear? There has been considerable discussion as to the relation of the Khazars to the Huns on the one hand and to the West Turks on the other. The prevalent opinion has for some time been that the Khazars emerged from the West Turkish empire. Early references to the Khazars ap-

[4] *Noms turcs*, 207-224 (special article on Khazar).

[5] *Mél. Émile Boisacq*, Annuaire de l'Institut de Phil. et d'Hist. Or. et Slaves, v (1937), Brussels, 295-312.

pear about the time when the West Turks cease to be mentioned. Thus they are reported to have joined forces with the Greek Emperor Heraclius against the Persians in A.D. 627 and to have materially assisted him in the siege of Tiflis. It is a question whether the Khazars were at this time under West Turk supremacy. The chronicler Theophanes (died circa A.D. 818) who tells the story introduces them as "the Turks from the east whom they call Khazars."[6] On the other hand, the West Turks appear in the Greek writers simply as Turks, without special qualification.

The Syriac historians mention the Khazars earlier than A.D. 627. Both Michael Syrus[7] and Bar Hebraeus[8] tell how, apparently in the reign of the Greek Emperor Maurice (582-602), three brothers from "inner Scythia" marched west with 30,000 men, and when they reached the frontier of the Greeks, one of them, Bulgariōs (Bar Hebraeus, Bulgarīs), crossed the Don and settled within the Empire. The others occupied "the country of the Alans which is called Barsalia," they and the former inhabitants adopting the name of Khazars from Kazarīg, the eldest of the brothers. If as seems possible the story goes back to John of Ephesus[9] (died circa A.D. 586), it is contemporary with the alleged event. It states pretty explicitly that the Khazars arrived at the Caucasus from central Asia towards the end of the 6th century.

In the Greek writer Theophylact Simocatta (circa 620) we have an almost contemporary account of events among the West Turks which can hardly be unrelated to the Syriac story just mentioned.[10] Speaking of a Turkish embassy to Maurice in 598, this author describes how in past years the Turks had overthrown the White Huns (Hephthalites), the Avars, and the Uigurs who lived on "the Til, which the Turks call the Black River."[11] These Uigurs, says Theophylact, were

[6] Ed. Bonn, 485.
[7] Ed. Chabot, 381, col. 1, line 9.
[8] Ed. Budge, 32b, col. 1, line 15.
[9] So Barthold, *E.I.*, art. Bulghār.
[10] Ed. Bonn, 282ff, Chavannes, *Documents*, 246ff.
[11] Unidentified. *Til* is apparently the same as *atil*, *itil*, "river." Cf. Atil,

descended from two chiefs called Var and Hunni. They are mentioned elsewhere as the "Varchonites."[12] Some of the Uigurs escaped from the Turks, and, appearing in the West, were regarded by those whom they met as Avars, by which name they were generally known. The last part of this is confirmed by another Greek author, according to whom Justinian received representatives of the pseudo-Avars, properly Uigurs, in A.D. 558,[13] after which they turned to plundering and laying waste the lands of eastern and central Europe. If the derivation from Uigur is right, the word "ogre" in folklore may date from this early period.

Theophylact also tells us that about the time of the Turkish embassy in 598 there was another emigration of fugitives from Asia into Europe, involving the tribes of the Tarniakh, Kotzagers, and Zabender. These were, like the previous arrivals, descendants of Var and Hunni, and they proved their kinship by joining the so-called Avars, really Uigurs, under the Khaqan of the latter. It is difficult not to see in this another version of the story given by Michael Syrus and Bar Hebraeus. The Kotzagers are undoubtedly a Bulgar group,[14] while Zabender should be the same name as Samandar, an important Khazar town, and hence correspond to Kazarīg in the Syriac. Originally, it seems, Samandar derived its name from the occupying tribe.[15] We appear to have confirmation that the Khazars had arrived in eastern Europe by the reign of Maurice, having previously been in contact with the West Turks and destined to be so again.

On the other hand, the older view implied that the Khazars were already on the outskirts of Europe before the rise of the Turks (circa A.D. 550). According to this view, the affinities of

---

Itil=the Volga. Zeuss (*Die Deutschen*, 713n.) denied that the Volga was meant. Marquart, followed by Chavannes (*Documents*, 251), suggested the Tola, a tributary of the Orkhon, which is probably too far east.

12 Menander Protector, ed. Bonn, 400.

13 Menander, *ibid.*, 282.

14 Cf. Marquart, *Streifzüge*, 488.

15 Similarly, another important Khazar town, Balanjar, seems to have been originally the group-name of its inhabitants. See below.

the Khazars were with the Huns. When Priscus, the envoy to Attila in 448, spoke of a people subject to the Huns and living in "Scythia towards the Pontus" called Akatzir,[16] these were simply Aq-Khazars, i.e., White Khazars. Jordanes, writing circa 552, mentions the Akatzirs as a warlike nation, who do not practice agriculture but live by pasturing flocks and hunting.[17] In view of the distinction among some Turkish peoples between the leading clans of a confederacy as "white" and the remainder as "black," when we read in the Arab geographer Iṣṭakhri that the Khazars are of two kinds, one called Qara-Khazars (Black Khazars), the other a white kind, unnamed,[18] it is a natural assumption that the latter are the Aq-Khazars (White Khazars). The identification of the Akatzirs with "Aq-Khazars" was rejected by Zeuss[19] and Marquart[20] as impossible linguistically. Marquart further said that historically the Akatzirs as a subject race correspond rather to the Black Khazars. The alternative identification proposed is Akatzirs=Agacheri. But this may not be very different from the other, if Zeki Validi is right in thinking that the relation between the Agacheri and the Khazars was close.[21]

There are one or two facts in favor of the older view which have not been explained away effectively. If the Khazars had nothing to do with the Akatzirs and appeared first as an offshoot of the West Turks at the end of the 6th century, how do they come to be mentioned in the Syriac compilation of circa 569,[22] going under the name of Zacharias Rhetor? The form Kasar/Kasir, which here comes in a list of peoples belonging to the general neighborhood of the Caucasus, refers evidently to the Khazars. This would fit in well with their existence in the same region a century earlier. We have also the testimony of the so-called Geographer of Ravenna (? 7th century) that the Agaziri (Acatziri) of Jordanes are the Khazars.[23]

16 Priscus, ed. Bonn, 197.

17 Ed. Mommsen, 63.

18 Iṣṭakhri's account of the Khazars is translated in Chapter V.

19 *Die Deutschen*, 714-15.

20 *Streifzüge*, 41, n. 2.

21 *Ibn-Faḍlān*, xxxi.

22 Rubens Duval, cited Chavannes, *Documents*, 250, n. 4.

23 Ed. Pinder and Parthy, 168.

The Khazars, however, are nowhere represented simply as Huns. The question arises, If they were subjugated by the latter shortly before A.D. 448, as Priscus tells, how long had they existed previously? Here we must consider the views of Zeki Validi, which are put forward exclusively on the basis of Oriental sources and are quite independent of the considerations which have just been raised. He believes that he has found traces of one and the same *Urgeschichte* of the Turks, not only in Muslim but also in Chinese sources, the latter going as far back as the Wei dynasty (366-558).[24] In the story the Khazars play a leading part and even claim to be autochthonous in their country.[25] Zeki Validi cites a story in Gardīzi, according to which the eponymous ancestor of the Kirgiz, having killed a Roman officer, fled to the court of the Khazar Khaqan, and later went eastward till he found a permanent settlement on the Yenissei. But as the Kirgiz in early times are believed to have lived in eastern Europe and to have been south of the Urals before the beginning of the Christian era, Zeki Validi would assign a corresponding date to this episode and is unwilling to allow that the mention of Khazars thus early is an anachronism.[26] These are remarkable claims to make for the antiquity of the Khazars. The principal Muslim sources which Zeki Validi relies on are relatively late, Gardīzi, circa A.D. 1050, and an anonymous history, the *Mujmal al-Tawārīkh w-al-Qiṣaṣ*,[27] somewhat later (though these doubtless go back to ibn-al-Muqaffaʿ in the 8th century, and through him to pre-Islamic Persian sources), nor does his Chinese source mention the Khazars explicitly. But the view that the Khazars existed anterior to the Huns gains some confirmation from another quarter.

The Armenian History going under the name of Moses of Chorene (5th century) has a story which mentions the Khazars

[24] The Later Wei is meant (Zeki Validi's dates).

[25] *Ibn-Faḍlān*, 294. Yet on the basis of the same tradition, the original home of the Khazars is represented as the lower Oxus, cf. *ibid.*, 244, 266.

[26] *Ibid.*, 328.

[27] *Ibid.*, 311.

in the twenty years between A.D. 197 and 217.[28] According to this, the peoples of the north, the Khazirs and Basilians, made an agreement to break through the pass of Chor at the east end of the Caucasus "under their general and king Venasep Surhap."[29] Having crossed the river Kur, they were met by the Armenian Valarsh with a great army and driven back northward in confusion. Some time later, on their own side of the Caucasus, the northern nations again suffered a heavy defeat. Valarsh was killed in this second battle. His son succeeded him, and under the new king the Armenians again passed the Caucasus in strength, defeating and completely subjugating the Khazirs and Basilians. One in every hundred was taken as a hostage, and a monument in Greek letters was set up to show that these nations were under the jurisdiction of Rome.

This seems to be a very factual account, and by Khazirs certainly the Khazars are to be understood. It is, however, generally held that the Armenian History is wrongly ascribed to Moses of Chorene in the 5th century and should be assigned to the 9th, or at any rate the 8th, century.[30] This would clearly put quite a different complexion on the story of the Khazar raid. Instead of being unexceptionable evidence for the existence of the Khazars at all events in the time of Moses of Chorene, it would fall into line with other Armenian (and also Georgian[31]) accounts which, though they refer to the Khazars more or less explicitly in the first centuries of the Christian era, and even much earlier, we do not cite here. Though interest-

[28] The chronology of the text is confused, suggesting both these dates and an intermediate one. *Enc. Brit.* (14th ed.), s.v. Khazars, has the date 198. Carmoly (*Khozars*, 10, in *Itinéraires de la Terre Sainte*, Brussels 1847) must refer to the same incident when he speaks of the Khazar Juluf, who ruled seventeen nations on the Volga, and, pursuing some rebel tribes, burst into Armenia between A.D. 178 and 198. The source of Carmoly's information is quite unknown to me.

[29] In the Whistons' 18th century translation, II, 62 (65) "sub duce ac rege eorum Venasepo Surhaco." Kutschera thought that the two kings of the Khazars were intended (*Die Chasaren*, Vienna 1910, 38).

[30] For a summary of the views about Moses of Chorene, see an article by A. O. Sarkissian, *J.A.O.S.*, Vol. 60 (1940), 73-81.

[31] A favorable example of the Georgian accounts in Brosset, *Inscriptions Georgiennes* etc., *M.R.A.*, 1840, 329.

ing in themselves, these accounts, in view of their imprecision and lack of confirmation, cannot be regarded as reliable.

The Muslim writers provide us with a considerable amount of material which may be expected to throw light on the date of the emergence of the Khazars. As already indicated, some of this demonstrably derives from Pehlevi sources, composed before the Arab conquest of Persia. What the Arabic and Persian writers have to say about the Khazars deserves careful scrutiny, as liable to contain authentic information from an earlier time. It is not surprising that these accounts, written when the Khazar state north of the Caucasus was flourishing, distinguish them from the Turks encountered by the first generations of Muslims in central Asia. But a passage like the following, where the Khazars are set side by side with the leading types of contemporary humanity, is somewhat remarkable. In a discussion between the celebrated ibn-al-Muqaffaʿ and his friends the question was raised as to what nation was the most intelligent. It is significant for the low state of their culture at the time, or at least for the view held by the Arabs on the subject (ibn-al-Muqaffaʿ died 142/759), that the Turks and Khazars were suggested only after the claims of the Persians, Greeks, Chinese, Indians, and Negroes had been canvassed. Evidently in this respect the Turks and the Khazars shared a bad eminence. But they are given quite different characteristics: "The Turks are lean dogs, the Khazars pasturing cattle."[32] Though the judgment is unfavorable, we get the impression of the Khazars as a distinct, even important, racial group. How far this corresponds with the fact is not certain. Suggestions have been made connecting the Khazars with the Circassian type, taken to be pale-complexioned, dark-haired, and blue-eyed, and through the Basilians or Barsilians already mentioned, with the so-called "Royal Scyths" of Herodotus.[33] All this is evidently very speculative. Apart from the passage where the

[32] Ibn-ʿAbd-Rabbihi, *al-ʿIqd al-Farīd*, ed. of A.H. 1331, II, 210. The anecdote is commented on by Fr. Rosenthal, *Technique and Approach of Muslim Scholarship*, *Analecta Orientalia*, 24 (1947), 72.

[33] IV, 59.

Black Khazars are mentioned, described as being dusky like the Indians, and their counterparts fair and handsome,[34] the only available description of the race in Arabic sources is the following, apparently from ibn-Sa'īd al-Maghribi: "As to the Khazars, they are to the left [north] of the inhabited earth towards the 7th clime, having over their heads the constellation of the Plough. Their land is cold and wet. Hence their complexions are white, their eyes blue, their hair flowing and predominantly reddish, their bodies large and their natures cold. Their general aspect is wild."[35] This reads like a conventional description of a northern nation, and in any case affords no kind of support for Khazar affinity with the "Circassian" type. If we are to trust the etymology of Khalīl ibn-Aḥmad,[36] the Khazars may have been slant-eyed, like the Mongols, etc. Evidently nothing can be said positively in the matter. Some of the Khazars may have been fair-skinned, with dark hair and blue eyes, but there is no evidence that this type prevailed from antiquity or was widely represented in Khazaria in historical times.

A similar discussion on the merits of the different races is reported from the days before Muḥammad, in which the speakers are the Arab Nu'mān ibn-al-Mundhir of al-Ḥīrah and Khusraw Anūshirwān. The Persian gives his opinion that the Greeks, Indians, and Chinese are superior to the Arabs and so also, in spite of their low material standards of life, the Turks and the Khazars, who at least possess an organization under their kings. Here again the Khazars are juxtaposed with the great nations of the east.[37] It is consonant with this that tales were told of how ambassadors from the Chinese, the Turks, and the Khazars were constantly at Khusraw's gate,[38] and even that he

[34] See Iṣṭakhri's account of the Khazars in Chapter V, *infra.*

[35] Bodleian MS., I, 874, fol. 71, kindly communicated by Professor Kahle.

[36] Yāqūt, *Mu'jam al-Buldān*, s.v. Khazar.

[37] Ibn-'Abd-Rabbihi, *op.cit.* I, 166.

[38] Ṭabari, I, 899. According to ibn-Khurdādhbih, persons wishing access to the Persian court from the country of the Khazars and the Alans were detained at Bāb al-Abwāb (*B.G.A.*, VI, 135).

kept three thrones of gold in his palace, which were never removed and on which none sat, reserved for the kings of Byzantium, China, and the Khazars.[39]

In general, the material in the Arabic and Persian writers with regard to the Khazars in early times falls roughly into three groups, centering respectively round the names of (a) one or other of the Hebrew patriarchs, (b) Alexander the Great, and (c) certain of the Sassanid kings, especially Anūshirwān and his immediate successors.

A typical story of the first group is given by Ya'qūbi in his History.[40] After the confusion of tongues at Babel, the descendants of Noah came to Peleg, son of Eber, and asked him to divide the earth among them. He apportioned to the descendants of Japheth China, Hind, Sind, the country of the Turks and that of the Khazars, as well as Tibet, the country of the (Volga) Bulgars, Daylam, and the country neighboring on Khurāsān. In another passage Ya'qūbi gives a kind of sequel to this. Peleg having divided the earth in this fashion, the descendants of 'Āmūr ibn-Tubal, a son of Japheth, went out to the northeast. One group, the descendants of Togarmah, proceeding farther north, were scattered in different countries and became a number of kingdoms, among them the Burjān (Bulgars), Alans, Khazars, and Armenians.[41]

Similarly, according to Ṭabari,[42] there were born to Japheth Jām-r (the Biblical Gomer), Maw'-' (read Mawgh-gh, Magog), Mawdāy (Madai), Yawān (Javan), Thūbāl (Tubal), Mash-j (read Mash-kh, Meshech) and Tīr-sh (Tiras).[43] Of the descendants of the last were the Turks and the Khazars. There is possibly an association here with the Türgesh, survivors of the West Turks, who were defeated by the Arabs in 119/737,[44] and disappeared as a ruling group in the same century. Ṭabari says curiously that of the descendants of Mawgh-gh were

[39] Ibn-al-Balkhi, *Fārs Nāmah* (*G.M.S.*), 97.
[40] Ed. Houtsma, I, 17. [41] *Ibid.*, I, 203, cf. Marquart, *Str.* 491.
[42] I, 217-18. [43] Cf. *Gen.* 10.2.
[44] H. A. R. Gibb, *Arab Conquests in Central Asia*, London 1923, 83ff. Cf. Chapter IV, n. 96.

Yājūj and Mājūj, adding that these are to the east of the Turks and Khazars. This information would invalidate Zeki Validi's attempt to identify Gog and Magog in the Arabic writers with the Norwegians.[45] The name Mash-kh is regarded by him as probably a singular to the classical Massagetai (Massag-et).[46] A. Bashmakov emphasizes the connection of "Meshech" with the Khazars, to establish his theory of the Khazars, not as Turks from inner Asia, but what he calls a Japhetic or Alarodian group from south of the Caucasus.[47]

Evidently there is no stereotyped form of this legendary relationship of the Khazars to Japheth. The *Tāj-al-'Arūs* says that according to some they are the descendants of Kāsh-ḥ (? Māsh-ḥ or Māsh-kh, for Meshech), son of Japheth, and according to others both the Khazars and the Ṣaqālibah are sprung from Thūbāl (Tubal). Further, we read of Balanjar ibn-Japheth in ibn-al-Faqīh[48] and abū-al-Fidā'[49] as the founder of the town of Balanjar. Usage leads one to suppose that this is equivalent to giving Balanjar a separate racial identity. In historical times Balanjar was a well-known Khazar center, which is even mentioned by Mas'ūdi as their capital.[50]

It is hardly necessary to cite more of these Japheth stories. Their Jewish origin is a priori obvious, and Poliak has drawn attention to one version of the division of the earth where the Hebrew words for "north" and "south" actually appear in the Arabic text.[51] The Iranian cycle of legend had a similar tradition, according to which the hero Afrīdūn divided the earth among his sons, Ṭūj (sometimes Tūr, the eponym of Turan), Salm, and Īraj. Here the Khazars appear with the Turks and the Chinese in the portion assigned to Ṭūj, the eldest son.[52]

Some of the stories connect the Khazars with Abraham. The tale of a meeting in Khurāsān between the sons of Keturah and the Khazars where the Khaqan is mentioned is quoted from

[45] *Ibn-Faḍlān*, 196ff. [46] *Ibid.*, 244, n. 3.
[47] *Mercure de France*, Vol. 229 (1931), 39ff.
[48] *B.G.A.*, v, 289.
[49] Ed. Reinaud and De Slane, 219.
[50] *Tanbīh*, 62. [51] "Conversion," §3. [52] Ṭabari, I, 229.

ibn-Sa'd and al-Ṭabari by Poliak.[53] The tradition also appears in the Meshed manuscript of ibn-al-Faqīh, apparently as part of the account of Tamīm ibn-Baḥr's journey to the Uigurs, but it goes back to Hishām al-Kalbi.[54] Zeki Validi is inclined to lay some stress on it as a real indication of the presence of the Khazars in this region at an early date.[55] Al-Jāḥiẓ similarly refers to the legend of the sons of Abraham and Keturah settling in Khurāsān but does not mention the Khazars.[56] Al-Dimashqi says that according to one tradition the Turks were the children of Abraham by Keturah, whose father belonged to the original Arab stock (al-'Arab al-'Āribah). Descendants of other sons of Abraham, namely the Soghdians and the Kirgiz, were also said to live beyond the Oxus. Dimashqi himself does not favor these genealogies.[57]

Quite typical of the Alexander stories of the second group is an account of how the conqueror, after advancing from Egypt to north Africa (Kairouan) and meeting Qandāqah, a kind of Queen of Sheba to Alexander's Solomon, passes northward to the "Land of Darkness." He returns, founds two cities "on the frontier of the Greeks," and then proposes to go back to the east. His viziers represent the difficulty of passing the "Green Sea," of which the waters are fetid. But in spite of viziers and obstacles he crosses the Greek territory and arrives in the land of the Ṣaqālibah, who submit to him. He passes on, reaches the Khazars, who also submit, and continues through the country of the Turks and the desert between the Turks and China, etc., etc.[58]

In view of this kind of thing, when we meet a statement connecting Alexander with the Khazars which is not palpably

[53] *Loc.cit.*; *Khazaria*, 23, 142, 148; Cf. ibn-Sa'd, I, i, 22; Ṭabari I, i, 347ff.

[54] Hishām ibn-Muḥammad, the authority given by ibn-Sa'd=Hishām ibn-Lohrāsp al-Sā'ib al-Kalbi in ibn-al-Faqīh's text (in V. Minorsky, "Tamīm ibn-Baḥr's Journey to the Uyghurs," *B.S.O.A.S.*, 1948, xii/2, 282).

[55] *Ibn-Faḍlān*, 294.

[56] *Faḍā'il al-Atrāk*, transl. C. T. Harley Walker, *J.R.A.S.*, 1915, 687.

[57] Ed. Mehren, 262.

[58] Dīnawari, *Al-Akhbār al-Ṭiwāl*, ed. Guirgass and Kratchkovsky, 37ff.

absurd, such as that from Wahb ibn-al-Munabbih, to the effect that the conqueror found the Khazars in the region of Merv and Herat,[59] we cannot begin to consider it. Ṭabari remarks similarly that the meeting-place or a meeting-place of Alexander and the Persian ruler was in Khurāsān, near the Khazar border, where a great battle was fought.[60] If this could be accepted, if even it could be regarded as an anachronism, it would be very important as evidence of the extension of Khazar activity far east of the Caspian at some time. But so remote from fact are many of the Alexander stories that we can infer little or nothing from the statement, much less accept it at face value.

We may in fact say roundly that all references to the Khazars in the time of Alexander are fanciful. This is obviously the case for Niẓāmi's Sikandar Nāmah, where the Khazars are usually coupled with the Russians as the conqueror's enemies in the north.[61] Mention of the Russians is a glaring anachronism. The idea was no doubt suggested to the poet, writing at the end of the 12th century, by what he knew of the historical raids of the Russians down the Volga and across the Caspian.[62] He was familiar with local circumstances in the Caucasus region.[63] It is clear that Niẓāmi gave his own turn to the story of Alexander in other directions.[64] The conqueror's battles with the Russians seem to be mentioned by no writer before this time. There is no question of a genuine tradition.

So far we have not learned much from the Arabic and Persian sources about the antiquity of the Khazars. It remains to be seen whether any greater light will be thrown on this

[59] Cited Zeki Validi, *Ibn-Faḍlān*, 294.

[60] I, 699.

[61] E.g., Qanṭāl, chief of the Rūs, "from the multitudes of Burṭās, Ālān and Khazarān raised up an army like a sea or mountain." Alexander says, "From the Khazar mountain to the China sea I view the land—all Turk on Turk." In another place, the army of the Rūs is "arrayed with the men of Khazarān."

[62] These are discussed below, Chapter IX.

[63] As was also the poet Khāqāni. See Chapter IX.

[64] Cf. Nöldeke, *Beiträge zur Geschichte des Alexanderromans*, *Denkschriften d. Wien. Akad*, B. 38, No. 5, 51-53.

problem and on the Khazars in general by the third group of passages from Muslim writers, connecting the Khazars with various Persian kings, particularly Khusraw Anūshirwān.

We have an account of a great expedition against the Turks in the time of Kay Khusraw under four commanders, one of whom is said to have advanced on the enemy by way of the Khazar country. But the date of this (Kay Khusraw=Cyrus) would be long before the Alexander stories, when mention of the Turks is a demonstrable inaccuracy. The story which is found in Ṭabari[65] as well as ibn-al-Balkhi[66] is surely a late invention.

A hitherto unknown legend of the Khazar court is found in a Persian text belonging to the Leyden University Library.[67] The author is a certain Muḥammad ibn-ʿAli al-Kātib al-Samarqandi, who lived in the 12th century and dedicated his book to one of the Qara-Khānids. It bears the title Aʿrāḍ al-Siyāsah fi Aghrāḍ al-Riyāsah and was known to Ḥajji Khalīfah.[68] Barthold spoke of it as a historical work[69]—the one historical work written in Transoxiana under the Qara-Khānids, he says—but it is rather of the "Mirror of Princes" order of literature. The relevant passage begins in the elaborate, high-flown style of much Persian writing: "Khaqan, king of the Khazars [was] that sovereign, the eagle of whose majesty had hunted down the *sīmurgh* of happiness, and the falcon of whose kingdom-adorning, state-nurturing wisdom had made a prey of the peacock that was the high rank of world-dominion."[70] After some observations on the ways of kings, the writer tells that "once the Khaqan gave a feast and sat alone with his boon companions." To him enters one of the sons of Ḍaḥḥāk-i Tāzi, i.e., evidently an Arab (al-Ḍaḥḥāk is the typical Bedouin marauder

[65] I, 609.

[66] *Op.cit.*, 45.

[67] *Catalogus Codicum Orientalium Bibl. Acad. Lugduno-Batavae*, III, 14, No. 927. I owe the reference to Professor A. M. Honeyman, St. Andrews University.

[68] I, 368.

[69] *Turkestan* (*G.M.S.*), 18.

[70] Professor Minorsky kindly provided a translation of the difficult sentence.

of the old Iranian cycle of legend) and, having paid respectful greeting to the Khaqan, is invited to drink with him. As the two sit drinking, musicians begin to play and the conversation turns on the subject of music. Two questions in succession are put to the Arab prince, to which he replies: "What do you understand by audition [listening to music]?" and "Why is the hearer sometimes carried away and confused as he listens?" Thereafter, being apparently satisfied as to the discretion and knowledgeability of his visitor, the Khaqan asks a third question: "Why has prosperity turned its back on you [i.e., the Arabs] after the kings of the earth bore the saddle-cloth of obedience to you upon the shoulders of submission, and the stars of heaven laid their foreheads on the dust of your threshold?" The son of Ḍaḥḥāk replies suitably that this was owing to bad government. Some moralizing by the author follows and the episode closes.

This is quite clearly an apologue in the Oriental manner and not history. Ḍaḥḥāk, as already indicated, belongs to legend. The observations of his son on audition reflect the musical theory of the time. The story has been invented or adopted by the 12th century author in order to edify his patron.[71]

The interest for us therefore is how Samarqandi here presents the Khazars. Other sources, as we have seen, both Persian and Arabic, speak of the Khazar Khaqan in pre-Islamic times as a great king, whose position as head of an important section of humanity entitles him to rank with the Sassanid rulers and the emperors of China. Of all such more or less apocryphal references to the ancient grandeur of the Khazar Khaqan, none presents him more distinctly than the present passage. Here he is a heathen, or at least a non-Muslim, given over to wine and the delights of music. He is surrounded by courtiers, unlike the Khaqan of later date, who, we are credibly informed, lived in more or less seclusion. He is treated deferentially by

[71] Had the Qara-Khānids (Īlek Khans) a special interest in the Khazars? Cf. Chapter VI, n. 125 *ad finem*.

the Arab prince. Further, he is well-informed and affable and discourses with simple wisdom about the affairs of men. How far all this corresponds with historical reality it is of course impossible to say.

Something much more positive seems to be indicated by an incident reported by Mas'ūdi as having taken place at the court of Shīrūyah (Shīrwayh) in the 7th century, but relating to an earlier period. According to Mas'ūdi's story,[72] while out riding this king happened to ask one of his suite if he remembered the famous stratagem which his ancestor Ardashīr ibn-Bābak had practised on the king of the Khazars. To flatter and amuse Shīrūyah, the courtier feigned ignorance of the story and, pretending to be absorbed in the king's recital, allowed his horse to fall into a canal. It is clearly intended that the tale was common knowledge. We are thus given to understand that the Khazars existed in the time of Ardashīr (A.D. 226-240). Now, although the Arabic historians refer briefly to the activity of Ardashīr in their direction,[73] particularly mentioning his occupation of Ṣūl (Darband), the important post at the east end of the Caucasus, it is difficult to discover what Mas'ūdi meant by the "famous stratagem." Nothing which can be so described, nor indeed any explicit connection of Ardashīr with the Khazars, seems to be related elsewhere. Certainly what Mas'ūdi says here cannot be accepted as evidence for their existence in the 3rd century A.D. Why are the circumstances, if well-known and authentic, not to be found in the Kārnāmak, a work in Pehlevi devoted to the history of Ardashīr, which has been translated by Nöldeke?[74] The most probable opinion is that the reference in Mas'ūdi is to some other Persian sovereign, as we shall see.

There is a brief, anachronistic mention of the Khazars as having marched against Shāpūr (Sapor), the son of Ardashīr, in the armies of the Emperor Julian,[75] after which the Muslim

[72] *Murūj*, VI, 124ff.
[73] Cf. ibn-Khaldūn, ed. of A.H. 1284, II, i, 169.
[74] *Beiträge zur Kunde der indogermanischen Sprachen*, IV (1878), 22ff.
[75] Ṭabari, I, 840.

sources have little or nothing to say about them till considerably later. According to Ṭabari,[76] the Persian Fīrūz (457-484) erected a work of stone in the neighborhood of Ṣūl[77] and the Alans, to protect his country from the northern nations. According to the Greek author Priscus, Peirozes (Fīrūz) some time before A.D. 465 sent to Kounkhas (? Qūn Khān), king of the Kidarite Huns, saying that he wished for peace and an alliance and would give the Kidarite his sister in marriage. Kounkhas agreed, but there was sent to him from Persia, instead of the sister of Fīrūz, another woman got up to impersonate her. When peace had been duly made, the woman divulged the fraud to the Kidarite, who insisted on going through with the marriage. To avenge himself, he induced Fīrūz to send him a number of leading Persians, some of whom he put to death, and the rest he sent back mutilated to their master.[78] There is no reason to doubt that the facts, including the ferocious dénouement, are in the main as Priscus relates them. He is writing practically contemporary with the events, and we may see his authority in a certain Constantius, an envoy from the Byzantine court, who met Fīrūz in A.D. 465. Here is a stratagem practised by a Persian against a northern ruler. Is it Mas'ūdi's famous example?

Before proceeding, we must glance at the question, Who are the Kidarites? The usual view is that Priscus meant the Hephthalites, or White Huns, to whom in the sequel Fīrūz owed his death. Bury remarked that "the Kidarites proper seem to have been Huns, who had settled in the trans-Caspian country and threatened the Pass of Dariel."[79] Priscus mentions that the Persians in 465 held the fortress of Yuroeipakh (?),[80] apparently at the east end of the Caucasus, against the Kidarites and wanted the Romans to contribute to its upkeep. Elsewhere he says that when the Saragurs in 468 marched against the Per-

[76] I, 895.

[77] It is the Greek Tzour (Procopius, *Hist.* VIII, iii, 4) from Armenian tsur, "door" (=Chor).

[78] Ed. Bonn, 220ff.

[79] Bury, *Theodosius*, II, 7, n. 5.

[80] *Ibid.*, 159, with the var. Uroeisakh.

sians, they met at the Caspian Gates (Darband) the Persian garrison which formerly had held the pass against the Kidarites.[81] A little later, in 472, a Persian embassy to Constantinople announced a victory over the Kidarites and the capture of the town of "Balaam," which may have to be looked for north of the Caucasus. The name as it stands is surely due to a copyist.[82]

From all this the question suggests itself, Are the Kidarites in the 5th century simply the Khazars? The view which connects the Kidarites with the Hephthalites does not exclude this, for it appears that there may be affinity between Hephthalites and Khazars. The institution of polyandry is said to be characteristic of the Khazars, or at least attested among them, as well as among the Hephthalites.[83] But unless the text of Priscus is seriously defective, the Kidarites are perfectly distinct from the Akatzirs (Akattirs, Akatirs), of whom he also speaks. If the Kidarites are the Khazars, the Akatzirs apparently are not.

To resume the argument, Qubād (488-531), like his father Fīrūz, was concerned with the defense of Darband. It is repeatedly mentioned that he built a brickwork defense in the region of the Caucasus.[84] He sent one of his generals against the Khazars, who at that time occupied Jurzān (Georgia) and Arrān (Albania),[85] south of the range. Much of this territory is said to have been wrested from them. Then Qubād, following his general, himself built in Arrān the cities, afterwards important, Baylaqān, Bardha'ah, and Qabalah. This notice is due to Balādhuri, usually regarded as a good early authority (died 279/892). More remarkable is the following from Ya'qūbi (died after 278/891): "The Khazars were they who conquered all the lands of Armenia. Over them was a king called Khaqan. He had a representative [*khalīfah*] called Y-z-?-d ?-lāsh over

81 *Ibid.*, 161.

82 *Ibid.*, 165.

83 Marquart, *Historische Glossen*, 200; cf. Zeki Validi, *Ibn-Faḍlān*, 131.

84 Balādhuri, 194; ibn-Khurdādhbih, 123. According to Balādhuri it stretched between the province of Shirwān (on the Caspian) and Bāb al-Lān (pass of Darial in the middle Caucasus).

85 Balādhuri, *loc.cit.* Cf. ibn-Khurdādhbih, 122: The provinces of Arrān, Jurzān, and Sīsajān were in the Khazar kingdom (*mamlakah*).

Arrān, Jurzān, Busfurrajān and Sīsajān. These provinces were called the Fourth Armenia, which was conquered by Qubād, king of Persia, and passed to Anūshirwān [i.e., his son], as far as Bāb al-Lān for a thousand parasangs, including three hundred and sixty towns. The Persian king conquered Bāb al-Abwāb, Ṭabarsarān and Balanjar. He built the town of Qālīqala and many others, and colonized them with Persians. Then the Khazars reconquered what the Persians had taken from them, and it remained in their hands for a time, till the Romans defeated them and appointed a king over the Fourth Armenia."[86] The first part of this notice apparently refers to the time of Qubād. We seem to be told that the Khazar Khaqan's deputy, i.e., presumably the Beg, until defeated by the Persians, was in control of part of Armenia. At first sight, there is no reason to doubt the historic character of the notice, supported as it is by Balādhuri and ibn-Khurdādhbih. As to the title or personal name of the deputy, it should certainly be Turkish, like the rest of the Khazar nomenclature known to us. (Houtsma's restoration of the first part as Yazīd is not at all satisfactory.) The second part of the notice refers to the situation on the Khazar frontier at a later period, shortly before the coming of the Arabs. On this showing, the notice would give the first certain appearance of the Khazars, raiding or migrating en masse south of the Caucasus, as we meet them later on various occasions. The date would be not later than 531 (death of Qubād). Moreover, the notice would give the existence of the Khazar Khaqanate, and even the double kingship, at this time.

This is very difficult. It is not simply that the Khazar Khaqan and his representative are not named distinctly in the existing sources till much later. The existence of a Khaqan among a Turkish people is usually understood to mean their sovereignty and independence. When next the Khazars appear, it is as part of the West Turk confederation, marching under West Turk leadership. In addition, if the notice in Ya'qūbi is to be taken at its face value, the Khazars, complete with Khaqan and

[86] *Historiae*, ed. Houtsma, I, 203-204.

deputy, make their appearance while as yet there is no such thing as a West Turk empire, before even the original Turkish federation had come into being (A.D. 552). While the Khazars may have existed in the west before this time, it seems practically certain that their emergence as a power was connected with the decline of the West Turks. The rule of the West Turk Kagans (Khaqans) lasted till A.D. 657 or 659, when they were crushed by the Chinese.[87] It is from this point onward that one would expect to find a Khaqanate among the Khazars.[88] Later investigation may confirm the surprising statements of Ya'qūbi. Meanwhile, an explanation of them may be suggested along the lines of what we already know. The context of Ya'qūbi's notice is a genealogy of the northern peoples, of which the source is not stated,[89] but which links up with genealogies given by Hishām al-Kalbi.[90] It is reasonable to suppose that the latter is Ya'qūbi's authority, especially as elsewhere Hishām al-Kalbi mentions the Khaqan of the Khazars.[91] This gives us a much more credible order of dating for the existence of the Khazar double kingship. Al-Kalbi's principal authority was his father, who died in 146/763. He himself survived till 204/819.[92] A date three centuries before this is almost certainly much too early. On the other hand, it is hardly by chance that the Khazars begin to be mentioned in the reigns of Qubād and Anūshirwān (531-579). The growing number of increasingly precise indications seems to prove that they are indeed upon the scene.[93]

Ṭabari[94] tells us that Anūshirwān divided his empire into

[87] Chavannes, *Documents*, 267-268.

[88] Zeki Validi (*Ibn-Faḍlān*, 293) claims that the tradition of the Khaqanate among the Khazars is older than the West Turks, on the basis of the "Urgeschichte" of the Turks (see above) and archaic features in the Khazar constitution.

[89] Cf. Marquart, *Streifzüge*, 491. [90] E.g. Ṭabari, I, 218ff.

[91] See *supra*, nn. 53, 54.

[92] Dates from Brockelmann, *G.A.L.*, I, 139.

[93] A genuine Pehlevi reference to the Khazars may be in the *Bahman Yasht*, dated to about this period. See H. W. Bailey, "Iranica," *B.S.O.A.S.*, XI, i (1943), 1-2.

[94] I, 894-895, apparently part of an official directive to the Persian

four great provinces or satrapies, one of which was Ādharbayjān and its neighborhood, "the country of the Khazars." He was engaged with "a nation called Ṣūl," surely inhabitants of the eastern extremity of the Caucasus, in the neighborhood of the "pass of Ṣūl" (Darband). He defeated the B-n-j-r,[95] Balanjar and another people who may be the Khazars[96] (if so, as yet distinct from the others), when they raided Armenia, and settled 10,000 of the survivors in Ādharbayjān. He built Bāb al-Abwāb, to call the place by its later Arabic name, a fortress and city whose purpose was to stem the tide of northern invasion—a purpose which on the whole it served well in succeeding centuries.

The figure of Anūshirwān attracted the interest of storytellers. In Qudāmah[97] and Yāqūt[98] we find the following. Anūshirwān feared the hostility of the Khazars and wrote to their king, asking for reconciliation and an alliance. To this end he requested a Khazar princess in marriage and offered to send his own daughter in exchange. The Khazar agreed to the overture. Anūshirwān in due course received his bride. But the girl he sent in return was not of royal race. The two rulers then met at a place called Barshalīyah, where entertainments went on in apparent friendliness for several days. Then Anūshirwān caused part of the Khazar camp to be set on fire and, when the king complained, denied all knowledge. He then ordered his own camp to be fired and the next day went to the Khazars in pretended anger, declaring that they suspected his good faith. Finally he said that though there might be friendship between himself and his brother, there could never be peace between

governor of Ādharbayjān and Armenia (cf. *ibid.*, 892), and in any case from a Pehlevi source (see below).

95 Perhaps to be read with Marquart (*Streifz.*, 16) as Burgar, a Pehlevi form for Bulgar, or right as it stands for the people elsewhere called W-n-nd-r. The meaning in either case would be much the same. See Chapter III.

96 Text of Leiden ed. of Ṭabari (here Nöldeke) has "Abkhāz," but cf. Marquart, *Streifzüge*, 16 and the references in n. 3, *ibid.*

97 *B.G.A.*, VI, 259ff. The same text practically *verbatim* in Balādhuri, 195-196, with "Turks" for "Khazars."

98 *Buldān*, s.v. Bāb al-Abwāb.

the armies, and it was therefore best that a wall should be built to separate them. The Khazar king agreed and left the Persians free to fortify Darband. Later he was told that Anūshirwān had deceived him in the matter of the marriage and had built the wall against him. But in spite of his rage he could do nothing.

It seems very probable that this story or something like it is the "famous stratagem" to which Mas'ūdi refers. It is demonstrably not historical. The incident reported by the Greek Priscus as having happened in the reign of Fīrūz is the basis of the first part of the story.[99] It is transferred to Anūshirwān, because he married a daughter of the Kagan of the West Turks, Sinjibu (Istämi).[100] That Anūshirwān was responsible for building the "Wall of Darband" as part of his defense arrangements on the Caucasus is not doubtful, but the circumstances given in the second part of the story are fictitious. The difference between legend and historical record is shown by another quotation from Ṭabari.[101] "Sinjibu Khāqān was the strongest and bravest of the Turks and possessed the best-equipped armies. It was he who killed W-z-r, king of the Hephthalites, in spite of their numbers and power.[102] Having slain their king and the greatest part of their armies, he took possession of their territories. He won over [*istamāla*] the B-n-j-r, Balanjar and the Khazars[103] (?), who accorded him their obedience, and informed him that the kings of Persia were in the habit of paying them money, on condition of their not raiding Persian territory. Subsequently, Sinjibu advanced with a large army until he was near Ṣūl [Darband] and sent a message to Khusraw Anūshirwān demanding the money which had formerly been paid to the three peoples already mentioned, threatening that if it was not quickly forthcoming he would invade Persian territory. But Anūshirwān, having already fortified the pass

[99] See above.
[100] Cf. Marquart, *Historische Glossen*, 199.
[101] I, 895-896, continuing the Pehlevi source referred to in n. 94.
[102] Cf. Chavannes, *Documents*, 226.
[103] Text "Abkhāz," cf. n. 96.

of Ṣūl and secure in the knowledge that he could defend the frontier of Armenia with 5,000 men, made no reply. When news reached Sinjibu Khāqān of the fortification of the frontier he and his troops retired to their own country."

This undoubtedly has an air of authenticity which is lacking in the tale in Qudāmah, etc. On the basis of it, one may affirm that certain groups later within the Khazar empire, and perhaps the Khazars themselves, were ranged under West Turkish leadership against the Persians at a time which is determined by the defeat of the Hephthalites, circa A.D. 567,[104] and the death of Sinjibu, A.D. 575 or 576.[105] In the latter year a West Turkish force was sent by the son of Sinjibu to join the Utigurs, then besieging the Crimean town of Bosporus[106] (Panticapaeum, Kertch). Clearly at this period the West Turks were operating extensively north of the Caucasus. But the meeting at Barshalīyah of Anūshirwān and a king of the Khazars or Turks, as described in the composite narrative of Qudāmah, is not confirmed.

Other stories are told of Anūshirwān. When the Wall of Darband had been built, a throne was set upon a spur of the mountain, overlooking the sea, and as Anūshirwān sat upon it, there appeared a monster, gifted with speech, which addressed him and declared that it had seen this frontier closed seven times and laid open as often, but Anūshirwān was he who was destined to close the pass forever. Scarcely less wonderful is the tale that after completing the Wall, Anūshirwān made enquiries about the Caspian. He learned that al-Bayḍā' of the Khazars lay four months' distance along the coast and determined to see this for himself. Undissuaded by those who told him that in the Caspian to the north was a dangerous whirlpool, the Lion's Mouth, which no ship might escape, he set sail and reached the whirlpool. Here he was in danger of perishing, but was miraculously delivered, reached his goal,

[104] Chavannes, *loc.cit.*
[105] Chavannes, 242.
[106] Menander Prot., ed. Bonn, 404; cf. Chavannes, 241.

and in due course returned safely.[107] These stories in the best style of Oriental romance are simply embellishments of the fact that Anūshirwān fortified the pass of Darband. The place-names will meet us later.

Anūshirwān was succeeded by his son Hormuz (579-590). Not only did Hormuz make war against Sinjibu Khāqān during his father's lifetime,[108] but later, when himself king of Persia, he was called on to meet a great coalition, headed, we are told, by the Shāhān-Shāh of the Turks, and including the Greeks and the Khazars.[109] Hormuz wrote to the Greek Emperor, offering in exchange for peace the return of towns which his father had conquered, and the proposal was accepted. He next directed his generals to advance against the chief of the Khazars (*ṣāḥib al-Khazar*), who was driven from Persian territory. Hormuz was thus left free to turn his attention to the Turks. The interest of this narrative is chiefly in the relation of the Khazars to the Turks. They appear to march at Turkish orders, and to belong to the West Turkish empire. There is at all events no reason to suppose that at this date they were independent. The attack on Persia is put in the 11th year of the reign of Hormuz, i.e., something like A.D. 589.

With the reign of Hormuz we have reached a point where references to the Khazars have begun in other sources, notably the Syriac writers Michael and "Zacharias Rhetor."[110] Let us see what the Greek author Procopius has to say about the inhabitants of the lands north of the Caucasus in his own time, the first half of the 6th century. According to Procopius, the Alans and the Abkhazians, who were Christians and had long been friends of the Romans, lived in this region together with the Zichs (Circassians), and beyond were the Sabir Huns,

[107] Ibn-al-Faqīh, 289.

[108] Dīnawari, 69ff. Mīrkhwānd, who quotes Dīnawari by name, substitutes for Sinjibu Khāqān "the Khaqan of China" (transl. Rehatsek, I, ii, 375). Cf. below.

[109] Dīnawari, 81. Ṭabari (I, 991) adds that at the same time the Arabs attacked in the south.

[110] See above.

mentioned with other Hunnic nations. During the reign of the Emperor Anastasius (491-518), the Hun Ambazuk held the Caspian Gates (Darband) and was succeeded on his death by one Kabad. Procopius speaks of the Sabirs as living in the neighborhood of the Caucasus in very large numbers and divided into many separate groups.[111] Of the Khazars as such he appears to know nothing.

The term Sabir is new in our discussion, but Procopius is neither the first nor the only author to mention the Sabirs. According to Priscus,[112] they made their appearance on the confines of Europe in the 5th century (before 465), having been forced from their territories in the east by the Avars. In the next century Jordanes refers to them as one of the two great branches of the Huns.[113] What Procopius says of them is so far confirmed by Theophanes, according to whom they passed through the Caspian Gates about 514 and invaded Cappadocia and Galatia.[114]

The Sabirs then should be the enemy opposed to the Persians along their northwest frontier for a considerable period, before the appearance of the West Turks, and even later. After the second half of the 6th century they are no longer mentioned in the sources as a national group, and it is probably significant that about 576 a section, or perhaps the remnants of them, were transplanted south of the Kur river by the Greeks.[115] The suggestion is that about this time the Khazars asserted their leadership of the tribes north of the Caucasus, for while there remains some doubt as to the earlier references to the Khazars in this quarter, there can be none later. Masʿūdi (10th century) says that the Khazars are called in Turkish Sabīr,[116] and this identification is perhaps implicit in Maḥmūd al-Kashgari[117] (11th century). Originally

[111] Procopius, *Hist.* II, XXIX, 15; VIII, iii, 5; I, x, 9-12; VIII, XI, 23.

[112] Ed. Bonn, 158. Cf. D. Sinor, "Autour d'une migration de peuples au Ve siècle." *J.A.*, t. 235 (1946-1947), 1-77.

[113] *Getica*, ed. Mommsen, 63.

[114] Ed. Bonn, 249.

[115] Menander Prot., 394.

[116] *Tanbīh*, 83.

[117] Cf. Zeki Validi, *Ibn-Faḍlān*, 203.

the two groups were different.[118] That they could later be identified is perhaps best explained by assuming that the Khazars submerged the Sabirs. In any case, an important reconstitution of the tribes seems to have taken place north of the Caucasus at the end of the 6th or the beginning of the 7th century. Not only the Sabirs, but apparently others also, cease to appear in the sources under their old names (Saragur, Utigur, Samandar, Balanjar, etc.). This can hardly be fortuitous. It is no doubt to be connected with the increasing prestige of the Khazars.

For the events which brought them into contact with the Greek Emperor Heraclius we are comparatively well informed from a variety of sources, Greek, Armenian, and Georgian. In A.D. 627 Heraclius was at Tiflis, on one of his expeditions against Persia which he had undertaken as a diversion to the Persian invasion of his own country. Here he was met by the Khazars, who, under their chief Ziebel, second in dignity to the Khaqan, had forced the Ċaspian Gates and marched to the rendezvous. Gibbon has given a description in brilliant colors of the reception of Heraclius by the Khazars.[119] Ziebel presented his son to Heraclius, assigned 40,000 men to the Emperor's service, then withdrew to his own country. Heraclius himself pressed on with the Khazar contingent into Persian territory. As winter approached, and the allies were being sharply attacked by the Persians, the Khazars with Heraclius gradually fell away, perhaps impatient of the Greek method of conducting the war. Heraclius continued to advance with the imperial troops, until, when he was within three days' march of Ctesiphon, the Persian capital, a revolution broke out which precipitated the death of Khusraw. His son hastened to treat with Heraclius, who in 628 began his return march.[120]

The Armenian account is somewhat different.[121] In 625 the

[118] Chazirk' and Savirk' quite distinct in the Armenian Geography ascribed to Moses of Chorene (Marquart, *Streifz.*, 57ff).

[119] *Decline and Fall of the Roman Empire*, c. 46.

[120] Theophanes, ed. Bonn, 485ff.; cf. Chavannes, *Documents*, 252ff.

[121] Moses of Kaghankaytuk (Kalankatuk). See Patkanian in *J.A.*, VI,

Khazars broke into Armenia and, having amassed great booty, returned by way of Darband. In consequence the Khazar king decided the next year to take the field in person. Orders were given to all under his authority, "tribes and peoples, inhabitants of the mountains and the plains, living under roofs or the open sky, having the head shaved or wearing their hair long," to be ready to march at a given signal. When the time came, the Khazars put themselves in motion. They took and destroyed the fortress of Tzur (Darband), to construct which the Persian kings had spared no effort or expense, and, proceeding southward, massacred the inhabitants and plundered the wealth of the country till they reached Tiflis. Here, as already mentioned, they met Heraclius. The two armies, acting in concert, set siege to Tiflis, which was on point of yielding when a strong reinforcement succeeded in entering the town. The allies decided to retire, on the understanding that they should join forces again the following year. After this, apparently in 626, the Emperor sent Andreas, one of his lords, to negotiate with the Khazars. In order that agreement might be reached on the final conditions, a corps of 1,000 Khazar horsemen visited Constantinople. These negotiations, if authentic, should evidently be set before the meeting at Tiflis. In the next year, A.D. 627, the "King of the North" sent the troops promised under the command of his brother's son, who was called Shath (Shad), and they ravaged Arrān and Ādharbayjān.

In 628, according to the same account, the Khazars entered Arrān and, having taken Bardha'ah, turned west towards Tiflis, under the command of Jebu Khaqan and his son. They surrounded and set siege to the Georgian city, and were soon joined by Heraclius and his Greeks, fresh from their triumph in Persia. But the city resisted the combined assault, and both armies withdrew. Some time later under Jebu Khaqan and his son Shath the Khazars actually took Tiflis. When it fell, two of the chiefs were brought before Jebu Khaqan, who treated them

vii (1866), 205ff.; Chavannes, *ibid.* Moses of K. wrote in the 10th century (Minorsky, *Ḥudūd*, 398).

with abominable cruelty, causing them to be blinded and racked, with other tortures, and finally exposing them on the walls of the city. The source adds that the "King of the North" took tribute from the smelters of gold and silver (?), the miners of iron and the fishers of the river Kur, and that in 629-630 the Khazar king prepared a great invasion, sending in advance 3,000 horses commanded by the general Chorpan Tarkhan. Ten thousand Persians were defeated, and the invaders spread through Armenia, Georgia, and Arrān.

It is not necessary to attempt to bring these accounts into strict agreement. Of considerable importance to our investigation is, however, the identification, if possible, of the leaders on the Khazar side. After mentioning that Heraclius sought an alliance with "the Turks from the East, whom they call Khazars," Theophanes says that the "Khazars" broke through the Caspian Gates under "their general Ziebel, being second to the Khaqan in dignity." Ziebel at Tiflis presents his son, a beardless boy, to Heraclius. Later in the account the Khazars are referred to simply as "Turks." The Armenian account says that the "King of the North" sent troops under his brother's son, who was called Shath (Shad), and that later Jebu Khaqan and his son Shath ravaged Georgia and Arrān. On this showing, Ziebel is for Jebu, Ziebel's son is Shath (Shad) and the "King of the North" is the Khazar Khaqan. As there is no doubt that Jebu (cf. Georgian Jibghu)[122] is the Turkish title Yabgu, assigned to brothers and sons of the sovereign, we get Ziebel as a Khazar Yabgu. But there are serious objections to this. If Ziebel is precisely second in rank to the Khazar Khaqan (whose existence has not been established up to this time), he corresponds to the Khazar Beg, who should be of a different family from the Khaqan, as we know from later Arabic sources.[123] Ziebel is identified with Jebu Khaqan. How does a subordinate bear the supreme title? It seems, moreover, that

[122] The Georgian Chronicle gives an account of these events (in Brosset, *Histoire de la Géorgie*, I, 227-229), but as Marquart remarks (*Streifz.*, 394, n. 2) it is secondary.

[123] See Chapter V.

the Armenian account only in appearance distinguishes between Jebu Khaqan and the "King of the North,"[124] the king of Khazaria. This is not reconcilable with Theophanes, according to whom Ziebel/Jebu is "second in dignity to the Khaqan." Ziebel, in fact, is neither the Khaqan of Khazaria nor bearer of a subordinate title among them (Beg, Yabgu).

The writer of the Armenian account knows of a single chief, whom he calls Jebu, i.e.,Yabgu, Khaqan and erroneously identifies with the king of the Khazars. But Yabgu Khaqan was the title of the rulers of the West Turks,[125] from the days of Sinjibu (Sin, or Sir, Yabgu). Ziebel then is the ruler of the West Turks, a paramount chief, but still second in dignity, as Theophanes says, to the supreme Khaqan of the Turks. He is perhaps to be identified with the Khaqan of the West Turks mentioned in the Chinese sources as T'ong che-hou (T'ong Yabgu), whose headquarters were in the region of the Chu and Ṭarāz (Talas) valleys, north of Tashkent.[126] The situation in 627 is then as we seem to have seen it before: Khazars marching under West Turkish leadership. There is no evidence in the passage for the existence as yet of the Khazar Khaqan or Beg.

This conclusion will be reinforced by the observation that while the title Yabgu may be traced back to the Hiung-nu (Huns) and is found apparently among the Avars, as well as the West Turks and other Turkish nations,[127] it scarcely appears among the Khazars. In the extensive Arabic accounts of wars with the Khazars, not to mention any of the other sources, the title, so far as the present writer is aware, does not occur. The only reference to a Yabgu among the Khazars seems to be a passage in the Persian historian Mīrkhwānd (15th century), where in connection with the rise of the Seljuks mention is made of "the king of the Khazars designated Payghu," for

[124] Cf. Chavannes, *Documents*, 255, n. 3.
[125] Chavannes, 38, n. 5.
[126] Marquart, *Streifz.*, 498; Chavannes, *Documents*, 52.
[127] Pelliot, "L'origine des T'ou kiue," *T'oung Pao*, 1915, 688, n. 5; Zeki Validi, *Ibn-Faḍlān*, 140.

"Yabghu."[128] Mīrkhwānd, however, is no authority on such matters. In an earlier version of the same story an ancestor of the Seljuks (Tuqāq, a chief of the Ghuzz) quarrels with "Paighu, king of the Turks."[129] There is no doubt that this is his own superior, the Yabgu of the Ghuzz.[130]

There is one other point. The Armenian writer Sebeos mentions a "Khaqan of the Northern Lands," together with his general, the latter designated Chepetukh (evidently Yabgu) of Chenastan (China), as receiving certain Armenians who later passed Darband, going to the help of Heraclius.[131] This appears to be an obscure reference to the events of A.D. 627. In the expression "Chenastan Chepetukh" we seem bound to see the same original form as in "Sinjibu." Sebeos appears to have interpreted the first part of the latter name as Sin=China. This is interesting as affording an explanation of references in the *Darband Nāmah* to a mysterious Khāqān-i Chīn (Khaqan of China), who is said to have assisted the Khazars against the Muslims circa A.H.32/A.D.652.[132] But apart from these two texts there is no evidence of the existence of any Turkish ruler Sinjibu after the 6th century. Mention of the name later should be due to anachronism.

In summing up the results of this chapter, we may say that a survey of the available evidence brings to light no positive trace of the Khazars before the 6th century. In the second half of the century—i.e., coincident with the rise of the Turkish power—they are first unmistakably mentioned. In the first half of the 7th century they are still under West Turkish domination. Later, but within the same century, they enjoy full in-

128 Cited Von Stackelberg, *W.Z.K.M.*, XVII, 58.

129 Ibn-al-Athīr, IX, 162, *s. ann.* 432.

130 See below, Chapter IX.

131 Patkanian, *ibid.*, 196; cf. Chavannes, *Documents*, 255, n. 3.

132 Ed. Kasem Beg, 494. Kasem Beg states (*ibid.*, 501) that according to "Ṭabari" the Khazars about twenty years later, having invaded Ādharbayjān, solicited the aid of the Emperor of China against the Arabs. Kasem Beg's "Ṭabari" is a Turkish version of Balʿami, where the passage in question is given, referring to the expedition of Jarrāḥ (considerably more than "twenty years later"). See below, Chapter IV.

dependence of action, as we shall see. The Khazar connection with the West Turks is not unambiguous, but in view of what has been said there is no doubt that it existed. This cannot be affirmed with confidence of a possible relation through the Akatzirs with the Huns or the conjectured affinity with the Hephthalites.

CHAPTER II

A THEORY OF THE UIGUR ORIGIN OF THE KHAZARS

THE NAME Turk first became known through the rise in the 6th century of the great power to which we have already referred. It is applied legitimately to groups belonging to the same racial family which have appeared at different times. That the Khazars were Turkish in this broader sense, and not Finnish (Finno-Ugrian) as used to be thought,[1] nor Japhetic, proto-Caucasian,[2] etc., admits of no doubt. The titles of their leaders, the existence of a double kingship, and much else besides are not otherwise to be explained. We have to enquire if there is one or more of the kindred peoples to which the Khazars are more particularly to be attached.

A good deal of evidence appears to connect the Khazars with the Uigurs. The latter people existed before and after the empire of the Turks in the east, and we know about them from Chinese records as well as from the old Turkish inscriptions. For the existence of the Uigurs in the west we have a number of passages in the Byzantine writers. It is convenient to examine some Chinese sources first.[3]

According to Gibbon, the Khazars were known to the Chinese as Kosa, and he quotes for this at first sight surprising statement the well-known *Histoire des Huns* by De Guignes.[4] De Guignes derived the equation Kosa=Khazars from the *Wên-hsièn t'ung-k'ao*, the final redaction of which is dated A.D.

1 E.g., Klaproth in *J.A.*, I, iii, 160, but also much later.

2 Bashmakov, *loc.cit.*, cf. N. Slouschz in *Mélanges H. Derenbourg*. Even Dubnov (*Weltgeschichte des jüdischen Volkes*, Berlin, n.d., IV, 247) thinks of the Khazars as coming from the south of the Caucasus, but rightly regards them as Turks.

3 Professor Haloun was kind enough to supply practically all the following information about the Chinese sources.

4 *Decline and Fall of the Roman Empire*, c. 46.

1322. This gives an article on Fu-lin or Rūm, the Byzantine empire, taken verbally from an earlier Chinese work, the *T'ung-tien*, written in the period 766-801. The source quoted for this part of the Fu-lin article is the narrative of a certain Tu Huan, who had fallen into Arab captivity at the battle of Ṭarāz (Talas) in 751 and returned to China in 762.[5] Tu Huan had evidently heard about the Khazars as northern neighbors of the Arabs and distinctly refers to them as the K'o-sa Turks, in connection with Chan[6] (Shām, Syria) as well as Fu-lin[7] (Rūm). Similarly in the *T'ang-shu*, in 945 or 1060 according to the date of its two versions, the K'o-sa Turks are mentioned as lying to the north of the Byzantine empire,[8] Khwārizm[9] and Persia.[10] In the notice relative to Khwārizm the name appears with a somewhat different orthography as Ho-sa Turks.[11]

In the Chinese sources there appears to be nothing which would lead us to suppose that the expressions already mentioned "Chenastan Chepetukh" and "Khaqan of China" indicate Chinese activity in the vicinity of the Caspian, or are to be explained otherwise than as due to confusion with Sinjibu (?Sin Yabgu). But we learn from these sources that the sixth of the nine primitive Uigur tribes was called Ko-sa.[12] Is Ko-sa the same as K'o-sa=Khazars? This is a very attractive equation. It has been made in effect by E. H. Parker, who, speaking of the Ko-sa in connection with certain Shado Turks, says, "They would seem to have mostly migrated west, for the History of the T'ang dynasty [he means the passages from the

5 Hirth and Rockhill, *Chao Ju-kua*, 108ff; Pelliot, "Les artisans chinois à la capitale abbaside en 751-762," *T'oung Pao*, XXVI (1928-1929), 110ff.

6 *Wên-hsièn t'ung-k'ao*, 339, 19b=*T'ung-tien*, 193, 24a. Professor Haloun translated: "The country of Chan is situated on the western borders of the Ta-shih [Abbasids] . . . in the north it is limitrophe to the K'o-sa Turks. To the north of the K'o-sa there are still other Turks."

7 *Wên-hsièn t'ung-k'ao*, 339, 3a=*T'ung-tien*, 193, 11b, translated by Hirth, *China and the Roman Orient*, 83.

8 *T'ang-shu*, 221, translated Hirth, *ibid.*, 56.

9 *T'ang-shu*, 221b, 27, translated Bretschneider, *Researches*, II, 93, and Chavannes, *Documents*, 145.

10 *T'ang-shu*, 221b, 64, translated Chavannes, *ibid.*, 170.

11 This may possibly point to a tradition independent of Tu Huan.

12 Chavannes, *Documents*, 94.

T'ang-shu quoted above] gives a Khazar race northwest of the Arabs."[13] It may be remarked that according to Parker the Shado Turks were West Turks.[14] More recently Paul Pelliot said explicitly that in his opinion we have the same name in Khazar and Ko-sa, the Uigur tribe, citing other authorities and a number of relevant facts.[15]

From the inscriptions, we know that the Uigurs existed in the time of the Turkish empire. In 742 they formed part of the coalition which destroyed the East Turkish power, and thereafter took the leadership on the river Orkhon till 840.[16] But they certainly are to be found in the records of the Far East much earlier, at the head of a great confederation under the later Wei,[17] and possibly even before this at the time of the first Wei (227-264).[18] According to one of the versions of the *T'ang-shu*, they were descended from the Hiung-nu[19] (Huns). These facts are to be connected with what is said by the Byzantine authors. We have already alluded to the passage in Priscus about the appearance of the Sabirs circa 463. At that time the ambassadors of three peoples, the Saragurs, Onogurs, and another, probably the Uigurs,[20] felt themselves threatened, and applied to the Greeks for assistance. They are evidently represented as in the neighborhood of Byzantium, and are presumably still there a century later, when the tribes descended from Var and Hunni, calling themselves Avars but really Uigurs, first arrived from the east in 558.[21] For we hear that the newcomers caused great alarm on their appearance among the Barselt (Barsilians) Onogurs and Sabirs,[22] and in a

13 *A Thousand Years of the Tatars*, ed. 2, 198.

14 *Ibid.*, 180.

15 *Noms turcs*, 208, n. 1.

16 Minorsky, *Ḥudūd*, 264.

17 Chavannes, *Documents*, 87-89.

18 Marquart, *Streifz.*, 45.

19 Chavannes, *loc.cit.*

20 Priscus, ed. Bonn, 158 *Ourōgoi*, hence Artamonov, 135, Urogs, but rather read *Ougōroi*. It seems superfluous to suppose that these tribes are Ogurs(?) not Uigurs, when we have Sari Uigurs and On Uigurs vouched for in the Far East later (cf. e.g. Minorsky, *Ḥudūd*, 264-5, 509).

21 See Chapter I.

22 Theophylact Sim., ed. Bonn, 284 (correct *Sarsēlt*).

parallel account they attack the Utigurs and Sabirs.[23] It looks uncommonly like a situation in which successive groups of Uigurs from before 465 have migrated westward, till they are well within the boundaries of Europe. Certainly we read of Uigurs west of the Volga in 569,[24] and of a force of Utigurs besieging Bosporus (Kertch) in 576,[25] in both cases as subject to the West Turks. Apparently the process was not complete till 598, when other "Varchonites" arrived in Europe, as we have seen.[26]

Certainly not all the Uigurs withdrew to the west. What we seem to find is that within the territory controlled by the Turks, and perhaps beyond it, there was a population which was alien, and which appears moreover to have had a great defeat and massacre to avenge.[27] It is hardly fortuitous that the destruction of the West Turks in 652-657, as of the East Turks later, was brought about by a coalition of which the Uigurs formed part. We know that the West Turk power was replaced by that of the Khazars not long afterwards. It appears that the Khazars, supported by other groups, e.g., Zabender (Samandar), Kotzagers (Bulgars),[28] now made rapid strides to empire.[29]

[23] Menander Prot., 284. [24] *Ibid.*, 301. [25] *Ibid.*, 404; cf. 399.

[26] It is here assumed that such names as Saragurs, Onogurs, Utigurs involve the same component and could be rendered respectively "Yellow Uigurs," "Ten Uigurs," "Three (?) Uigurs." Cf. Zeki Validi, *Ibn-Faḍlān*, 271.

[27] Theophylact, 285, where the proper name Kolkh should refer to the chief of the Uigurs, as Gibbon took it (*Decline and Fall*, c. 42), rather than to an unknown Turkish nation. Cf. Marquart, *Historische Glossen*, 170; Chavannes, *Documents*, 251.

[28] See Chapter I.

[29] The problem of the Khazar Khaqanate seems connected with the Khaqanate of the Avars (pseudo-Avars), who since circa 558 had been devastating the lands of Europe. The "Varchonites" who came in 598 are said to have joined the Avar Khaqan, but not all can have done so. Either *1*, there was a ruling family among the Khazars in the west from an early period (? of the Achena house, cf. *Ḥudūd al-'Ālam*, 162); or *2*, the Khazar Khaqanate is connected with the second influx of "Varchonites" in 598; or *3*, the Khazars invented a Khaqanate (? in imitation of the Avars). Of these, *2* seems likeliest, cf. Samandar (*Zabender*) as the first Khazar capital (text of Mas'ūdi in Chapter VII). The date of the Khaqanate should no doubt be *post* rather than *ante* the events of 652-657. On the other hand, the Ya'qūbi notice of the Khazar Khaqan

It is conceivable that the *de facto* Khazar leadership before and after 657 was more readily acquiesced in if they represented a tribe (Ko-sa) of an earlier ruling race. The doubtful heredity of the "Varchonites" connects them with less honorable progenitors.[30]

The argument that the Khazars may be the Ko-sa Uigurs is offered tentatively, in the absence of demonstrative proof. It is supported by a variety of considerations, which cumulatively, perhaps, have a certain weight and may now be considered.

Corroboration of an earlier stratum of Uigurs in what came to be known as Khazaria is perhaps to be found in the story from Michael Syrus and Bar Hebraeus, mentioned in the previous chapter. A people called Puguraya or Panguraya is there represented as one of the nations which before the advent of the Khazars and Bulgars had occupied eastern Europe. Nothing can be made of the form as it stands, and various attempts have been made to render it intelligible. The early editors of Bar Hebraeus, Bruns and Kirsch, rendered "Hungarians," Wallis Budge "Pangurians" (?) and Marquart proposed a modification of the text to give "the people of Balanjar."[31] Of these much the most plausible is the last, but since elsewhere Bar Hebraeus has a similar word for Uigurs, it should perhaps also be read here.[32] These Uigurs would be those already settled in Europe, as we seem to find them in the Greek sources.

Again, among the high dignitaries of the Khazar state, according to ibn-Faḍlān, we find the holder of the title Jāwshygh-r. It is possible that the last part of the term is precisely Uigur, and it has been explained as Chāvush Uigur, perhaps "marshal of the Uigurs." The alternative explanations seem labored.[33]

---

and his deputy could refer to the years before the coming of the Arabs (circa 642). As there was apparently no Khazar Khaqan in 627-630 (see Chapter I), the office may have arisen, if not post 657, in the decade 630-640.

[30] Cf. Chavannes, *Documents*, 88n. [31] *Streifz.*, 491.

[32] Bar Hebraeus, ed. Budge, fol. 126a, 1.7 infra: Īguraya.

[33] Zeki Validi (*Ibn-Faḍlān*, 261) suggests Jāwlishagir, a combination

There are some parallels between the ceremonial of the Khazar Khaqan, as described by ibn-Faḍlān,[34] and an account of the king of the Toghuzghuz,[35] which may be adduced here. It is generally allowed that Toghuzghuz in Arabic sources means the Uigurs.[36] Here the Uigurs of the Tien Shan (from circa 860) seem to be intended.[37] Their king, like the Khazar Khaqan, does not rule himself. "All the affairs of his kingdom are in the hands of his viziers and chamberlains." The Khazar Khaqan has sixty slave-girls, the king of the Toghuzghuz (three hundred and) sixty. The king of the Toghuzghuz sees the common people once a year. According to ibn-Faḍlān, the Khazar Khaqan appears in public only once in four months. When this happens, he like the king of the Toghuzghuz receives the prostrations of his subjects. If what is here said was actually the practice among the Tien Shan Uigurs we should probably be entitled to allow a connection with the Khazars.

As to a possible linguistic connection between Uigurs and Khazars, the existing monuments of the Uigur dialect offer no support for it. It is commonly accepted that the Khazar dialect belonged to the so-called aberrant branch, conveniently called "Lir" Turkish, as opposed to "Shaz" Turkish,[38] represented by nearly all known Turkish dialects. The Uigur dialect as known is "Shaz" Turkish.[39] There is no evidence that it ever was anything else. It is conceivable, however, that the "Lir" Turkish at a remote period was widely spoken, and if the Uigur/Khazar

---

of two titles found among the Qara-Khānids, Jawli Bek and Jagri Bek. Zajączkowski, *Studies*, 34-35, 97 offers *jarashgir*, from *yarash*, *jarash*, "reconcile," a nominal form in *-gir* in the sense of "arbiter," "judge."

[34] See translation in Chapter V.

[35] From a Risālah fi-al-Aqālīm (Treatise on the Climes), MS. Köprülü 1623, cited Zeki Validi, *Ibn-Faḍlān*, 263, 268.

[36] Marquart's view, corroborated by Minorsky's findings, *Tamīm*, 304.

[37] Cf. Zeki Validi, *Ibn-Faḍlān*, 197n.

[38] The terms are derived from the correspondences in the system sh(a)z ∼ l(i)r, taken to represent the principal phonetic changes between the two groups of languages, cf. Zeki Validi, *Ibn-Faḍlān*, 105. The principle goes back to Ramstedt, see N. Poppe, "Gustav John Ramstedt," *Harvard Journal of Asiatic Studies*, 14 (1951), 319.

[39] E.g.,Samoylovitch in *E.I.*, art. Turks.

relationship was otherwise acceptable, the linguistic argument would not be determinative against it.[40]

We cannot omit mention of the view that the national names of the Bulgars and the Bashkirs are originally the same,[41] corresponding to the differences between "Lir" and "Shaz" Turkish. *Bil* or *biel* is "Lir" Turkish for "Shaz" Turkish *bash*, and the last part of both names is the same *-gur*, *-gir*. Both are interpreted as "Five Ogurs (Uigurs)." If the proposed derivation is right, it gives interesting confirmation of the theory discussed in this chapter, for there is no doubt that the relations between the Khazars and the Bulgars were at all times close.

40 The question of the Khazar language is discussed in later chapters.
41 Munkacsi's view, cited Zeki Validi, *Ibn-Faḍlān*, 147.

CHAPTER III

THE CONSOLIDATION OF THE KHAZAR STATE AND THE FIRST ARAB-KHAZAR WAR (642-652)

THE KHAZARS at first evidently nomadized within relatively narrow limits. We have already met them in the Caucasus. A notice in the *Armenian Geography* speaks of them at an unspecified date as in winter-quarters on the Volga, thereby causing alarm to the Barsilians who fortify themselves on an island in midstream.[1] At one time the Khazars were in close alliance with the Bulgars.[2] We have to think of the Khazars in the territory between the Volga and the Causasus occupying the coastal lands, while the Bulgars are situated farther to the west, with their center in the Kuban river valley. Relations between the two groups did not always remain the same. We must now speak of a great expansion of the Khazars at the cost of the Bulgars, which took place in the course of the 7th century and gave the Khazars direct control of a wide region, at least as far west as the Don and Kuban rivers.

According to the story in Theophanes, the Bulgars (Onogundurs) in the Kuban region had been strongly organized by their ruler Kubrat. On his death towards 650 he left his dominions to five sons, enjoining them to keep together and not seek separate kingdoms. This sound advice they rejected, for, while the eldest brother Batbaias remained in his inheritance, the others separated, the second brother Kotragus crossing the Don and settling opposite Batbaias, the third, Asparukh, occupying lands west of the Dniester, the fourth and fifth going yet farther afield, beyond the Danube. Whereupon the Khazars, described by Theophanes as "a great nation from the in-

[1] Ed. Soukry, 26, 16 (quoted Marquart, *Streifz.*, 57, 154).
[2] Cf. the story of Michael Syrus in Chapter I.

terior of Berzilia in the first Sarmatia," advanced and possessed themselves of all the territory as far as the Black Sea, and rendered tributary those of the former inhabitants who remained.[3] The change of position was complete in 679, when Asparukh crossed the Danube and conquered present-day Bulgaria.[4]

We may remark that this story affords a basis for the view that the name Bulgar means the Five (? Uigurs). According to Constantine Porphyrogenitus, after the events just recorded, the name Onogundur was replaced by Bulgar.[5] This puts the change too late. Plainly, the Onogundurs did not adopt the new name after one or more of their hordes had been subjugated by the Khazars. The Bulgars are distinctly mentioned before this time.[6] The other name is paralleled in an independent account of the events described. It is perhaps an alternative form of Onogur.[7]

The earliest recorded event in the sketch of Khazar history offered by the "Reply of Joseph," a Hebrew document of great interest which will concern us later, is a great Khazar victory over a people called in this source W-n-nt-r. The W-n-nt-r, though more numerous than the Khazars, were unable to stand against them and were pursued by the Khazars as far as the river Dūna (Danube apparently). The survivors were still living on the river Dūna "near Constantinople," beyond the limits of Khazar rule, in the writer's own time. There is no doubt that this is a version of the story given by Theophanes. It is not

[3] Theophanes, ed. Bonn, 544ff; cf. Nicephorus, ed. Bonn, 38ff. Bury (*L.R.E.*, II, 332) thought that this notice puts the events too late by nearly two centuries, cf. also Marquart, *Streifz.*, 505. It seems best to retain the 7th century date with Minorsky, *Ḥudūd*, 467; cf. an indication of Bury's, *ibid.*, 336.

[4] The Armenian Geography, following the same tradition (Marquart, *ibid.*, 529), says that Aspar-hruk (Asparukh) in his flight from the Khazars settled on the island of Peuke in the Danube (ed. Soukry, 17,5;25,25, cited Marquart, *Eranshahr*, 4).

[5] *De Them.*, ed. Bonn, 46.

[6] "Zacharias Rhetor" has Burgārē (Marquart, *Streifz.*, 505).

[7] So J. Moravcsik, *Ungarische Jahrbücher*, x, 72-73 (cited Pritsak in his review of Zajączkowski, *Studies*, *Der Islam*, B. 29, 102).

necessary to show that the change from Onogundur to W-n-nt-r in Hebrew script is feasible, since there is a people W-n-nd-r in the Caucasus, according to the *Ḥudūd al-'Ālam* (10th century), whose presence is best explained as a remnant of the Bulgars.[8] Connected with W-n-nd-r are N-nd-r in Gardīzi,[9] perhaps also W-b-nd-r in ibn-al-Athīr,[10] corresponding to N-ndh-rwayh in Ḥāfiẓ-i Abru,[11] and W-l-nd-r in Mas'ūdi.[12] It seems likely that some or all of these words retain the old name of the Bulgars.

The Reply of Joseph gives no indications as to where the Khazars were before they came to occupy the newly-conquered territory. According to Theophanes they proceeded against the Onogundurs, as already quoted, "from the interior of Berzilia in the first Sarmatia." For Berzilia a parallel account in Nicephorus gives Berylia.[13] Both forms are unknown to classical geography, but the name, which we have already met, can be explained from the Oriental sources.

"Basilians" are mentioned with Khazirs by the *Armenian History*. According to Michael Syrus, the eponymous ancestor of the Khazars came to occupy "the country of the Alans, which is called Barsalia." In the story told by Qudāmah of the meeting between Anūshirwān and the king of the Khazars (according to Balādhuri the king of the Turks) this took place at Barshalīyah or Barsalīyah. These names [14] are to be brought into relation with the Berzilia of Theophanes, and seem to point to a locality in the Caucasus. In the *Armenian Geography* there is mention of a "kingdom of the Huns" north of Darband,[15] with its capital "to the west"[16] at Varach'an. In

[8] Marquart, *Ungarische Jahrbücher*, IV, 275, cited by Zeki Validi, *Völkerschaften*, 48, who, however, finds the identification very questionable. Cf. the long discussion in Minorsky, *Ḥudūd*, 465-471.

[9] Ed. Barthold, 98.

[10] *S. anno* 104.

[11] Cited Dorn, *Bal'ami*, 468n.

[12] The passage is given in translation and discussed below, Chapter VII.

[13] Marquart, *Streifz.*, 490, n. 3, proposed to read Ber(z)ylia.

[14] See Chapter I.

[15] Ed. Soukry, 27, 14 (quoted Marquart, *Streifz.*, 58).

[16] Apparently "west" is south, as "east" is north in the source (the river Atil east of Darband).

Bīrūni later we find a place situated apparently between Baku and Darband called Warathān,[17] and this may be the same. It appears to be mentioned also as War(a)ṣān in one of the Hebrew accounts of the conversion of the Khazars to Judaism.[18] Varach'an (Warathān) may be the same as Barshalīyah. Minorsky has already characterized the identification as very probable.[19] How in this case two forms should have arisen in Arabic is not perfectly clear. Perhaps Warathān represents the native pronunciation of the name, which gave also Armenian Varach'an, while Barshalīyah is an attempt, like Berzilia and Barsalia, to accommodate it to another language. It seems right with Zeki Validi to regard both Varach'- and Barsh- as the name of a tribe.[20]

The available notices, though regrettably vague, do not permit us to restrict Barsilia and the Barsilians to a small territory at the east end of the Caucasus. Apart from the town in Daghestan, there is unmistakable evidence of the name on the Volga, as we have seen. Michael Syrus identified Barsalia with Alania, i.e., the neighborhood of the pass of Darial in the middle Caucasus. The pseudo-Avars in 558 brought alarm to peoples already occupying the southeastern fringe of Europe, among which are mentioned the Sarselt. We may confidently read this name Barselt and connect it with Berzilia. The Barsilians were apparently to be found in widely separated parts of the later Khazaria. If it is thus difficult to determine what Theophanes meant by his Berzilia, a certain light has been thrown on the situation before the Khazar advance against the Bulgars. The Khazars seem in fact to have mastered the Barsilians at an earlier date. They are perhaps represented as on the point of doing so in the first-quoted passage of the *Armenian Geogra-*

[17] Cited Zeki Validi, *Ibn-Faḍlān*, 298n. Another town of similar name, Warathān or Warthān, lay farther south on the Araxes (Minorsky, *Ḥudūd*, 395).

[18] See Chapter VI.

[19] *Ḥudūd*, 453, n. 1.

[20] Ibn-Faḍlān, 156-157. The Bulkhk' (Bughkhk') mentioned in the Armenian Geography as forming a single people with the Khazars are perhaps the same (ed. Soukry, 26, 16, Marquart, *Streifz.*, 154, cf. 57).

phy. This is doubtless the explanation of another passage of that work in which the "King of the North" is explained as "the Khaqan, the lord of the Khazars," while the Queen, sc. of the North, is "the Khatun, of the people of the Barsilians."[21]

There can be no doubt in regard either to the fact that the Khazars overcame the Bulgars or to its importance for their subsequent development. The sources amply attest that on the middle Volga the Bulgars were subject to the Khazar Khaqan in the 9th and 10th centuries,[22] and though we cannot say for certain when this state of affairs came about, it is a reasonable conjecture which would relate it to the events which we have mentioned. If, as seems likely, the Volga Bulgars were fugitives from the south, some time may have elapsed before they were obliged to acknowledge Khazar supremacy. This would account for their retaining the individuality which their kinsmen who survived between the sea of Azov and the Caucasus (the horde of "Batbaias") largely lost.[23] In any case, it is evident that the opening up of the new territory must have presented the Khazars with opportunities and responsibilities such as they had not hitherto known. By their emergence on the Black Sea, which cannot have been long delayed after the defeat of the Bulgars, they entered for the first time a sphere where the influence of Byzantium was paramount. They must now, if not indeed earlier, have taken the road to the Crimea, where by the end of the 7th century we shall find Khazar garrisons firmly established.[24] In the Crimea, as probably elsewhere, they were in direct contact with the Greeks. In wealth and power the Khazars can only have gained by their new situation. It is likely also that they gradually came to be impressed by the intellectual aspects of a civilization superior to anything which they had yet known.[25]

But meantime, in another part of the world, a fresh chain

[21] Marquart, *Streifz.*, 58-59. [22] See Chapter V.

[23] For differences between Bulgars and Khazars, cf. ibn-Faḍlān's *Riḥlah, passim.*

[24] See Chapter VII.

[25] Possibly the Khazars took their Judaism from Greek Jews. Cf. *infra.*

of events had been set in motion. By A.D. 641 or even before this date Arab armies operated in the neighborhood of the southern approaches to the Caucasus, and inevitably in the prevailing temper of the Muslims invasion of the country north of the mountains was not likely to be long delayed. The great westward expansion of the Khazars of which we have just spoken had perhaps not yet taken place, for, though hardly the result of a mere year or two's campaigning, it has to be placed in the third quarter of the 7th century rather than the second. It is at all events certain that in 642 when the invading Muslims first debouched into the country north of Bāb al-Abwāb (Darband), the Khazars were already in possession.

It was of capital importance for subsequent history that at the moment when the victories of Islam brought the Arabs to the Caucasus barrier, they met the Khazars, then vigorous and expanding. Though the great mountain range would doubtless have caused the invaders from the south much difficulty in any case, sooner or later they would have overrun any but a strong and well-organized resistance. Such they appear to have met in the Khazars. For though in the next hundred years Muslim armies repeatedly attempted to advance beyond the Caucasus and were sometimes successful, the Arabs were never able to get firm foothold north of the mountains. In spite of their efforts they were effectively held, except on one occasion—to be described later—when circumstances did not permit them to make full use of their victory.

The situation on the Caucasus in the early days of Islam in general resembles that on the line of the Pyrenees, reached somewhat later by the Muslim armies. Like the Franks, the Khazars were strong enough to check the impetus of the invaders. In the west a decision was reached as the result of one great battle, the memorable field of Tours (732), while in the east, against the Khazars, the issue remained for long in doubt. Yet when the aggressive strength of the Caliphate was spent, Khazaria still existed. Having gained the former Persian lands as far as the Caucasus, the Arabs showed themselves unable to push their conquests farther. On several occasions they marched and counter-marched in Khazar country, but no permanent settlement was ever established. Beyond the Caucasus an independent Khazaria emerged after years of intermittent war, shaken perhaps, yet possessing a wider territory than when the Arabs first appeared, and with reserves of power which were later to be shown. Here Islam might later flourish,[26] but it was as a tolerated religion (like Khazar Christianity), not imposed by conquering armies. The implications of the Khazar defense are very wide-reaching, as we have already remarked. If the nation had been unable to maintain itself in the wars which we must now describe, there is little doubt that the history of eastern Europe and particularly of the Russian state would have been completely different.

The first Arab commander reported in the neighborhood of Bāb al-Abwāb (Darband) is Bukayr ibn-ʿAbdullāh, who with another officer was sent to Ādharbayjān in 21/641.[27] In the next year Surāqah ibn-ʿAmr was directed to Darband by the Caliph, and ʿAbd-al-Raḥmān ibn-Rabīʿah al-Bāhili, in command of Surāqah's van, found Bukayr already near the town.[28] He subsequently joined Surāqah and received a subordinate command. The main incident reported in the proceedings of the Muslims, now in force at the Caucasus for the first time, is the interview between ʿAbd-al-Raḥmān and the Persian commandant at Darband called Shahrbarāz, who is said to have written to ʿAbd-al-Raḥmān, on the arrival of the latter at Bāb, requesting protection. At a subsequent meeting Shahrbarāz explained his position. He had nothing in common, he said, with the surrounding barbarians and would give them no help against the Arabs, between whom and his own people, the Persians, was the natural kinship of noble races. He proposed therefore to join the Muslims, requesting that he and his followers in return for their services should not be required to pay the capitation-tax (*jizyah*). When the matter was re-

[26] Cf. the texts translated in Chapters V and VII.
[27] Ṭabari, I, 2635, 2661. [28] *Ibid.*, 2663.

ferred by ʿAbd-al-Raḥmān to Surāqah, he decided to remit the tax in the case of men who actually marched with the Muslims, but all others were to pay. The Caliph ʿUmar afterwards approved of Surāqah's decision, and it became the regular practice in those parts where there was much fighting to be done.[29] It seems indeed that the Persian system had already completely broken down. According to Balādhuri, the Greeks and the Khazars partitioned Armenia.[30] This was a return to an earlier situation. The western part had been ruled before the coming of the Persians by a Greek governor, while Arrān with Georgia had belonged to the Khazars.[31] Whether or not it is right to speak of the Khazars as south of the Caucasus at this juncture, we can readily believe that the situation of a Persian governor in Darband, surrounded by disaffected Armenians and threatened by yet more powerful enemies, was untenable.

There is an interesting version of the speech of Shahrbarāz in Balʿami,[32] whose work, as is now understood, represents more than an abbreviated translation of Ṭabari into Persian.[33] Shahrbarāz, or Shahriyār as he is here called, complains that he is between two enemies, the Khazars and the Russians. It is difficult to see what this can mean, particularly as we associate the rise of the Russian power with a later century, the 9th rather than the 7th. Presumably it is no more than an anachronism to speak of Russians at this early time. The geographical position envisaged is also far from clear. Zeki Validi, however, regards the Balʿami passage as indicating that the Russians were already taking part in the Khazars' wars, as is stated for the 10th century by Masʿūdi.[34] Marquart, it should be said, decided against the historicity of the whole Shahrbarāz story, perhaps too hastily.[35] The treaty cited by Ṭabari as having been granted to him and "the inhabitants of Armenia [? Persian colonists] and the Armans [? the natives of the

[29] *Ibid.*, 2663-2665, cf. Ibn Khaldūn, Muqaddimah, ed. Beirut-Cairo, 142.
[30] Balādhuri, 197. [31] *Ibid.*, 194. Cf. Chapter I. [32] Ed. Dorn, 500.
[33] R. Paret, *E.I.* art. Ṭabari, cf. Zeki Validi, *Ibn-Faḍlān*, 254.
[34] *Ibn-Faḍlān*, 253-254; "Völkerschaften," 54-56. [35] *Eranshahr*, 107.

country]" is credibly said to have been witnessed to by 'Abd-al-Raḥmān ibn-Rabī'ah, Salmān ibn-Rabī'ah and Bukayr ibn-'Abdullāh, all of whom are known to have been active in this region. Salmān ibn-Rabī'ah, or Salmān of the Horses, was the younger brother of 'Abd-al-Raḥmān ibn-Rabī'ah. There seems indeed to be an element of the fabulous in the story of Shahrbarāz, who is said to have been with 'Abd-al-Raḥmān ibn-Rabī'ah at Darband, when a man, previously sent by him, returned from the Dyke of dhū-al-Qarnayn and described what he had seen. But the picture of the Persian governor harassed by a native population, who were perhaps assisted by the Khazars from the other side of the Caucasus, may well be authentic.[36]

When Bāb had been occupied, the lieutenants of Surāqah were sent out in different directions. The Caliph, when informed of what had been done and of the successes already gained, was greatly surprised and pleased. Surāqah's lieutenants, however, had little success. Shortly afterwards, Surāqah died, and 'Abd-al-Raḥmān ibn-Rabī'ah took his place. No more appears to be heard of Bukayr. 'Abd-al-Raḥmān was confirmed in his command by 'Umar and instructed to proceed north against the Khazars.[37]

Ṭabari reports a conversation which 'Abd-al-Raḥmān ibn-Rabī'ah had about this time with the former Persian commandant at Bāb. Asked by the latter where he was going, 'Abd-al-Raḥmān said, "To Balanjar." This was an important Khazar center,[38] lying on a river of the same name,[39] within easy distance of the pass of Darband.[40] "But we Persians were con-

[36] Ṭabari, I, 2665-2671; Balādhuri, 198; ibn-'Abd-al-Barr, *Istī'āb*, 400.

[37] Ṭabari, I, 2666-2667; ibn-Ḥajar, *Iṣābah*, II, 134.

[38] Mas'ūdi (*Tanbīh*, 62) says that Balanjar was the earlier capital of Khazaria.

[39] Balādhuri, 204. It is identified by Zeki Validi as the Qoy-su.

[40] Balanjar is probably to be identified with the ruins of Endere near Andreyeva, as Artamonov (*Études*, 93) has it. Artamonov's further equation Balanjar=Samandar is not right. Samandar is consistently represented in the Arabic sources as farther from Bāb (Darband), and in the two most detailed itineraries which we have for Khazaria (the campaign of Jarrāh ibn-'Abdullāh in 104/722 and Marwān ibn-Muḥam-

tent if the barbarians left us alone at Bāb," Shahrbarāz is supposed to have replied. "Well," returned 'Abd-al-Raḥmān, "the Arabs are not content with that, and, by Heaven! we have people with us who have entered into this affair with all their heart. They were men of honor and scruple in the time of the Ignorance and are so now, more than before. They will not change nor cease to conquer, till they are defeated and changed by their conqueror." And so, we are told, the Muslims advanced for the first time into Khazaria.[41]

Balanjar was attacked, says Ṭabari, without loss on this first raid (22/642), and the Arab cavalry even got as far as al-Bayḍā', 200 parasangs from Balanjar.[42] The statement may be doubted. Al-Bayḍā' is the name given by the Arabs, especially in the earlier period, to Atil (Khazarān-Atil), the Khazar capital on the Volga, which should be intended here. No doubt the Khazars already had a settlement there in 642, but it was scarcely as yet their capital.[43] In any case, to speak of the Muslims as having penetrated so far on their first expedition seems exaggerated. On the other hand, there is no doubt that the Khazar opposition was unexpectedly light—a surprising fact, we may add, in view of their stout resistance later. On this occasion the Arab army found that their antagonists shut themselves in strong points and refused to engage on any scale. According to the Arab historian, the Khazars quickly reached the conclusion that their enemies were exempt from death and, if not actually supernatural, at least divinely helped. This is unlike

---

mad in 119/737, for which see *infra*) Balanjar and Samandar are distinct. It is a fact that Mas'ūdi says in the *Murūj al-Dhahab* (see translation in Chapter VII) that Samandar is an old Khazar capital and in the *Tanbīh* that Balanjar is an old Khazar capital (cf. n. 38), using the same phrase "dār mamlakah," but this does not mean that he identified them. Marquart at first thought (*Streifz.*, 16, cf. 492) that Balanjar was the same as Varach'an, cf. Bulkhk' as above, n. 20. Artamonov, who also takes Balanjar=Varach'an, adduces the strange name Balkh in the *Darband Nāmah*. There is relevant material in Zeki Validi, *Ibn-Faḍlān*, 298-299nn.

41 Ṭabari, I, 2667.

42 *Ibid.*, 2668.

43 According to Mas'ūdi (*Murūj*, II, 7, translated *infra*) the Khazar capital was transferred to Atil on the Volga from Samandar in the days of Salmān ibn-Rabī'ah.

the language which is used of Muslim victories elsewhere, and possibly represents the reaction of a simple race to unprecedented and unforeseen calamity. Given these circumstances, a rapid drive on the part of the invaders, even as far as the Volga, is perhaps not excluded. The sources seem to be unanimous in regard to the distance covered.[44]

Marquart not only denies that al-Bayḍā' was reached, but thinks that the advance on Balanjar is wrongly dated by Ṭabari. It took place, according to Marquart, in 32/652.[45] Ṭabari happens to repeat the story of the invulnerability of the Muslims under A.H. 32, while on the other hand Balādhuri knows nothing of any Muslim attack on Balanjar in 22/642. Marquart, as is occasionally the case, gives no reason for his opinion as to the date when Balanjar was first attacked. Ibn-Khaldūn, however, has a definite statement to the effect that 'Abd-al-Raḥmān was constantly raiding Khazaria and constantly raided Balanjar.[46] It is also perfectly clear from Ṭabari himself, not only that 'Abd-al-Raḥmān advanced on Balanjar in A.H. 22, but that attacks on Khazaria in which Balanjar must have been a first objective, and is so mentioned, were repeated in the next and subsequent years.[47] Against this testimony the silence of Balādhuri and Marquart's *obiter dictum* have no weight whatever.

Where we must part company with the Muslim sources is in their assertion that the Arabs suffered no casualties against the Khazars until the great battle at Balanjar in which 'Abd-al-Raḥmān ibn-Rabī'ah was killed. This is of course quite beyond the bounds of credibility. Bal'ami mentions Arab blood shed by the Khazars on the first expedition,[48] as it must have been. Subsequent raids may have been on a small scale, and the losses of the invaders inconsiderable, but on this point, as

[44] Cf. Bal'ami, 503. (In Zotenberg's translation, III, 495, "vingt parasanges," for which no manuscript authority appears.) Ḥāfiẓ-i Abru (Dorn, 581) says that "Turkestan" was entered for 200 parasangs.

[45] *Streifz.*, 491.

[46] II, ii, 138.

[47] Ṭabari, I, 2668, 2889-2891.

[48] Dorn, 505.

on others, the main Arab tradition evidently bears traces of patriotic exaggeration.

A little later, perhaps in A.H. 24,[49] Walīd ibn-'Uqbah, 'Uthmān's half-brother, was appointed to the governorship of Kufah. Walīd, like his father 'Uqbah, had an unenviable reputation in Islam, and it is said that the Qur'ān verse: "O ye who have believed, if a reprobate come to you,[50] etc." was revealed with reference to him. While governor, his appearance to lead the morning prayer, while still intoxicated from a night's debauch, was notorious. 'Uthmān seems to have appointed his relative in the hope that his strong hand (for this merit was not denied to Walīd) would be effective in curbing the Kufans. Ṭabari records an expedition into Ādharbayjān and Armenia undertaken by Walīd, shortly after his appointment. He is said to have summoned Salmān ibn-Rabī'ah, presumably from the neighborhood of Bāb, and thereafter sent him towards the frontier in command of his van. For the numbers of Muslims engaged on this occasion, Ṭabari preserves a notice to the effect that at Kufah at this time there were 40,000 fighting men, who campaigned in rotation once in four years. Of the 10,000 thus available each year some were regularly diverted elsewhere, but there were always 6,000 in Ādharbayjān.[51] When Walīd left Kufah in person, additional troops were no doubt raised from the city's military population. He is said to have sent out a column of 4,000 men under one officer, which was apparently strong enough to reduce the whole of Ādharbayjān, and at the close of this operation he gave Salmān ibn-Rabī'ah a force of 12,000 to go into Armenia. Salmān's task was evidently the collection of tribute from a recalcitrant population. No action against the Khazars is recorded. The Armenian expedition was successful. Salmān rejoined Walīd, and the whole army withdrew to the neighborhood of Mosul. The numbers of the troops involved are not large. The record of the earlier expedition to Bāb and beyond, lacking figures, does not allow a comparison in this respect with the campaign of Walīd ibn-'Uqbah, but it

[49] Ṭabari, I, 2804. [50] Sur. 49, 6. [51] Ṭabari, I, 2805.

is perhaps to be assumed that the strength of the Muslim forces on the two occasions was not greatly different.

On his return Walīd received a letter from the Caliph, saying that in the west the Greeks were pressing hard on the Muslims and directing that 8,000 or 9,000 men should be sent immediately to their help from the troops of Kufah. At a meeting with his men Walīd explained the situation and invited them to volunteer for the Greek front. Within a short time 8,000 were ready to start under Salmān ibn-Rabī'ah. Salmān and his soldiers made their way to a junction with Ḥabīb ibn-Maslamah, commander of the Syrians, and the whole force proceeded against the Greeks.[52]

It is unlikely that the command of 'Abd-al-Raḥmān at Bāb was interrupted by Walīd's expedition of 24/644. In the following years he appears to have had assistance from Kufah[53] and to have raided the Khazars repeatedly. To this period refers the remark of a grandson of Walīd ibn-'Uqbah, who spoke of the good old days of his grandfather, when 'Abd-al-Raḥmān was in command at Bāb.[54] Very probably Salmān ibn-Rabī'ah was associated with his elder brother during this time. The traditionist ibn-'Abd-al-Barr mentions a certain Shaqīq ibn-Salamah, who related that when he raided Balanjar under Salmān's orders, the men were strictly forbidden to take away booty on baggage animals, i.e., they might have what they could carry by hand or on their own backs.[55] This or a similar occasion is referred to by Zuhayr ibn-al-Qayn, who was with Ḥusayn at Kerbela, and there quoted words spoken by Salmān a generation before when engaged on a successful expedition against Balanjar. "Are you content with your victory and the booty you have gained?" Salmān had asked his men. "Indeed we are," answered they. Salmān then went on, "If you are alive in the days of the young men of Muḥammad's family, may you be yet more glad of the booty that you gain when you fight with them."[56] We find Salmān cited also for the reaction

[52] *Ibid.*, I, 2807, cf. II, 977. [53] *Ibid.*, I, 2891.
[54] *Ibid.*, I, 2844. [55] Istī'āb, 558. [56] Ṭabari, II, 291.

of the Khazars to the Arab attacks.[57] But these operations were doubtless on a small scale. Between 22/642 and 32/652 the Muslims appear to have been sufficiently occupied in settling their affairs in Armenia and Ādharbayjān. In any case, no exploit in Khazar country during these years has left a detailed record.

Ṭabari mentions that in 30/650 Hudhayfah ibn-al-Yamān, previously stationed at Rayy, was sent to Ādharbayjān.[58] ʻAbd-al-Raḥmān at Bāb apparently was in difficulties and needed support. The situation of the Muslims vis-à-vis the Khazars is unfortunately quite obscure. On the other hand, we do know something of the disputes which were beginning to vex the Arabs on this frontier. It was while operating in the neighborhood of Bāb that Hudhayfah ibn-al-Yamān reached the conclusion, from what he saw of the disagreement of the Muslims about the wording of the Qur'ān, that a new, uniform text was a necessity.[59] Later he persuaded the Caliph to take action in the matter. We can appreciate that arguments as to the true reading of the sacred text might lead to serious consequences, if Kufans and Syrians were the contending parties, for already at Kufah disaffection to ʻUthmān and his government was coming to a head. There was no rupture at Bāb till later,[60] but Hudhayfah's report in A.H. 30 suggests a strained situation there, from which no doubt the Khazars profited.

No details are available of a letter said to have been sent about this time by Yazdagird, titular king of Persia, to the "king of the Khazars."[61] After years of exile and humiliation, the last of the Sassanids, shortly before his obscure death in A.H. 31, sent out appeals to various Oriental rulers, but without success. The statement that the Khazar king was applied to comes in ibn-al-Athīr and ibn-Khaldūn, as well as in Ṭabari, and is in itself quite probable. The Spanish poet ibn-ʻAbdūn

57 *Ibid.*, I, 2668.

58 *Ibid.*, I, 2856.

59 Ibn-al-Athīr, *s. anno* 30; cf. Nöldeke-Schwally, *Geschichte des Qurans*, II, 47ff.

60 Ṭabari, I, 2893-2894.

61 *Ibid.*, I, 2876.

knew the story, and spoke of Yazdagird and the Khazars in his famous *qaṣīdah* on the fall of the Afṭasids[62] (485/1092).

The most serious attempt hitherto on the part of the Arabs to coerce the Khazars was made in 32/652, and for the circumstances we have relatively full information. The initiative appears to have come from ʿAbd-al-Raḥmān ibn-Rabīʿah. Disregarding the instructions of ʿUthmān to take no risks, ʿAbd-al-Raḥmān led what was evidently a strong Muslim force into Khazaria. The immediate objective, as on previous occasions, was Balanjar. The legend that the Muslims had so far been immune from casualties in their clashes with the Khazars has already been mentioned. We are told that in A.H. 32, apparently for the first time, the Khazars determined to test the vulnerability of their enemies, and from ambush killed a small party, or a single man, who according to one form of the tale was bathing.[63] Thus emboldened, they risked a general encounter, in which the Muslims were totally defeated. The detail of the ambush should perhaps refer to an earlier raid but is represented as an incident of the siege to which Balanjar was now subjected by the invading army. The town appears to have resisted strongly. It was evidently fortified at this period, for we read of a tower from which much execution was done among the Muslims. Both sides had artillery. The Muslims used both *majānīq* and *ʿarrādāt*, i.e., large and small ballistae, while the Khazars had the latter at least.[64] This is particularly interesting in view of a passage in Procopius, in which he tells us that the Sabirs, a kindred race to the Khazars, had earlier in the same Caucasus region light rams of their own invention, which they showed the Greeks how to construct.[65]

A considerable part of Ṭabari's narrative is taken up with the fate of a group of Kufans, most of whom are named earlier as in the entourage of ibn-Masʿūd.[66] Ibn-Masʿūd was the Kufan religious chief whose opposition to the new recension of the

[62] Ibn-Badrūn, ed. Dozy, 140.
[63] Ṭabari, I, 2891; cf. 2668; *Darband Nāmah*, 494.
[64] *Ibid.*, 2892.
[65] VIII, xi, 27ff.
[66] Ṭabari, I, 2896.

Qur'ān in A.H. 30 had been exceptionally bitter. The significance of their deaths is not clear, but possibly it is represented as the penalty of disobedience. The phrase "the rebellion of the Kufans" occurs in the prayer of 'Uthmān when he was told of the disaster at Balanjar, and similar expressions occur elsewhere.[67] The bare presence of troops in Khazaria was contrary to the Caliph's express command.

After some days of sharp fighting round the city, the Khazars within made a general sortie and at the same time a relieving force appeared, apparently of cavalry.[68] That the joint attack was well-timed and brilliantly successful seems plain, though we do not have details of the action. According to one account,[69] as the Muslim general tried to rally his troops, a voice was heard calling, "Courage! men of 'Abd-al-Raḥmān. Your rendezvous is Paradise." When 'Abd-al-Raḥmān fell, his death was the signal for the flight of the Muslims. But his brother took up the standard, and the voice was heard again through the din of battle, "Courage! men of Salmān ibn-Rabī'ah." To which Salmān responded, "Are you grieved to see us?" According to others, the death of al-Qarthā', one of the Qur'ān-readers from Kufah, was the point at which the rout began.[70] Four thousand of the Muslims were slain. Survivors told how at the end the cry *Allāh akbar*, "God is greatest," was raised time and again from the stricken field.[71] Some escaped to Bāb with Salmān ibn-Rabī'ah. Others are said to have continued in their flight through Jīlān and even farther.[72] Among the latter are mentioned abu-Hurayrah and Salmān al-Fārisi, two well-known Companions of the Prophet. The body of 'Abd-

[67] *Ibid.*, I, 2893, cf. 2669 n., where ibn-Ḥubaysh is quoted.

[68] Balādhuri, 204. There is no reason to think, in spite of ibn-al-Athīr (*s. anno* 32) that West Turkish forces were engaged, though this would be theoretically possible. Ṭabari's narrative of the event sometimes speaks of the Khazars as Turks (e.g., I, 2890), and ibn-al-Athīr, misunderstanding this, has "Turks and Khazars."

[69] Ṭabari, I, 2668-2669.

[70] *Ibid.*, I, 2892.

[71] Balādhuri, *ibid.*

[72] Jurjān, mentioned in the parallel accounts, Ṭabari, I, 2669 and 2890. A third account (Ṭabari, I, 2891) is garbled.

al-Raḥmān had to be abandoned. It was taken by the Khazars, placed in a suitable vessel, and preserved, they judging that intercession might be made in times of drought for rain, and in war for victory, through the efficacy of the fallen enemy.[73]

The repulse at Balanjar practically marks the end of the first phase of Arab-Khazar relations, though Muslim contingents are mentioned shortly after this at Bāb.[74] The troubles which involved the Caliphate after the death of 'Uthmān turned men's thoughts away from the frontiers. So far as the Arabs are concerned, the Khazars were left in peace for long. The initial advantage rested no doubt with them. But it is significant for the future that at about this time the Khazar capital was transferred to a less dangerous situation on the banks of the Volga.[75]

[73] Ṭabari, I, 2669, 2890, referred to also by Balādhuri (*ibid.*), who cites verses linking the grave of 'Abd-al-Raḥmān (according to Balādhuri, Salmān) ibn-Rabī'ah at Balanjar with that of the more famous Qutaybah ibn-Muslim in "Ṣīnastān" (actually Farghānah, cf. H. A. R. Gibb, *Arab Conquests*, 56), by a poet of Bāhilah, i.e., a fellow-tribesman of both heroes. (For Balādhuri, Salmān ibn-Rabī'ah was the Muslim general killed at Balanjar. He knows nothing of 'Abd-al-Raḥmān ibn-Rabī'ah.) Cf. also ibn-al-Faqīh, 287.

[74] Ṭabari, I, 2894.

[75] Cf. n. 43.

CHAPTER IV

THE SECOND ARAB-KHAZAR WAR (722-737)*

To JUDGE from our sources, the peace which now descended on the Caucasus frontier remained unbroken for nearly thirty years. Among the Arabs new interests supervened and political partisanship absorbed the energies which had previously been turned against the outside world. The Khazars were also preoccupied, for in this interval fall their successes at the expense of the Bulgars and the great westward expansion already

* BIBLIOGRAPHICAL NOTE TO CHAPTER IV: In the latter part of the chapter, considerable use has been made of what is often called Bal'ami's Persian version of Ṭabari. A few words of explanation are perhaps desirable. It is quite clear that Bal'ami does more than translate Ṭabari. Occasionally he supplements him to a notable extent. Sometimes other authors (ibn-al-Athīr, Balādhuri, Ya'qūbi) also give Bal'ami's additional material. But the correspondence seems to be closest between Bal'ami and ibn-A'tham al-Kūfi, who no doubt is yet more copious in certain places. The question of these additions to Ṭabari has never, I believe, been gone into systematically but some unfavorable opinions have been expressed in regard to them. To credit what Ṭabari tells us and reject out-of-hand additional information offered by this or that other source is evidently methodologically wrong, and this is generally admitted, at all events in the case of ibn-al-Athīr and Balādhuri. Bal'ami's narrative of the closing years of the Arab-Khazar wars invites use because of the detail which it offers, but at the same time it presents serious difficulties. It is carelessly put together and sufficient attention has not been given to proper names. Numbers seem to be consistently exaggerated. (We have generally given these as in Dorn's text with a qualification.) Certain incidents, e.g., the exploits of Sa'īd ibn-'Amr, seem in part fictitious. On the other hand, some of these difficulties are no doubt owing to the transmission, rather than to Bal'ami himself, and surprisingly often what he says finds confirmation elsewhere. Where there is no confirmation, if what has been related by Bal'ami or another of the group which uses his material seems reasonable, we are no doubt right to adopt it. At this point, in deciding what is reasonable, a subjective element unavoidably enters. In attempting to reconstruct the course of events, we have taken the view that, as much as credulity, undue skepticism was to be avoided. A relevant consideration is that the exploits of Maslamah, Marwān ibn-Muḥammad, and the Umayyads in general evoked little sympathy or interest among the partisans of the succeeding dynasty, for whom principally the histories which we have were written.

characterized. The process was perhaps complete towards 60/679. A year or two later, they were ready to take the offensive in the Caucasus.

We hear first of an attack directed by a certain Alp, chief of the "Huns of Varach'an" on Albania (Arrān) before 62/681-2.[1] Perhaps Alp was a Khazar, or his further appellation "Ilutver" (cf. Yaltawar, Elteber of the Bulgars) may mean that he was a semi-independent ruler of Varach'an (Warathān) under the Khazars.[2] A letter sent by the king of the "Huns" to the Armenian archbishop Sahak and the latter's reply are mentioned.[3] The "Hun" king's envoys are named as Zirdkin-Khursan and Chat-Khazar, where, as Minorsky notes, the second element of the names should refer to the ambassadors' nationality.[4] In A.D. 682 an Albanian bishop went north and preached Christianity successfully to Alp and his army. Heathen shrines, especially that of a deity Spandiat or Aspandiat, identified by the people with their supreme god Tengri Khan,[5] are said to have been destroyed and sacred trees cut down. The priests of the native religion (*shamans*) were executed or burned to death. The account of this mission affords a striking glimpse of the religious practices of a group who, if not actually Khazars, were at least nearly related to them, before the Khazar conversion to Judaism. Here we have an early contact with Christianity, clear traces of which are found among the Khazars during the whole historical period. The source does not mention the results of the mission in A.D. 682, but no see was erected,[6] and they can scarcely have been permanent.

Alp's expedition is to be distinguished from another and greater Khazar invasion which was launched on the lands south of the Caucasus a little later, probably in 65/685.[7] In the first years of 'Abd-al-Malik (685-705), Arab control of the region

[1] Marquart, *Streifzüge*, 114, 302, citing Moses of Kalankatuk, ed. Shahnazarean, II, 36.

[2] Zeki Validi, *Ibn-Faḍlān*, 106.

[3] Marquart, *Streifz.*, 514.

[4] *Ḥudūd*, 411, n. 1.

[5] Marquart, *Streifz.*, 429.

[6] *Ibid.*, 302.

[7] *Ibid.*, 443, citing Stephan Asolik (Asoghik), transl. Dulaurier.

was relaxed.[8] In consequence of this, or for some other reason, the Khazars now attacked and overran Georgia, Armenia, and Albania, apparently forgetful of the religious link which had recently been forged with the latter. The inhabitants offered resistance, but were powerless to stop them. The native prince of Georgia and Grigor Mamikonian, prince of Armenia, were killed in battle with the invaders. We must assume that the result of this campaign was victory for the Khazars on a great scale. It is notable, however, that the attempt does not seem to have been made to hold territory south of the Caucasus. The threat of the armies of the Caliphate, still in abeyance, evidently deterred the Khazars from this step. We read simply that having laid waste the country, they collected their prisoners and withdrew north again.

Yet not many years later, in 89/707 according to Ṭabari, Maslamah ibn-ʿAbd-al-Malik, half-brother of the reigning Caliph Walīd I, conquered fortresses and towns in Ādharbayjān and fought his way to Bāb against the "Turks."[9] If the notice is reliable, it looks as if the Khazars were temporarily in possession here. There is a report of the capture of Bāb in A.H. 90 by Muḥammad ibn-Marwān.[10] But in A.H. 91, in which year he succeeded Muḥammad ibn-Marwān, Maslamah is said to have been engaged in Ādharbayjān and to have reached Bāb.[11] The notice suggests that another account may be right, according to which it was Maslamah in 95/713 who captured Bāb.[12] In any case, it seems evident that for a period the fortress-town, at least, was under Khazar control.

In the Caliphate of ʿUmar ibn-ʿAbd-al-ʿAzīz (717-720) the Khazars made what was perhaps their first attack against Islam.[13] The year was A.H. 99/A.D. 717. Ādharbayjān was invaded and a number of the Muslims were killed. The Caliph sent Ḥātim ibn-al-Nuʿmān, like the sons of Rabīʿah, a member

[8] *Ibid.*, 514, citing Levond (Ghevond), ed. Shahnazarean, 34, 35.
[9] Ṭabari, II, 1200.
[10] Caetani, Chronographia, 1088.
[11] Ṭabari, II, 1217.
[12] Ibn Taghrībardi, I, 255.
[13] So Kmosko, *Araber und Chasaren*, 361.

of the Bāhilah clan.[14] This commander defeated the invaders with heavy loss and returned to the Caliph having fifty Khazar prisoners in his train.

These seem to be the first recorded Khazar prisoners. Later individual Khazars are occasionally mentioned within the Muslim empire. Perhaps the best known is Isḥāq ibn-Kundāj (Kundājiq) al-Khazari.[15] He was a contemporary of the poet Buḥturi and repeatedly the subject of his praise. Buḥturi says that ibn-Kundāj had gained in Iraq glory additional to that which he enjoyed in al-Bayḍā' and Balanjar.[16] Elsewhere he refers to the ancient race of Isḥāq ibn-Kundāj, and declares that his ancestors were the generals of kings before the time of dhū-Ru'ayn.[17] This at once transfers the existence of the Khazars to a remote period, for dhu-Ru'ayn is a Himyarite king. Buḥturi may well be in error or exaggerating, but the case is somewhat different from the anachronisms which were referred to earlier. His words may be intended to suggest that ibn-Kundāj counted Begs of Khazaria among his ancestors. In another poem Buḥturi says that the subject of his panegyric has performed an exploit which would entitle him to be "king of al-Bayḍā' who wears the crown." We gather from the same piece that his father's name was that good Muslim one, Ayyūb[18] These passages at least indicate what we should expect, that there was some common knowledge of Khazaria among contemporary subjects of the Caliphate. We shall have occasion to mention other Khazars among the Muslims in later chapters.

To return to the course of events, in 103/721-722 the Khazars attacked the Alans.[19] The frontier was evidently set in motion, and the second Arab-Khazar war may be said to have

[14] Ṭabari, II, 1346.

[15] A distinguished general in the wars between the Egyptian Khumārawayh and Mu'tamid (Caliph 870-892).

[16] *Dīwān*, ed. of 1329/1911, II, 21-22. Cf. Marquart, *Streifz.*, 18. The same poem refers to the origin of ibn-Kundāj in "the land of the Khaqan."

[17] *Ibid.*, II, 294.

[18] *Ibid.*, I, 104; cf. l. 9.

[19] Ṭabari, II, 1437; Ya'qūbi, II, 378. Kmosko (*ibid.*) thinks that this was the Khazar reaction to the check of the Arabs at Constantinople a year or two previously.

begun when in the next year a Muslim army under Thubayt al-Nahrāni met the Khazars[20] at Marj al-Ḥijārah in Armenia,[21] where a great battle was fought. The Khazars, who are said to have numbered 30,000,[22] gained a complete victory over the Muslims, whose camp fell into the hands of the enemy. The beaten army escaped to Syria. The Caliph Yazīd ibn-ʿAbd-al-Malik (720-724) was much distressed and upbraided Thubayt, who is said to have replied: "Commander of the Faithful, I played no coward's part, nor turned aside from meeting the enemy. Horse clove to horse and man to man. I thrust with my lance till it was broken and struck with my sword till it shivered in pieces. But God, Who is blessed and exalted, does what He wills."[23] It is noticeable that Ṭabari has nothing to say of this reverse.

The threat to the lands of Islam was now considerable. The Khazars prepared to occupy the territory uncovered by the retreat of the Muslim army, and assembled all their forces. Jarrāḥ ibn-ʿAbdullāh al-Ḥakami was hastily appointed governor of Armenia, with orders to attack the enemy in their own territory (A.H. 104).[24] When news came that Jarrāḥ was marching against them with a strong army, the Khazars fell back on Bāb, where a Muslim garrison still held out. Meanwhile Jarrāḥ reached Bardhaʿah and rested his men there for several days, finding time, apparently, to regulate the weights and measures of the place. At all events, a "Jarrāḥi" measure, said to have dated from this visit, was still in use when Balādhuri wrote.[25]

Jarrāḥ then advanced across the Kur river and eventually halted at a smaller stream called Rūbās a few miles from Bāb. Word had been sent to the local chiefs to join him with their levies, but Jarrāḥ learned that one of them had warned the

20 Ibn-al-Athīr (v, 41) says that the Khazars were supported by the Qipchaqs and other Turks. This must be an anachronism; cf. Chapter IX, n. 125.

21 Apparently in Armenia (Balʿami, 509), but cf. ibn-al-Athīr, *loc.cit.*

22 Balʿami, 510.

23 Ibn-al-Athīr, *loc.cit.*

24 Ṭabari, II, 1453; ibn-al-Athīr, *s. anno.*

25 Ed. De Goeje, 206.

Khazars of his approach. Accordingly he ordered his muezzin to proclaim to the army that the general would remain on the Rūbās for several days. The Khazars were informed, as Jarrāḥ had foreseen would happen. Their main forces under "the son of the accursed Khaqan"[26]—possibly the Beg of Khazaria is meant—were already north of the mountains. The local commander was willing to avoid an encounter and made no hostile move. When night came, Jarrāḥ countermanded his previous order, and advanced rapidly towards Bāb. He and his men reached the town while it was still dark without meeting opposition. They entered by the wooden gate of the Nārīn citadel, and marching through, encamped a short distance north of the Bāb al-Jihād[27] (Gate of the Holy War). That morning two strong raiding columns were sent out by Jarrāḥ, with instructions to proceed into enemy territory and rendezvous within twenty-four hours at a point some twenty miles ahead. During the day the main Muslim force advanced to the place agreed on. At dawn the following morning they were joined by the raiding columns, bearing a great booty of sheep and cattle and many prisoners. Some were from the Khazar dependency of Khaydhān[28] (Qaytaq).

Next day under "Bārjīk,[29] son of the Khaqan" a Khazar force, of 40,000 men it is said, arrived from Ḥamzīn,[30] to con-

[26] *Darband Nāmah,* 464 n.

[27] Persian *Darband Nāmah,* Dorn, 464 n.; Bal'ami, 511, cf. Turkish *Darband Nāmah,* ed. Kasem Beg, 544.

[28] Khaydhān is perhaps a Persian, Qaytaq an Armenian form of the name (Zeki Validi, *Ibn-Faḍlān,* 191). The place appears as Khayzān (Balādhuri, 204, 206; De Goeje on Yāqūt, *Buldān,* IV, 251). Other forms are definitely wrong: Jīdān (Yāqūt, *loc.cit.,* Mas'ūdi, *Murūj,* II, 7); Ḥīda, Ḥabda, Janda, Jandāu (MSS. of Bal'ami, Dorn, 511); Khanda or Jabda (Zotenberg, IV, 562).

[29] Bal'ami's text offers Bārjīk, Bār-ḥbl, Bārḥīl, Bārḥīk. Dorn prefers Barjīl or Barjenk (466, n. 2), with Barjīk as another possibility (465). Zotenberg renders "Barkhebek" with a query (IV, 271). The Turkish version of the *Darband Nāmah* quoted by Dorn (463n.) has Pashenk.

[30] Bal'ami, ibn-al-Athīr, *Darband Nāmah* have Ḥaṣīn, which is not right. Elsewhere Bal'ami, speaking of Maslamah (Dorn, 534), has "wa-bigudhasht wa-ba-ḥ-ṣnīn [ḥ-ṣnain] shud wa-ān du hiṣār būd," i.e., he passed on and came to Ḥ-ṣnīn, which consists of two fortresses. This appears to be an attempt to explain a non-Arabic name. Balādhuri (206)

test the farther advance of the Muslims. A little speech ascribed to Jarrāḥ before the ensuing battle indicates respect for his opponents. "Men," he is supposed to have said, "you have no refuge to which to flee and no recourse, save God, Who is great and glorious. Each of you who is killed will go to Paradise, and all who are victorious will gain booty and a fair name."[31] After a fierce engagement the Khazars broke and fled. Great numbers of them were slain. As Jarrāḥ had promised, much booty was taken by the victors, after which the advance was resumed. Ḥamzīn and Targhu[32] successively fell. Jarrāḥ settled the inhabitants of these places elsewhere. It is interesting to read that some of them were removed to Qabalah, south of the Caucasus, which, according to Balādhuri, was occupied by Khazars, apparently in his day.[33]

Jarrāḥ then approached Balanjar, which had already been the object of repeated Muslim attacks and the scene of a formal siege in A.H. 32. At that date its strong fortifications were partly responsible for the repulse of the Arabs. But seventy years had passed, and in the interval the defenses seem to have been dismantled. The main obstacle in Jarrāḥ's time was an improvised barricade of common wagons, fastened together and drawn up on high ground round the fortress. When the assault was made, the attackers found themselves in great difficulties on this account. At last one of them raised his scimitar and cried, "Muslims, which of you will devote himself to God?" A number of his friends indicated that they would join him in any attempt and took an oath to the death, breaking the scabbards of their swords in token of this intention. Then they returned to the attack, forcing their way up-hill under a hail of arrows so thick that "the sun was darkened."

has Ḥamzīn. Zeki Validi (*Ibn-Faḍlān*, 298 n.) gives Ḥ-ṣnīn and identifies with Qaya Kent (Kand).

31 Bal'ami, 512-513.

32 Not Yarghu, as Kmosko, following the misreading in ibn-al-Athīr, *s. anno* 104. Targhu is not the same as Samandar, mentioned distinctly in the same account (Bal'ami, 513-514). Zeki Validi (*ibid.*) identifies Targhu with Makhach Qala, cf. Minorsky, *Ḥudūd*, 452.

33 Ed. De Goeje, 194.

Some of them succeeded in cutting the ropes which bound the wagons together, and began to drag them down the slope. Soon the way was clear for the attackers. Both sides fought desperately "till men's hearts were in their throats." At last the defenders weakened and gave way, and the Muslims took possession of the city.

It is significant for the wealth and general prosperity of the Khazars that when the booty was distributed after the fall of Balanjar each horseman in the Muslim army is said to have received 300 dinars.[34] If the number of the recipients is not grossly exaggerated—it is put as high as 30,000[35]—this represents a huge sum of money. To it must apparently be added the fifth, which belonged by law to the public treasury.

The Khazar governor of Balanjar[36] escaped with a handful of men to Samandar. His wife and son were captured and put up for sale as slaves. Jarrāḥ himself bought them for 100,000 dirhams, and then sent a safe-conduct to the Khazar, offering to restore all that he had lost—wife, child, fortress, with his belongings, great and small—evidently on the condition of his accepting Muslim rule. To this the Khazar is said to have assented, but it is difficult to see how the story can be authentic. In particular, what happened to Balanjar in the sequel, if it thus became a Muslim town?

The fact is, we do not have the whole story of what took place. After the fall of Balanjar, Jarrāḥ is said to have caused a number of the Khazars and their families to be drowned, presumably in the Balanjar river.[37] Many prisoners were taken. The neighboring fortresses were reduced, and most of the inhabitants are said to have emigrated. It is readily understandable that many of them moved north. Two hundred years after this the traveler ibn-Faḍlān came across several thousands of "Baranjār" among the Volga Bulgars. The identity

[34] Ibn-al-Athīr, *s. anno* 104.
[35] Ibn-al-Athīr's figure. Bal'ami makes 25,000 or only 20,000 before the battle.
[36] Bal'ami, 514; *mihtar Balanjar*; ibn-al-Athīr: *ṣāḥib Balanjar.*
[37] Ṭabari, II, 1453. Cf. Chapter III, n. 39.

Baranjār/Balanjar seems as certain as these things can be, and one may conjecture that the ancestors of the people seen by ibn-Faḍlān were from the Khazar town.[38] In ibn-Faḍlān's time, the Baranjār had recently been converted to Islam, but he found a non-Muslim with the name Ṭālūt (Saul). This may point to Judaism among them at an earlier period.

From Balanjar, Jarrāḥ advanced to the fortress and town of Wabandar[39] (? Wanandar), an important place with numerous defenders.[40] But they had no heart for fighting, preferring to capitulate and pay an indemnity. Jarrāḥ decided to continue his march to Samandar and had already reached its neighborhood when the former Khazar governor at Balanjar wrote urgently to say that farther advance was dangerous. Ahead of the Muslims lay another large enemy force, while their lines of communication were now threatened by unrest among the mountain chiefs. Orders were accordingly given to retreat. The Arab army repassed the Caucasus, and as the season was now advanced went into winter quarters in Shakki.[41]

Evidently Jarrāḥ hoped to resume operations the following year. He wrote to the Caliph and told him of the successes gained, but, pointing out that the Khazars were not yet beaten, he requested additional troops. In spring news came that Yazīd was dead (105/724). His successor Hishām, while confirming Jarrāḥ in his appointment, sent only promises of help.

When the campaigning season opened, Jarrāḥ invaded Khazaria again, this time by the Darial pass and the country of the Alans,[42] and operated against certain towns and fortresses beyond Balanjar. Details of the campaign are wanting, so that we are quite in the dark as to the Khazar reaction. In 106/725 he was engaged against the Alans and imposed the capitation

38 Following Zeki Validi, *ibid.*, 191-192; cf. ibn-Faḍlān, §70.

39 Ibn-al-Athīr, *loc.cit.* Cf. Chapter III, W-n-nd-r etc. and notes there.

40 Ibn-al-Athīr, *loc.cit.*, speaks of 40,000 families (!).

41 Otherwise Shakka, e.g. ibn-al-Faqīh, 288. This is "die Stadt Šaba" cited Kmosko, *ibid.*, from Elias of Nisibis. The Latin transl. (E. W. Brooks in *Corp. Script. Christ. Orient.*) has "urbem Shabbam," but it is incorrect.

42 Ṭabari, II, 1462; ibn-al-Athīr, *s. anno* 105.

tax.[43] The Khazars are not mentioned. Next year the Caliph recalled Jarrāḥ and assigned the governorship of Armenia and Adharbayjān to his own half-brother, Maslamah ibn-'Abd-al-Malik.

The appointment of Maslamah is itself an indication of the importance attached to the Khazar frontier at this period. The son of a slave-girl and hence excluded from succession to the throne, Maslamah for more than twenty years was one of the principal props of Umayyad power and a foremost actor on the stage of the East. He had already at this time commanded the great expedition against Byzantium, when the Arabs invested the capital of Christendom for more than a year (98/716-99/717), and had put down the rebellion of Yazīd ibn-al-Muhallab (102/720). Maslamah's chivalry, like his valor, was legendary.[44] His exploits and personality indeed captured the imagination not only of contemporaries[45] but distant generations.[46] Such was the man now chosen to vindicate the glory of Islam against the unbelieving Khazars.

At first the command was delegated to al-Ḥārith ibn-'Amr of the famous tribe of Ṭayy, who occupied Khazar territory and took a number of villages (A.H. 107).[47] These gains cannot have been very considerable. In 108 the Khazars appeared in Adharbayjān under the "son of the Khaqan." Al-Ḥārith went to encounter them, and a battle was fought in which the invaders were defeated and driven across the river Aras (Araxes). Here they made a stand, but were again beaten by the Muslims and lost great numbers killed.[48]

In the next campaigning season (109/727) Maslamah arrived in person. Advancing from Adharbayjān he reoccupied the pass of Darial, which had been lost, and marched into

[43] Ṭabari, II, 1472; ibn-al-Athīr, *s. anno* 106.

[44] Cf. *Mustaṭraf*, transl. Rat, I, 682, for Maslamah and a lady of Cairo; ibn-Qutaybah, *'Uyūn al-Akhbār*, ed. Brockelmann, 211.

[45] E.g. Kumayt in the *Ḥamāsah*, I, 774.

[46] Maslamah's expedition to Byzantium was treated in the *Muḥāḍarāt al-Abrār* ascribed to ibn-'Arabi and is an episode in the *Khamsah* of the Turkish poet Nargisi.

[47] Ibn-al-Athīr, *s. anno.*

[48] *Ibid.*, *s. anno* 108.

Khazaria. He is said to have been opposed by the Khaqan himself, but returned with prisoners and booty.[49] Maslamah, according to Mas'ūdi, at an unspecified date placed an Arab garrison in the fortress which defended the pass of Darial.[50] It was perhaps during this successful campaign that he did so. The fortress was built on a massive rock overlooking a bridge across a deep ravine and was, says Mas'ūdi, one of the most famous in the world.

Next year the fighting was more serious. Maslamah advanced as before from Darial (110/728) and engaged the armies of the Khaqan for nearly a month. Then, we are told, torrential rain descended, under cover of which the Khaqan fled.[51] Though the Muslims claimed a victory, another story seems to have been current.[52] Maslamah withdrew past the so-called "mosque of dhu-al-Qarnayn,"[53] a residence of the Georgian kings.

In spite of Maslamah's reputation and ability and the partial successes which he seems to have won, the Khazars evidently had not yet been effectively dealt with. They were back in Adharbayjān in the following year. Again they were repulsed by al-Ḥārith ibn-'Amr.[54] About this time Maslamah was recalled by Hishām, and Jarrāḥ ibn-'Abdullāh after an absence of several years returned as governor.

Jarrāḥ is said to have campaigned in Khazaria in the same year (A.H. 111). According to ibn-al-Athīr, he advanced from Tiflis (sc. through the Darial pass) and penetrated to al-Bayḍā', the Khazar capital, which he occupied. The exploit is at least seriously exaggerated. There can be no question at this time of a large-scale expedition, which alone would have been capable of such a feat, and that after heavy fighting and systematic

[49] *Ibid.*, *s. anno* 109, cf. Ya'qūbi, II, 395.

[50] *Murūj*, II, 43ff.

[51] Ṭabari, II, 1506; ibn-al-Athīr, *s. anno* 110. Ibn-Taghrībardi (I, 297) calls this the "Campaign of the Mud," apparently in error, cf. below.

[52] Michael Syrus, ed. Chabot, II, 501.

[53] Ibn-al-Athīr, *loc.cit.*, has "maslak dhī-al-Qarnayn," but cf. Marquart, *Streifz.*, 175.

[54] Ṭabari, II, 1526; ibn-al-Athīr, *s. anno* 111.

reduction of strong points. Khazaria was certainly not brought to its knees in 111/729. It is possible that a raid by a flying column actually got so far. On the other hand, how can a relatively small force have reached the Volga, on which al-Bayḍā' lay, and have returned safely through hostile country, as is stated by ibn-al-Athīr? It is important to note that the other authorities are silent about any invasion of Khazaria in this year. Almost certainly there is confusion with the great expedition of Marwān ibn-Muḥammad (later Caliph as Marwān II), which we have still to describe.

The year 112/730 was marked by perhaps the greatest defeat ever sustained by the Arabs at the hands of the Khazars—reason in itself for rejecting ibn-al-Athīr's notice of the events of A.H. 111. In A.H. 112 the Khazar forces poured through the pass of Darial[55] under the commander Bārjīk, already mentioned, to the number, it is said, of 300,000 men.[56] Jarrāḥ appears to have wintered as once before in Shakkī. Now he marched to Bardha'ah and thence to Ardabīl, where he awaited developments. Part of his forces were diverted to other districts, and he sent out columns into the surrounding country. The Khazars received word of his situation from the prince of Georgia,[57] and advanced as far as the southern Warathān, to which they laid siege. Jarrāḥ engaged the enemy near Warathān but was unable to relieve the town. We next find him back at Ardabīl in close proximity to the main Khazar army. Advised by a native of the country to hold a defensive position with his back to Mt. Sabalān, which rose nearby, the governor decided to risk a decisive encounter in the plain called Marj Ardabīl, near the town. The Khazars now came up with the Muslims, and both sides prepared for battle.

Of the action itself we have, as usual, little reliable information. Jarrāḥ had originally split up his available force. Yet the Syrians who remained with him and the local levies were in

[55] Ṭabari, II, 1530; ibn-al-Athīr, *s. anno* 112.
[56] Bal'ami, 517.
[57] *Ibid.*, 516. Dorn's translation (469) is not right.

sufficient numbers and good enough heart to hold their ground for two days in the most dreadful fighting which those who took part had ever seen.[58] Jarrāḥ seems to have been culpable in his decision to fight in the plain. The Khazars were greatly superior in number, and by evening on the second day this factor had told heavily. It was then seen that the situation of the Muslims was desperate. The veterans in the ranks, and especially the Qur'ān-readers, on whose encouragement the morale of a Muslim army in those days greatly depended, were mostly dead. Night fell, and many of the survivors slipped away under cover of darkness to their homes in Ādharbayjān, or elsewhere. At dawn on the third morning Jarrāḥ had but few men left, and these wounded or dispirited. The Khazars renewed the attack, and the Arabs turned to fly. Yet when one of Jarrāḥ's companions shouted, "To the Garden, Muslims, not the Fire! Follow the path of God, not Satan!" they retained the spirit to rally, and most of them fought on to the death. Jarrāḥ himself was killed commanding the shattered remnant. His head was struck off, and afterwards his women and children fell into the hands of the Khazars. The victory of the latter was complete. Much booty was taken, and only prisoners were wanting, for the Muslim army was dead or dying. A mere hundred escaped by flight. Ardabīl was immediately assaulted, and though it did not yield at once, the Khazars were soon in possession. All the city's fighting men were killed and the women and children taken.[59]

The effect of this disaster was widely felt among the Muslims. Jarrāḥ had been popular. His loss and the death of so many of his men made a deep impression. The brutality of the invaders excited indignant comment.[60] Jarrāḥ's defeat was

58 Ibn-al-Athīr, *loc.cit.*

59 The Khazar victory was also known to the Byzantines, cf. Theophanes, ed. Bonn, 626 under 720 (A.D. 728), who also speaks of the "son of the Khaqan" *'o 'uios Khaganou.* A tradition that Jarrāḥ was killed at Balanjar is referred to by Ṭabari (II, 1531) and ibn-al-Athīr (*loc.cit.*). It seems due to a confusion between his successful siege of Balanjar in A.H. 104 and the earlier debacle there (A.H. 32).

60 Bal'ami, 519.

talked about in central Asia the same year and considerably later.[61] The Caliph himself was concerned by the heavy losses. But more than all this, while measures were being taken at Damascus to deal with the situation, the Khazars continued to advance, and, overrunning Adharbayjān, reached Diyār Bakr and the vicinity of Mosul.[62] The alarming prospect of what seemed a mass migration of Khazars[63] was opening up before the Caliph and his advisers.

Al-Ḥajjāj ibn-ʿAbdullāh, the brother of Jarrāḥ, had assumed command in the north.[64] As once before, Hishām had recourse in the new emergency to Maslamah, and al-Ḥajjāj was set aside. But first, on the advice of the vizirs, the Caliph sent for Saʿīd ibn-ʿAmr al-Ḥarashi[65] from Manbij in Syria. This officer had previously held a command in Jurjān.[66] It was Hishām's intention to employ him in stemming the Khazar tide until such time as Maslamah was ready to take the field. According to ibn-al-Athīr, when Saʿīd reached Damascus, Hishām said to him, "I have heard that Jarrāḥ has fled from the polytheists [Khazars]." "Not so," replied Saʿīd. "Jarrāḥ had better knowledge of God than to fly. Rather he has been killed." "What then is your counsel?" asked the Caliph. "That you send me," was the reply, "with forty riders mounted on the horses of the post, and every day another forty, and that you write to the emirs of the armies to join me." So Hishām acted on his advice. According to another account, the Caliph with his own hand gave Saʿīd a standard and sent him north with 30,000 picked men, adequate supplies, and 100,000 dirhams for the expenses of the campaign.[67]

When he reached al-Jazīrah, Saʿīd came upon a few stragglers from the army of Jarrāḥ, and a painful scene of recognition followed. Proceeding to the Armenian town of Khilāṭ on

[61] Ṭabari, II, 1531 and 1595 (A.H. 119).
[62] Ibn-al-Athīr, *loc.cit.*
[63] Cf. Michael Syrus, II, 501.
[64] Ibn-al-Athīr, *loc.cit.*
[65] Or al-Jurashi. Wellhausen says that al-Ḥarashi is the nisbah to Ḥarīsh ibn-ʿĀmir (*Das arabische Reich*, 281).
[66] Ibn-Khaldūn, III, 82.
[67] Balʿami, 520.

Lake Van, he found the Khazars in possession. The Muslims attacked and took the town, then went on to Bardha'ah, reducing the fortresses en route. At Bardha'ah Sa'īd delivered a sermon, in which he urged the people to unite in face of the common danger; he appealed especially to the rich to relieve the needs of the poor. Then, having recommended all to pray for victory, he marched to Baylaqān.

While Sa'īd was encamped there, a local inhabitant complained that the "son of the Khaqan" had quartered one of his *ṭarkhāns*[68] in a neighboring village. The *ṭarkhān* had seized the man's daughters and was now drunk and helpless, and could easily be taken. Sa'īd accordingly sent an officer to the village. The detachment found the Khazar in a drunken sleep, with the young women sitting unharmed by him, and immediately despatched him where he lay. Then, killing or dispersing the other Khazars, they returned to Baylaqān and restored the girls to their father.

All this while, at Warathān, the Muslim garrison had held out, though heavily beleaguered. Sa'īd's next move was an attempt to raise the siege, in which he was successful with the help of a Khazar-speaking Persian, who passed through the Khazar lines and announced to the garrison that help was near at hand. The Khazars passed to the siege of Bajarwān, but on Sa'īd's advancing from Warathān, the Khazars raised the siege and moved again on Ardabīl with Sa'īd following. At Bajarwān he was approached by a cavalier in white,[69] who informed him that an army of Khazars, 10,000 strong with 5,000 Muslim prisoners, was encamped at a distance of four parasangs. Sa'īd accordingly sent one of his men to investigate. This was a certain Ibrāhīm ibn-'Āṣim al-'Uqayli. He was familiar with the

[68] Bal'ami, 522: *ṭarkhāni az ān khūd.* The title was in use among the Khazars, as among other Turkish peoples, and perhaps serves to connect them with the West Turks. The original meaning is said to be "descendants of the iron-smiths"; cf. Zeki Validi, *Ibn-Faḍlān*, 276.

[69] Bal'ami seems to intend a supernatural visitor. Ibn-al-Athīr (*loc.cit.*) speaks simply of a rider on a white horse. Ibn-Khaldūn (III, 89) rationalizes the story and renders "one of (Sa'īd's) spies."

Khazar language,[70] and, when disguised, had no difficulty in joining their camp. Meantime Saʿīd made ready to attack with a force of 4,000 men. Al-ʿUqayli returned with the news that the Khazars were indeed in the locality, and told how he had seen a girl belonging to the harem of Jarrāḥ molested by a *ṭarkhān*. When he heard her pray to God to save her, it was only with difficulty that he had refrained from coming to her help. Saʿīd and his men, much affected by what his officer had told him, started at once and reached the Khazar position before daybreak. They at once improvised an attack. Before any alarm was given, the Khazars were surrounded. The *takbīr*, raised by the assailants, was re-echoed by Muslim prisoners within the camp, and, thus stimulated, Saʿīd's men fell on the enemy, as they struggled out of sleep, with drastic effect. When the sun rose, we are told, a great part of the 10,000 had been massacred. The survivors fled to the "son of the Khaqan" and told him of the disaster.

Several similar incidents involving Muslim successes under Saʿīd's command are recorded. Finally the Khazars assembled to the number of no less than 100,000 under Bārjīk and lay encamped on a river at Baylaqān.[71] Saʿīd, with 50,000 men of Syria, Iraq, and al-Jazīrah, went to meet them. While the two armies were preparing to engage, the Muslims observed the head of Jarrāḥ, fixed above the throne or car from which the "son of the Khaqan" gave his orders, in the middle of the Khazar ranks. As he looked, Saʿīd's eyes filled with tears. "Truly we belong to God, and to God we return," said he. "Our life is dishonored while the head of such a Muslim brother as Jarrāḥ remains in the possession of unbelievers." Leading the charge, he fought his way to where the head was fixed. Bārjīk had descended from his car and was now on horseback. Saʿīd struck him to the ground.[72] He was saved by his guard, who

[70] Perhaps a *maula* (client) and of Khazar extraction. He is mentioned again (Ṭabari, II, 1594-1595) with the additional *nisbah* al-Khazari (needlessly altered by D. H. Müller *in loco*).

[71] Ibn-al-Athīr, *s. anno* 112.

[72] Some further details in Kasem Beg's Turkish "Ṭabari," *op.cit.*, 637.

dismounted and closed around their chief. According to another account, Sa'īd slew him and sent the head to Hishām.[73] It was at all events another Muslim victory. The Khazars were forced to flight, leaving countless dead and a great booty behind them. Sa'īd returned in triumph to Bajarwān, where the spoils were counted and a fifth sent to the Caliph. From what remained each man of the Muslim army received, it is said, no less than 1,700 *dinars*.[74]

As an authentic record of what took place, the narrative of Sa'īd's exploits against the Khazars is of course open to serious doubt. The mysterious character of the horseman who directs the Muslims and the numbers of the Khazar forces, rising progressively after each defeat, belong to romance rather than history. On the other hand, the account appears to contain indication of early date, e.g., the Khaqan or his son is called "the enemy of God,"[75] surely a contemporary description. Again, the exact hour of the day for one of the battles is given.[76] It is not credible that Bal'ami and ibn-al-Athīr, who give the same account, expanded the briefer notice in Ṭabari or filled up the remarks of Balādhuri, who confines himself to saying that Sa'īd raised the siege of Warathān and routed the Khazars. Rather, the whole story seems to have been known to Ṭabari, and also to Ya'qūbi, though not given by either of them in detail, and looks like an imaginative contemporary account.

For his services, which at any rate were considerable, Sa'īd was at first to reap little personal advantage. After distributing the booty, he marched to Maymadh in Adharbayjān, but had not yet engaged the Khazars when he received an angry letter from Maslamah, blaming him for having attacked them and announcing his supersession by 'Abd-al-Malik ibn-Muslim al-'Uqayli.[77] Sa'īd laid down his command and was by Maslamah's

[73] Ya'qūbi, II, 381. Al-Mufaḍḍal ibn-Salamah explains the proverb "He came with the head of the Khaqan" with reference to this exploit of Sa'īd ibn-'Amr (*Fākhir*, ed. Storey, 80). Cf. n. 96.

[74] Bal'ami, 531. The amount is evidently much too large.

[75] *Ibid.*, 529. [76] *Ibid.*

[77] Balādhuri, 206; Ya'qūbi, II, 381. Bal'ami and ibn-al Athīr differently.

orders confined at Qabalah. Here he had a conversation with his superior officer, reported by Balʿami. When Saʿīd was brought before him, Maslamah asked if he had not received instructions to desist from attacking the Khazars. Why had he acted independently and endangered the Muslims? To this Saʿīd answered that no word had reached him until God had already destroyed the unbelieving Khazars, by giving him the victory over them. "You lie," said Maslamah. "You wished to hear men speak of the numbers you had slain." "Not so," said the other. "I desired the glory of God and acted to secure it. The emir knows that it is the truth." But Maslamah's anger was not to be appeased. He caused Saʿīd to be insulted and manhandled. The Caliph's standard was broken over his head. Then he was removed to the public prison at Bardhaʿah. As soon as Hishām heard what had happened, he wrote to his brother, expressing serious displeasure. After taking action against Saʿīd, Maslamah had started out late in the season and advanced through rain and snow beyond Bāb into Khazaria.[78] But owing to the time already lost, a valuable opportunity for dealing a decisive blow had passed. It could not now be retrieved by Maslamah's unseasonable exertions. Hishām had learned what his brother was attempting and now in his letter wrote the verse:

Do you leave the Khazars at Maymadh when you see them,
and pursue them at the ends of the earth?[79]

Back from his expedition, Maslamah was obliged to make fair amends to his former lieutenant. He sent Saʿīd the Caliph's letter and asked his pardon, with regrets for what had occurred. Saʿīd was brought out of prison and, having been awarded a ceremonial dress and gifts for himself and his family, was given to understand that he was one whom the Caliph delighted to honor. Certain estates now assigned to him were later known by his name. In the face of all the material from a number of

[78] Ṭabari, II, 1531-1532; ibn-al-Athīr, *s. anno* 112.

[79] Balādhuri, 207; cf. Hitti, *Origins of the Islamic State*, New York 1916, 324.

sources, we must allow that Saʿīd's activities were of real importance, though somewhat obscured by legend. He should probably have a place among the most successful Arab commanders against the Khazars.

For the events of 112/730 our narrative gains confirmation once again from the Khazar side. The memory of the capture of Ardabīl appears to have been retained long afterwards. According to the Reply of Joseph, when the Jewish religion had already been established among them, the king of the Khazars was inspired to set up a place of worship, and for the purpose of obtaining the necessary means undertook an expedition by way of the Darial pass, into the country south of the mountains. The principal objective of this expedition was Ardabīl. The Khazar returned with a treasure of gold and silver, and this was dedicated and used for providing the furniture—ark, lamp-stand, table, etc.—of a tabernacle on the Biblical model. The Reply adds that these still existed (c. A.D. 960).[80] This story is no doubt legendary in its existing form. Yet there is nothing unnatural in the Jewish Khazars having a tent set apart for religious purposes. We find such later among Mongol Christians.[81] An instance has already been mentioned of precious metals from the lands south of the Caucasus being carried north.[82] We may safely say at least that the great victory of the Khazars over Jarrāḥ was not forgotten by them.

Maslamah's greatest effort was made in the next year 113/731.[83] The situation from his point of view was hardly improving. Fresh forces of Khazars had assembled north of the Caucasus. Al-Ḥārith ibn-ʿAmr al-Ṭāʾi, previously left by Maslamah at Bāb, had not been able to prevent them from occupying the place with 1,000 of their families.[84] Perhaps as serious as any-

[80] See Chapter VI.

[81] Cf. D. M. Dunlop, "The Karaits of East Asia," *B.S.O.A.S.* 1944, xi/2, 278-279, 286, 287.

[82] See Chapter I, *ad finem*.

[83] Ṭabari, II, 1560; ibn-al-Athīr, *s. anno* 113; cf. Yaʿqūbi, II, 381. Yaʿqūbi elsewhere (II, 395) gives A.H. 114. Lammens (*E.I.*, art. Maslamah) dates the retreat from Khazaria in A.H. 115.

[84] Balādhuri, 207: *alf ahl bayt min al-Khazar*. The expression "ahl

thing else was the attitude of the native rulers, who were giving the Muslims much trouble. We read of resistance at Khaydhān, where Maslamah dealt out severe measures. He then passed to Bāb with contingents from most of the former allies, who had made a virtue of necessity and joined him of their own accord. The Khazars in the fortress town were too few to delay him, so, leaving them unmolested, the Arab general passed into Khazaria, where he deployed his forces. This—probably a dangerous thing to do—was at first successful. Isolated detachments of the Khazars were either killed or put to flight, and several towns or forts, among them Ḥamzīn, fell into Maslamah's hands. The inhabitants of at least one place burned themselves to death rather than surrender. The Muslims proceeded to Balanjar and then over the "mountains of Balanjar"[85] to Samandar. Both these places, like Ḥamzīn, were very lightly defended, if at all, but they perhaps afforded plunder to the invaders.[86]

Samandar was the farthest point reached. Having information that the main body of the Khazars and their allies, "a multitude whose numbers God alone knew," was close at hand, like Jarrāḥ in a similar situation,[87] Maslamah decided that it was necessary to retreat. Now began a most spectacular march.[88] Maslamah gave orders that the campfires should be lighted before the withdrawal began, to deceive the enemy. The tents were left as they had been pitched. The heavy baggage was sacrificed. By then many of the men were in no condition to march and fight at the same time. They were set at the head of the column, while the freshest troops formed the

bayt," as Zeki Validi notes (ibn-Faḍlān, 190 n.) hardly by itself means "distinguished families." Bal'ami (533-534) has "a thousand men of the *ṭarkhāns*" (cf. 536, "a thousand families of Khazars").

85 Ṭabari, *loc.cit.* A "mountain of the Khazars" is mentioned in *Ḥudūd al-'Ālam*, §47. Zeki Validi ("Völkerschaften," 44) doubtfully identifies it with the Caucasus peak Bogos.

86 Zeki Validi, *Ibn-Faḍlān*, 305 (? from ibn-A'tham al-Kūfi).

87 See above.

88 The retreat of Maslamah's expedition was known to the Byzantines, cf. Theophanes, 626, under 721 (A.D. 729).

rear. By forced marches, covering two stages in the normal time for one, the Muslims retired by the way they had come. According to ibn-al-Athīr, they reached Bāb at their last gasp.[89]

Sometime later the Khazars, following through the passes, made contact with the Muslims.[90] Maslamah drew up his army with Sulaymān ibn-Hishām[91] on the left wing and Marwān ibn-Muḥammad on the right, while al-'Abbās ibn-al-Walīd[92] had command of the center. Local levies under native chiefs bore the shock of the Khazar attack. With the great standard of the Umayyads unfurled,[93] the Arabs and their allies held their position all day. Marwān specially distinguished himself in the action. Often he was lost to view and once was reported to Maslamah as dead. "No, by God!" said the general, "Not till he has attained the Caliphate!" Towards evening a Khazar deserter pointed out to Maslamah where the Khaqan sat in a tented car[94] and urged him to attack it. Marwān volunteered, but the task was given to another, Thābit al-Nahrāni.[95] This officer pressed forward, accompanied by a small picked force, and with a blow of his sword cut open the brocade of the

89 Ibn-al-Athīr's account (*loc.cit.*) is the most detailed. Ṭabari (*loc.cit.*) omits mention of the retreat (as does Ya'qūbi).

90 Ṭabari-ibn-al-Athīr, in this agreeing with Theophanes (n. 88), put the main engagement with the Khazars on this campaign, i.e., the engagement in which according to Ṭabari-ibn-al-Athīr the "son of the Khaqan" was killed, before the retreat from Khazaria. According to Yaq'ūbi (*loc.cit.*) the battle was fought at W-r-?ān (Houtsma, Warthān). This is almost certainly Varach'an, i.e. the northern Warathān (cf. Chapter III, n. 17). According to ibn-A'tham al-Kūfi the battle was at Darband (Zeki Validi, *Ibn-Faḍlān*, 305). It cannot be assumed that the account is fictitious on the general ground that Bal'ami and ibn-A'tham al-Kūfi, are unreliable, or because nothing is said about such a battle by Marwān, when giving his opinion of Maslamah's conduct to the Caliph (see below). There appears to be independent confirmation for the event (n. 96).

91 Son of the Caliph. His career was unfortunate and ended tragically at the advent of the Abbasids.

92 Son of al-Walīd I.

93 Bal'ami, 534.

94 Zeki Validi (*Ibn-Faḍlān*, 120) quotes from ibn-A'tham al-Kūfi a description of this car, which is called in the source *j-dādah* (perhaps a Khazar word, as Zeki Validi thinks probable). Its floor was spread with various carpets. The tent-cover was of silk brocade, and above was a pomegranate of gold. For other cars in the train of a Khazar princess see Chapter VII.

95 It seems unlikely that this was the commander of A.H. 103.

tented car. The Khaqan was wounded, but in the confusion managed to escape. Meanwhile the Muslims, having seen what was happening, made a general charge and were soon left in possession of the field.[96]

It was possible after the withdrawal of the Khazars to deal with the town of Bāb at leisure. The place proved too strong to take by assault, in spite of the artillery which Maslamah brought up for the purpose. He then had recourse to the old stratagem of poisoning the water supply. A single day of thirst convinced the Khazars of the hopelessness of their position. The next night they abandoned the town and fled northward. Maslamah and his army entered Bāb, which in the period that followed was thoroughly reorganized. Separate quarters were created for the men of Damascus, Kufah, al-Jazīrah, and Ḥimṣ. Granaries of wheat and barley were constructed, with a magazine for arms. A governor was appointed.[97] The fortifications were restored, and an iron gate was put in place.[98] It is evident

[96] Though Bal'ami's account mentions Bārjīk, the "son of the Khaqan," as well as the Khaqan, we cannot assume that the two Khazar kings are intended, as the account appears to be confused. According to ibn-Qutaibah (*Ma'ārif*, 185) Maslamah met and killed the Khaqan of the Turks (Khazars) and built Bāb in this year, A.H. 113. It seems more likely that there was a battle with the Khazars in 113, as we have given it, than that the reports of this (cf. also Balādhuri, 207, according to which Marwān was with Maslamah and greatly distinguished himself against the Khazars) refer to Sa'īd's victory the previous year, when according to Ya'qūbi, as already remarked, the son of the Khaqan was killed and his head sent to Hishām. On the other hand, it is a suspicious circumstance that in 113 another Khazar chief (the "son of the Khaqan" according to Ṭabarī-ibn-Athīr, the Khaqan according to ibn-Qutaybah) is said to have been killed during a campaign which was on the whole unsuccessful and appears to have cost Maslamah his governorship. Possibly Maslamah as at that time Sa'īd's superior officer got the credit for what happened in the previous year. Certainly the proverb "He came with the head of the Khaqan" (n. 73) or "Prouder than he who came with the head of the Khaqan" (Maydāni) should refer to an actual event. This was taken by Freytag to be what happened in central Asia in A.H. 119 (*Arabum Proverbia*, I, 195). In that year the Khaqan of the Turks (Türgesh) was killed after the Turkish defeat in a private quarrel and was buried by his own people (Ṭabari, II, 1613). The heads of some of the Turks with the insignia of the Khaqan were sent to Hishām (*id.*, II, 1616), but there is no indication that his corpse came into the possession of the Arabs.

[97] Bal'ami, 538.

[98] The Syriac chronicle cited by Kmosko, *ibid.* (MS. B.M. Add.

that these measures had the requirements of a future war in view and must have been directed in the first place against the Khazars. When all the arrangements had been made, Maslamah left his relative Marwān in charge and returned to Syria (A.H. 114).

The last phase of the second Arab-Khazar war is associated with the name of Marwān ibn-Muḥammad. Late in 114[99] (732) he assembled an army put at 40,000 men and advanced past Balanjar into Khazaria. Rain fell continuously. During the campaign Marwān is said to have given orders for the tails of the horses to be cut off because of the mud which clung to them—the mud from which this expedition got its name.[100] We do not read that much was accomplished. A number of the enemy were killed and prisoners and booty taken.

Some time later[101] Marwān presented himself, before his cousin Hishām, and when asked the reason of his coming, boldly criticized the measures which had been taken against the Khazars since the defeat of Jarrāḥ. In particular he spoke slightingly of Maslamah. The Caliph listened to Marwān when he proposed that he himself should be sent back to the frontier with full powers and an army of 120,000 men. Hishām seems to have been prompted to a decision by news from the north. Sa'īd ibn-'Amr, who was then in command, had developed a cataract and written to the Caliph to ask for a successor.[102] So Marwān had his way and departed for the Caucasus frontier with the Caliph's commission as governor of Armenia.

If Sa'īd, as we are told, was governor for two years,[103] Marwān can hardly have returned till 117/735. Soon after his arrival he established a new headquarters at Kasāk, forty parasangs from Bardha'ah and twenty from Tiflis.[104] From

---

14,642, ed. Brooks, 235), speaks of masons and other workmen in the army of Maslamah.

99 Ṭabari, II, 1562.

100 Bal'ami, *ibid.*, cf. n. 51.

101 Ibn-al-Athīr, *s. anno* 114. The indication here that Marwān returned with Maslamah appears to be wrong.

102 Bal'ami, 539.

103 Balādhuri, 207. Ṭabari ignores Sa'īd's governorship (II, 1563, 1573).

104 So Balādhuri, *ibid.* Balādhuri has Kisāl, Bal'ami Kasāl, but ibn-

the first it was his intention to take the offensive against the Khazars, yet this he was unable to do immediately. As usual, there were rebel chiefs in Armenia to deal with, and this entailed considerable fighting. An expedition was also necessary to the Alan country, where the Muslims took and perhaps held three fortresses.[105] These operations seem to have kept Marwān engaged for more than a year. It was not till 119/737[106] that he was free to undertake his main enterprise, the invasion and, if possible, the subjection of Khazaria.

When on the point of setting his army in motion against Khazaria, he announced that he was about to attack the Alans. A special envoy was sent to the Khazar Khaqan, who granted the Muslims a truce on this understanding. A Khazar ambassador came to Marwān to confirm the terms. He was delayed in the camp while the Muslims made their final dispositions.

Whatever may be thought of this negotiation—and it has to be remembered that Marwān's bad faith was at the expense of embittered and dangerous foes of his house and nation—the Muslim general's strategic conception is altogether admirable. The plan was at once simple and original—first, to ensure a surprise and then attack simultaneously through the passes of Darband and Darial. Its execution was wholly successful. Marwan now had at his disposal a large force, perhaps as many as 150,000 men,[107] volunteers as well as regular levies. He himself with the main body advanced through the Darial pass. At the same time another army proceeded from Bāb under abu Yazīd Usayd ibn-Zāfir al-Sulami. For long the Khaqan and his advisers must have remained uncertain of what was happening. Abu Yazīd had instructions to rendezvous at Samandar.

A'tham al-Kūfi's Kasāk is probably right (Zeki Validi, *Ibn-Faḍlān*, 296).

[105] Ṭabari, II, 1573.

[106] Ibn-al-Athīr's main account of Marwān's expedition is given *s. anno* 114, but this is too early. He has a short doublet *s. anno* 119. Ṭabari has nothing, beyond the fact that Marwān was governor of Armenia and Adharbayjān in 119 (II, 1635), but cf. ibn-Taghrībardi, I, 314. There is general agreement that Marwān's expedition was in 119/737 (Artamonov, 738).

[107] So Bal'ami, 539.

The place is significant. If Marwān, as is likely, had already been there, his memories cannot have been agreeable, for the great retreat in A.H. 113 had begun from Samandar. It had seen the discomfiture of Jarrāḥ as well as Maslamah. No Arab army had been able to go farther.[108] It seems to have been Marwān's intention on the present occasion to reach Samandar in such irresistible force as would carry the invaders over any obstacle to the heart of Khazaria.

Balanjar was by-passed by the northern army. The two columns converged on their objective against negligible opposition. When Samandar was reached[109] a great review was held. The army, we are told, was issued with white clothing—it was the Umayyad color—and brand-new spears.[110] How this could have been done so far from a base is not indicated. Possibly Marwān may have thought it worthwhile to convey a heavy baggage-train with him, in order to give the farther advance from Samandar the greater significance for every soldier in the ranks.

The Khazar envoy had been detained until the last possible moment. Then Marwān summoned him and, having abused the Khazars roundly, declared open war. Even after this, he was led back by a circuitous route, so that as much time as possible might be gained.[111] When at last the envoy reached his master, Marwān was already deep in the Khazar country. Filled with alarm, the Khaqan summoned his council and asked their advice.[112] They could recommend nothing better than an immediate flight from the capital, on the ground that it was hopeless either to oppose the Muslims as he was, or wait until larger forces could be assembled. The Khaqan therefore withdrew northeast towards the mountains (Urals). His capital was left screened by a picked force of considerable size. Marwān advanced from Samandar and in due course reached the

[108] Except possibly raiding columns, see above.

[109] Bal'ami, *ibid.*

[110] So ibn-A'tham al-Kūfi, cited Zeki Validi, *Ibn-Faḍlān*, 296 ff.

[111] Ibn-al-Athīr, *s. anno* 114.

[112] Ibn-al-Athīr, *loc.cit.*, who speaks of the "king of the Khazars," cf. Balādhuri, 208, who has the "chief of the Khazars" (*'aẓīm*). The council is to be noted, cf. below.

neighborhood of al-Bayḍā',[113] as the Khazar metropolis was then called by the Arabs, but did not attempt to blockade it. Instead he turned away and marched north, along the right bank of the Volga.

Above the Khazar country proper, settlements belonging to the people called Burṭās extended for some distance, as far as the Volga Bulgars.[114] Both peoples evidently at this time, as later, belonged to the Khazar empire. The Burṭās were now directly exposed to Muslim attack and suffered severely. It is said that 20,000 families were made prisoners and forced to emigrate south.[115] Great havoc was also caused by the invaders among the herds of horses in this region.[116]

Meanwhile the Khazar army already mentioned, under a certain Hazār Ṭarkhān, had followed Marwān along the opposite bank of the Volga.[117] The time came when the latter judged it proper to attack them. The crossing of the river was assigned to a Syrian, Kawthar ibn-al-Aswad al-ʿAnbari, who had instructions to keep a lookout for the enemy and ambush them when found. Marwān himself proposed to cross later, when they could take the enemy between them. Kawthar was reluctant to move (as well he might be), but the general would admit no delay. We gather that some kind of pontoon bridge[118] was constructed on the Volga, by means of which the first Muslims crossed over. A small party of Khazar huntsmen were overpowered and killed. On the first night, as they were preparing to bivouac on the outskirts of a wood—for by now the steppe had been left behind[119]—smoke was seen rising from its center, and the Muslims judged, rightly as it proved, that this was the Khazar army. Pushing forward, Kawthar and his men came on the enemy encampment and, thanks to the unexpectedness of their arrival, gained a rapid and decisive victory. From prisoners Kawthar learned that the leader of the hunting-party which they had earlier met was Hazār Ṭarkhān himself. There

[113] So ibn-al-Athīr, ibn-Taghrībardi, ibn-A'tham al-Kūfi.

[114] See Chapter V.

[115] Balādhuri, 208; ibn-A'tham al-Kūfi, *loc.cit.*

[116] Balʿami, 540.

[117] Ibn-A'tham al-Kūfi, *loc.cit.*

[118] Cf. Zeki Validi, *Ibn-Faḍlān*, 300, n. 1.

[119] The wooded character of the Burṭās country is confirmed by ibn-Rustah, 140.

was no further fighting east or west of the river. Kawthar rejoined the general. With his last available force destroyed, the Khaqan now sent a request for terms. Marwān offered him, it is said, a plain alternative–Islam or the sword. The envoy asked for three days in which to bring back a decisive answer. Evidently the Khaqan was not far away. At the expiration of the time he returned to say that the Khaqan was ready to become a Muslim.

In his message the Khaqan requested that someone should come to instruct him in Islam. Marwān sent two *faqīhs*, Nūḥ ibn-al-Sā'ib al-Asadi and 'Abd-al-Raḥmān al-Khawlāni.[120] The chief topic of the religious discussion was apparently the obligation to abstain from certain kinds of food–"impure" meat, blood, swine's flesh and wine. The Khaqan specially asked that the meat and wine might be permitted him, a request which led to a difference of opinion between the colleagues. Finally the Khaqan was told that the prohibition was absolute, and he expressed willingness to accept this ruling. There was no further obstacle, and the Khaqan professed Islam.

If we may conjecture Marwān's intention, it was to treat Khazaria like the small principalities of the Caucasus, which had become more or less amenable as soon as their rulers accepted the religion of the Caliph. Khazaria indeed was a different proposition. It appears that an Arab governor and a strong permanent army would have been necessary to hold the country. No doubt at this moment Marwān could have supplied both, but he did nothing of the kind. The considerations which weighed with him can only be guessed at. Perhaps it was that seeing domestic trouble ahead and not wishing to have a large number of troops committed far away, he hoped to be able to control Khazaria through a Muslim Khaqan. In any case, having superintended the return of the Khazar to his capital, he bade him farewell and marched southwards with his victorious army and a great train of prisoners.[121] So ended the famous "Raid of the Courser," as the campaign was called.[122]

120 Bal'ami, ibn-A'tham al-Kūfi.

121 The Khazar prisoners were settled "between the Samūr and Shābirān

It is difficult to avoid the feeling of anticlimax. More should have come of the Muslim successes. Marwān had no doubt good enough reasons for withdrawal. From one point of view his action was natural and proper. He applied to Khazaria the precedent with which he was familiar, that of the Caucasus principalities. He lived in other days than the first generation of Muslims, when new solutions of new problems were successfully applied. In accepting the precedent, Marwān showed, or so it seems, that his political insight was by no means on a level with his military genius. The Arabs at this time had a chance of removing what from the beginning had proved a perpetual obstacle to their advance and occasionally a menace to their own security. This chance seems to have been thrown away by the man who made it. It was never to come again. Khazaria was not destined to become a Muslim province, but to remain what it had been, an obstacle and potential threat to the Arabs, until it succumbed long afterwards to other hands.

The remainder of Marwān's governorship presents in general little of direct interest for Khazar history. The two or three years after 119/737 were spent in operations against the Avars of the Sarīr and other groups.[123] Meanwhile the Khaqan of the Khazars was evidently left to himself. An indication of what may have been happening in Khazaria is afforded by the action of one Ūpas ibn-Maḍār,[124] apparently chief of the Lakz (Lesgians), who, refusing submission to Marwān, shut himself up in his castle, where he was besieged, apparently in 122/740. In the end he left the castle by night with a few companions, intending to escape to the "king of the Khazars." Ūpas may have been in correspondence with some of the Khazar prisoners recently settled in his neighborhood.[125] It would appear that at that time the Khaqan was thought to be capable of pursuing

---

[rivers] in the lowland of al-Lakz." The Burṭās were sent to Khakhīṭ (Kakhetia), where they killed their (Muslim) emir and fled, but were overtaken and killed by Marwān (Balādhuri, *loc.cit.*)

[122] Ibn-Taghrībardi, *loc.cit.*

[123] Bal'ami, 541ff; Balādhuri, 208ff; ibn-al-Athīr, *s. anno* 114 and the doublet *s. anno* 121, with traces also in a third place, *s. anno* 118.

[124] Bal'ami, 545; ibn-al-Athīr, *s. anno* 114 and *s. anno* 118.

[125] Cf. n. 121.

an independent course. If the date A.D. 740 is right for the Khazar conversion to Judaism,[126] he certainly was. It follows from a remark of Balādhuri that Marwān at this time assigned the post of honor to the Shirwān Shāh "when the Muslims took the field against the Khazars," that hostilities were at least expected.[127]

At first sight, the statements that the Khaqan became a Muslim in A.D. 737 and Judaized three years later are, to say the least, remarkable.[128] It has already been suggested that they bear some relation to each other.[129] We have still to discuss elsewhere the date of the conversion of the Khazars to Judaism. Meantime, it may be noted that a phenomenon so rare in all history becomes rather more understandable if a year or two previously the religious and political situation in Khazaria had been violently disturbed. A consideration which may here be raised is that the story of the religious disputation which was held according to the Hebrew sources before the Khaqan, prior to his conversion to Judaism, is perhaps to be connected with the presence of the Muslim shaikhs sent by Marwān. The ingenious suggestion has been made[130] that a certain ʿAbd-al-Raḥmān ibn-Zubayr mentioned in a tradition as one of three persons who converted the king of the Bulgars to Islam, is the same as ʿAbd-al-Raḥmān al-Khawlāni, one of the two *faqīhs* who were with the Khaqan. It is not to be excluded that, having withdrawn from Khazaria after an unsuccessful mission, this man proceeded with better fortune to the Bulgars of the Volga.

As already noticed, Marwān was engaged for some time after his return from Khazaria in reducing the mountain kings, but apparently intended to resume operations against the Khaqan at a later date. We nowhere find that he did so. Disaffection had spread among the Muslim inhabitants of his province, so that he had to deal with a strong Khārijite movement. He re-

126 See especially Chapter VI.

127 Balādhuri, 209.

128 If he were already a Jew in 737, somewhat less so. Cf. above, events of 112/730.

129 Marquart, *Streifz.*, 13.

130 By Zeki Validi, *Ibn-Faḍlān*, 307.

tained his governorship till the death of Hishām (125/743) and later through the brief reigns of al-Walīd II and Yazīd III, but no action seems to have been taken against the Khazars. No doubt they made use of the respite to strengthen their position. Yet more fortunate for the Khaqan and his friends was the later course of events, from 126/744, the year in which Marwān left his province to contend for the Caliphate. It is probably no exaggeration to say that the subsequent dynastic struggle between the Umayyads and the Abbasids saved Khazaria. One of the effects of the revolution, as we can see from the sequel, was to hold up Muslim expansion on the Caucasus indefinitely.

The situation, however, had wider implications. As recently as 114/732, in Hishām's Caliphate, Muslim armies had been engaged in the same year both north of the Pyrenees and beyond the Caucasus. There is no proof of concerted action, determined and controlled by the Caliph in Damascus—the probability is in fact the other way—but it may be thought that the threat to Europe and Christendom was never so grave, even when Constantinople had fallen, or when Turkish armies stood at the gates of Vienna. The double attempt in that year failed. In the west the Franks of Charles Martel defeated "Abderame" ('Abd-al-Raḥmān ibn-'Abdullāh al-Ghāfiqi) at the battle of Tours and drove the invaders back towards the mountains.[131] On the Caucasus Marwān's attack was abortive. But, as we saw, in 119/737 Marwān was again in Khazaria, and this time, if we may trust our sources, he came within an ace of succeeding. Had Khazaria been permanently occupied by Marwān or one of his successors, the following years would doubtless have seen great Muslim campaigns on the Don and the Dnieper. Foiled in the west, the Arabs might have been victorious in eastern Europe. The margin by which Khazaria survived appears to have been narrow, but it did survive, and the boundary of Islam in this direction was permanently fixed on the Caucasus.

[131] Hitti, *History of the Arabs*, ed. 3, 501, points out that even after Tours the operations of the Muslims in other parts of France continued.

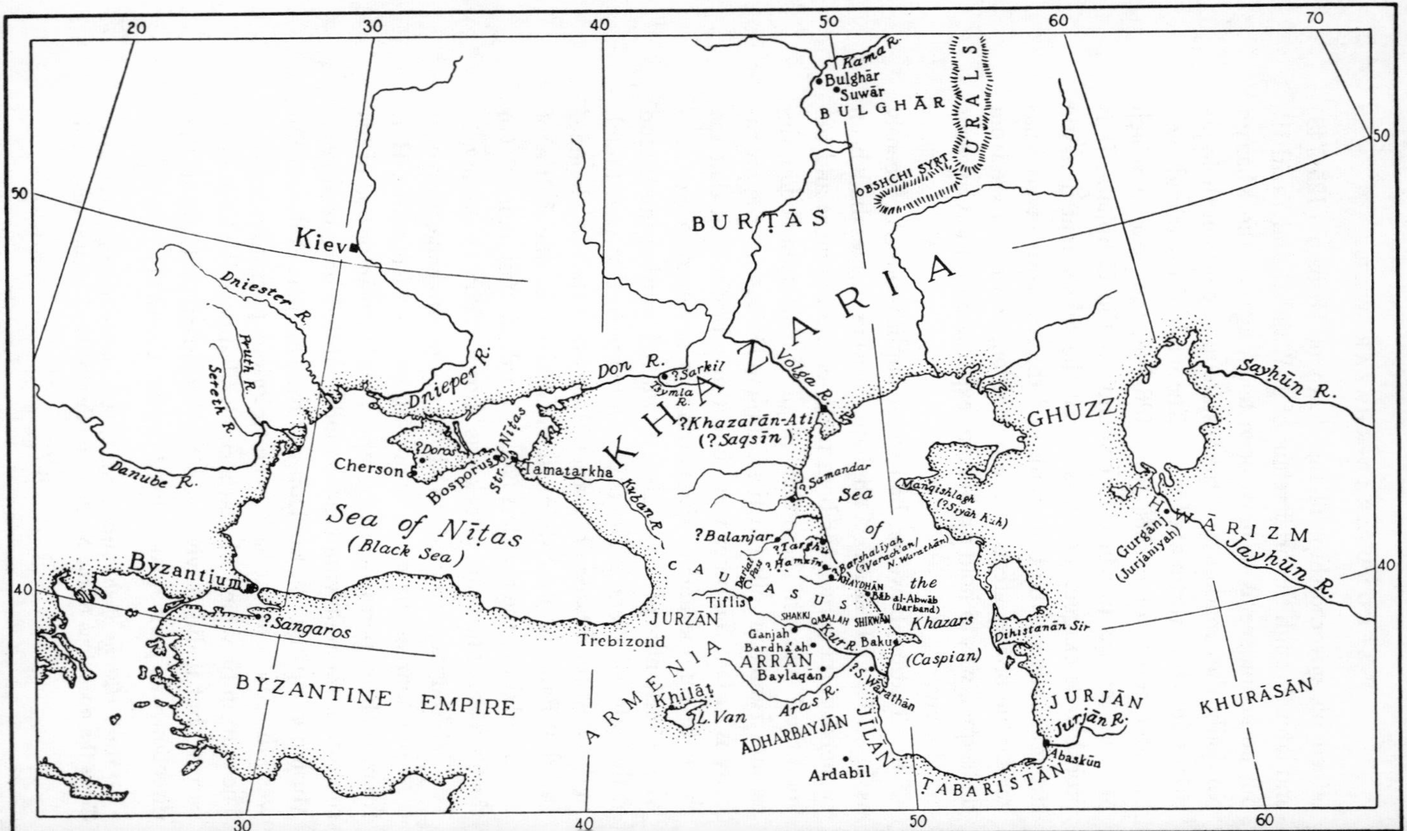
Kama R.
Bulghār
Suwār
BULGHĀR
URALS
OBSHCHI SYRT
BURṬĀS
KHAZARIA
Kiev
Dniester R.
Pruth R.
Sereth R.
Danube R.
Dnieper R.
Don R.
?Sarkil
Tsymla R.
Volga R.
?Khazarān-Atil
(?Saqsīn)
Cherson
?Doros
Bosporus
Str. of Nīṭas
Tamatarkha
Kuban R.
?Samandar
Sea of the Khazars
(Caspian)
Sea of Nīṭas
(Black Sea)
Byzantium
?Sangaros
BYZANTINE EMPIRE
Trebizond
JURZĀN
CAUCASUS
?Balanjar
?Targhu
?Ḥamzīn
Barshalīyah
(?Varach'an/N. Warathān)
KHAYDHĀN
Bāb al-Abwāb
(Darband)
Tiflis
SHAKKĪ
QABALAH
SHIRWĀN
Ganjah
Bardhā'ah
Kur R.
Baku
ARRĀN
Baylaqān
?S. Warathān
Aras R.
ARMENIA
Khilāṭ
L. Van
ĀDHARBAYJĀN
JĪLĀN
Ardabīl
ṬABARISTĀN
Abaskūn
Jurjān R.
JURJĀN
KHURĀSĀN
Dihistānān Sir
Manqishlagh
(?Siyāh Kūh)
GHUZZ
Sayḥūn R.
KHWĀRIZM
Jayḥūn R.
Gurgānj
(Jurjāniyah)
20
30
40
50
60
70

CHAPTER V

THE KHAZAR CONVERSION TO JUDAISM *ACCORDING TO THE ARABIC SOURCES*

THERE is no *locus classicus* in Arabic for the Judaizing of the Khazars, but perhaps the most frequently canvassed passage is the following, from the well-known *Murūj al-Dhahab* (Meadows of Gold) of Mas'ūdi, begun in 332/943 and completed in 336/947: "In this city [i.e., Atil, the capital of Khazaria on the Volga] are Muslims, Christians, Jews and pagans. The Jews are the king, his attendants and the Khazars of his kind [*jins*]. The king of the Khazars had already become a Jew in the Caliphate of Hārūn al-Rashīd, and there joined him Jews from all the lands of Islam and from the country of the Greeks. Indeed the king of the Greeks at the present time, A.H. 332 [=A.D. 943-944], Armānūs [i.e., Romanus Lecapenus] has converted the Jews in his kingdom to Christianity and coerced them. We shall give the history and numbers of the kings of the Greeks later in this book, with an account of this king and him who shares his empire with him [i.e., Constantine Porphyrogenitus] at this time in which our book is dated. Many Jews took flight from the country of the Greeks to Khazaria, aṣ we have described. An account is given of the Judaizing of the Khazar king which we do not mention here. We have already mentioned it in a previous work."[1]

It is a matter of conjecture which of his writings Mas'ūdi here refers to, and the account has not come to light. In a work of Dimashqi (*ob.* 727/1327) the following occurs. "Ibn-al-Athīr tells how in the days of Hārūn the Emperor forced the Jews to emigrate. They came to the Khazar country, where they found an intelligent but untutored race and offered them their

[1] *Murūj al-Dhahab*, II, 8-9. I have followed the arrangement of Bodleian MS., Marsh 243 (I, 792), collated by Professor Kahle.

religion. The inhabitants found it better than their own and accepted it."[2] Marquart, who had looked without success for the passage in ibn-al-Athīr here indicated, came to the likely opinion that Mas'ūdi is meant.[3] Further, the Spaniard Bakri (*ob.* 487/1094) has: "The reason for the conversion of the king of the Khazars, who had previously been a heathen, to Judaism was as follows. He had adopted Christianity. Then he recognized the wrongness of his belief and began to speak with one of his governors about the concern with which he was filled. The other said to him, O king, the People of the Book form three classes. Invite them and enquire of them, then follow whichever is in possession of the truth. So he sent to the Christians for a bishop. Now there was with him a Jew, skilled in debate, who disputed with the bishop, asking him, What do you say about Moses, son of Amram, and the Torah which was revealed to him? The other replied, Moses is a prophet, and the Torah is true. Then said the Jew to the king, He has admitted the truth of my creed. Ask him now what he believes. So the king asked him and he replied, I say that the Messiah, Jesus the son of Mary, is the Word, and that he has made known the mysteries in the name of God. Then the Jew said to the king of the Khazars, He confesses a doctrine which I know not, while he admits what I set forth. But the bishop was not strong in bringing proofs. So he invited the Muslims, and they sent him a learned and intelligent man who understood disputation. But the Jew hired someone against him who poisoned him on the way, so that he died. And the Jew was able to win the king for his religion."[4] Whatever may be thought of the content of this story, it gives us a tradition of a religious debate having preceded the Khazar conversion to Judaism, which is unique among the Arabic sources available. The part played by another prominent Khazar is to be noted. This is a feature of the Hebrew accounts.[5] Here it is he, not the king, who suggests that a debate should be held. If the story in Bakri is in the

[2] *Cosmographie*, ed. Mehren, 263.

[3] *Streifz.*, 6.

[4] Ed. Kunik and Rosen, 44 (transl. Marquart, *Streifz.*, 7-8).

[5] See Chapter VI.

main a reproduction of Mas'ūdi's lost account, as Marquart thought probable, we have by combination with the passages already cited that Mas'ūdi gave the conversion as having taken place, following a disputation before the Khazar king, not later than A.D. 809 (death of Hārūn). This result is in principle not inconsistent with Jewish tradition. According to Jehudah ha-Levi in *Cosri* (*Kuzari*), the conversion took place, after the debate on the merits of Judaism, Christianity, and Islam which is the setting of that work (and the theme of a large part of the Reply of Joseph), in A.D. 740. The difference in Mas'ūdi's account with regard to dating may amount to less than fifty years (Hārūn became Caliph in 170/786), and considering that Mas'ūdi wrote, no doubt in haste,[6] a century and a half after Hārūn's time, is not very serious.

We have now to show further evidence in Arabic sources for the date of the conversion, and the circumstances in which it took place. It is convenient to begin with Iṣṭakhri, whose account is as follows:[7] "As to Khazaria, it is the name of the region, and its capital is called Atil.[8] Atil is also the name of the river which flows to it from the Russians [al-Rūs] and Bulgars [Bulghār]. Atil is in two parts,[9] one west of the river called Atil, which is the larger, and the other east of it.[10] The king lives in the western part. The king in their language is called Bak and also Bāk. The extent of this part in length is about a league. It is

[6] Cf. Marquart, *Streifz.*, xxxv.

[7] Ed. De Goeje, 220-226. I have also used a Chester Beatty MS. in Professor Kahle's collation (K).

[8] De Goeje edited Ithil, but the most authentic form in Arabic is Atil, sometimes Ātil. In Hebrew '-t-l (Reply in L.V., ben-Daud), '-ṭil (Camb. Doc.), 'iṭ-l (Eldad ha-Dani), always with ' (and always of the river). Āmul of the Paris ed. of *Murūj al-Dhahab* is a serious blunder, which is still having its effect.

[9] According to others, the city was in three parts. Bury suggests that the western town included an island on which, according to Mas'ūdi (see below), the king resided (*Eastern Roman Empire*, 403).

[10] Ibn-Ḥawqal (ed. De Goeje, 278) adds the names—west part, Atil; east part, Khazarān. The second edition (Kramers, 389) gives west part, Khazarān; east part, Atil. Kramers, *in loco*, seems to have shown that De Goeje's reading was due to a misunderstanding. Elsewhere ibn-Ḥawqal says it was a small town (ed. Kramers, 15).

surrounded by a wall, though the buildings spread beyond. Their houses are felt tents except a small number built of clay.[11] They have markets and baths. In the town are people of the Muslims, more than 10,000, it is said. They have about thirty mosques. The king's castle is at a distance from the river-bank and is of brick.[12] No one else owns a brick building, the king not permitting anyone to build with brick. The wall already mentioned has four gates, one of which opens on the river and another on the steppe at the back of the city. The other two also open on the steppe.[13] Their king is a Jew. It is said that his attendants number about 4,000 men. The Khazars are Muslims, Christians[14] and Jews, and among them are a number of idolaters. The smallest group is the Jews, most of them being Muslims and Christians, though the king and his court are Jews.

"The predominating manners are those of the heathen. One man shows respect for another by prostrating himself before him. Their legal decisions [*aḥkām*] are peculiar, being according to old usages[15] contrary to the religion of the Muslims, Jews, and Christians. The royal army[16] consists of 12,000 men. When one dies another is put in his place. They have no regu-

[11] Earlier the houses of the double town are said to have been of wood. So at least Marquart (*Streifz.*, 18) and Bury (*loc.cit.*), I do not know on what authority (hardly Muqaddasi, 361).

[12] It seems a reasonable inference that this castle was built sometime after the building of Sarkil on the Don (see below, Chapter VII), and in imitation of its construction, out of brick. If the Khazars had no workmen skilled enough for this, we might suppose that Greeks were employed.

[13] Sentence added in K.

[14] Astēl (Atil) is mentioned as an episcopal town subject to a metropolitan at Doros under the Patriarch of Constantinople in an 8th century document known as the Notitia Episcopatuum (Kulakovsky, "The Gothic Eparchy," *Zh.M.N.Pr.*, 1898—in Russian; cf. Vasiliev, *Goths in the Crimea*, 97). The same document gives the Khazars as Khotzērōn (Khotzirōn), where -ōn is the gen. plur. suffix.— In the biography of Stephen of Sudak in the Crimea (8th cent.) a local Khazar chief, the *ṭarkhān* George, is an Orthodox Christian (ed. Vasilievsky, cited Poliak, *Conversion*, §2). The Khazars had the Christian church service in their own language (*Slavic Life of Constantine*, cited Marquart, *Streifz.*, 190).

[15] It is fairly plain from this and other passages that Turkish law, not Rabbinism, applied in Khazaria.

[16] Ibn-Ḥawqal (ed. Kramers, 390) has instead "all the army of Khazarān."

lar pay, except a pittance which comes to them at a long interval. When there is war or any disturbance occurs, they assemble.

"The king has no right to the property of the subjects.[17] His treasury depends on customs-dues [*arṣād*] and tithes on merchandise, according to certain usages of theirs, from every land-route and sea and river. To him[18] belong regular payments assessed on the people of the different places and districts, consisting of every description of food, drink, etc., which he requires. The king has seven judges[19] [*ḥukkām*] from the Jews, Christians, Muslims and idolaters. When the people have a lawsuit it is they who judge it. The parties do not approach the king himself but only these judges. Between the judges and the king on the day of the trial there is an intermediary, by whom they correspond with him about what is happening and have access to him. He transmits his orders to them, which they carry out.

"The city has no villages. But their farms are extensive. They go out in summer for about twenty leagues through fields to sow. They collect some of the crop on the river and some in the steppe, and bring in their produce either on carts or by the river. Their chief food is rice and fish. The honey and wax brought from their country are brought to them from the territory of the Russians and Bulghār. Similarly the beaver-skins which are taken to all parts of the world are found only in those rivers in the territory of Bulghār and the Russians and Kiev, and not anywhere else so far as I know.

"The eastern half of the [capital of the] Khazars contains most of the merchants, the Muslims, and the merchandise. The western is reserved for the king, his attendants,[20] his army and the pure-bred Khazars.[21] The Khazar language is not that of

[17] So in K.

[18] De Goeje "to them" (*wa-lahum*); K *wa-lahu*.

[19] Cf. Mas'ūdi, below, Chapter VII. Yāqūt (*Buldān*, ii, 437) has in error "nine judges."

[20] Added in K.

[21] Marquart (*Streifz.*, 41, n. 2) renders "eigentliche Chazaren," "real Khazars," identifying them with the "White Khazars" whose existence is perhaps indicated by Iṣṭakhri (see below), Aq-Khazars presumably

(cf. Akatzirs in Chapter I). Zeki Validi (*Ibn-Faḍlān*, 217 and n.) is definitely of opinion that the words should be referred to the Khwarizmians in Khazar service (Mas'ūdi), reading with ibn-Ḥawqal, ed. 2, "al-Khazar al-Khaliṣ" for "al-Khazar al-khullaṣ" (Iṣṭakhri and ibn-Ḥawqal, ed. 1). (It is inconsistent with this when he himself uses Marquart's expression "die eigentlichen Chazaren," *Ibn-Faḍlān*, 270, apparently in Marquart's sense.) Certainly the plur. *al-khullaṣ* coming immediately after its sing. *khaliṣah* in a different sense ("reserved") is awkward, though it may be noted that in the Chester Beatty MS. of Iṣṭakhri (K) al-Khazar al-khaṣṣ "the Khazar upper class" is read and may conceivably be right, while ibn-Ḥawqal, 1st ed., has *khāṣṣah* for *khaliṣah* (ibn-Ḥawqal, 2nd ed., is different). Perhaps *al-khullaṣ* as plural of *khaliṣ* means actually "White," cf. *Qāmūs*, s.v. If the form al-Khaliṣ is original, we may compare the people called Khwalis, mentioned twice in the Russian Chronicle (cc. 3, 79). Whether Khaliṣ/Khwalis is to be connected with Khwārizm (with interchange of l and r), as Zeki Validi thinks, there is no doubt that the name existed among the Khazars, cf. the Notitia Episcopatuum, where *'o Khoualēs* (Khwalis), like *'o Astēl* (n. 14) and *'o Tumatarkha* are sees subject to a metropolitan of Doros (Vasiliev, *Goths in the Crimea*, 99, 101-103). Vasiliev follows Kulakovsky, *op.cit.*, who thought that a city Khoualē lay in Khazaria near the mouth of the Volga, on the basis, according to Vasiliev, of Arabic accounts of the Russian campaigns in the Caspian, to be discussed below (Chapter IX). I do not know of any Khazar city called Khoualē, Khwalis, etc., in the Arabic sources for the expeditions of the Russians, nor indeed anywhere else. A locality Chwalynsk is mentioned on the Volga (Zeki Validi, *Ibn-Faḍlān*, 217). It seems likely that the Khwalis are also to be found, as Howorth observed (3rd Congress of Orientalists, II 139), in Menander Protector (300, 383) who mentions *Khliātai* or *Kholiatai* perhaps correctly *Khoalītai* (but according to Marquart *Kholiatai*=Khalaj (Kholach), cf. Minorsky, *Ḥudūd*, 347). But, further, the name and also apparently the people survived the eclipse of the Khazar state. The *Khalisioi* are mentioned as fighting against Manuel Comnenus in the 12th cent. (John Cinnamus, ed. Bonn 107, cited Vasiliev, *Goths*, 99). Up to this time they had retained "the Mosaic laws, but not in their pure form," as Vasiliev translates the Greek, while the other "Huns" i.e., Hungarians, have adopted Christianity. In another passage of the same author (ed. Bonn, 247) it is indicated that the Khalisioi were subject to the Hungarians. There seems to be little doubt that they were Khwalis who at some time had passed from Khazar to Magyar rule (for a case of this, see Chapter VII). The point that they observed only some of the Mosaic laws agrees very well with what we know or can infer about the Khazars. None of the names of tributary peoples in the Reply of Joseph as we have it is immediately identifiable with Khwalis/Khaliṣ/Halis but the Arīsu there mentioned may be the same. If so, the seats of the people in Khazar times were on the Volga. It is tempting to make the further equation of Arīsu and the Khwarizmian Arsīyah (var. Arīsīyah in Mas'ūdi's text translated below), for which the current rapprochement with Ās (the Alans) is far from certain. No clarification of the obscure relations of the Khazars and the Khwarizmians is possible from the expression Ḥalīs Ṭarkhān, which is a figment, cf. Chapter VII, n. 43.

the Turks and not Persian, nor does the language of any section of humanity coincide with it.[22]

"As to the river Atil, from what I have heard, it emerges from the vicinity of the Kirgiz and flows between the Kaymaks and the Ghuzz, being the boundary between the two. Then it proceeds west behind Bulghār, and turns back in its course eastwards till it passes by the Russians. Then it goes past Bulghār, then Burṭās, and turns back in its course till it falls into the sea of the Khazars [Caspian]. It is said that more than seventy streams branch out from this river. The main body of it flows by the Khazars till it falls into the sea. It is said that if this river's upper course were collected into one, its waters would exceed the Oxus. Its size and weight of water are such that when it reaches the sea it continues to flow as a river for two days' journey, prevailing over the water of the sea, so that in winter it freezes owing to its freshness and sweetness, and its color may be seen distinct from the color of the sea-water.

"The Khazars have a city called Samandar between [the capital][23] and Bāb al-Abwāb. It has many gardens. It is said that it contains about 4,000 vineyards towards the frontier of the Sarīr.[24] The principal fruit is the grape. Here are people of the Muslims, and they have mosques. Their dwellings are made of wood, arranged crisscross, and their roofs are domed. Their king is a Jew, related to the king of the Khazars.[25] From them to the frontier of the Sarīr it is two leagues.[26] Between them and the lord of the Sarīr is a truce.

"The people of the Sarīr are Christians. It is said that the

[22] K adds *jumlah kāfiyah,* apparently a gloss "complete sentence," or "completely" (?).

[23] Text "fīma baynaha," without explicit antecedent, suggesting compilation (see below).

[24] I.e., the Avar principality, cf. Minorsky, Ḥudūd, 447.

[25] He was perhaps a *tudun*, as Marquart suggested (*Streifz.* 21), i.e., a governor appointed by the Khazar central authority, rather than a hereditary prince (*elteber*, Zeki Validi, Ibn-Faḍlān, 106). Cf. the governor of Balanjar (Chapter IV, n. 36).

[26] Assuming that Samandar is present-day Qizlar on the Terek (Zeki Validi, "*Völkerschaften,*" 47), the distance seems very short. Cf. Minorsky, *Ḥudūd*, 452.

throne [*sarīr*] belonged to one of the kings of Persia, and is of gold. When their rule ceased, it was brought to the Sarīr, carried by one of the kings of Persia. I have heard that he was a son of Bahrām Chūbīn.[27] The kingship to the present day is among them. It is said that this throne was made for one of the Khusraws over many years[?]. Between the Sarīr and the Muslims is a truce, and each of them is wary of the other.[28] I know of no agglomeration of people in Khazar territory except Samandar.[29] The Burṭās are a nation bordering on the Khazars. Between them and the latter is no other nation. They are a people spread out along the valley of the Atil [Volga]. Burṭās is the name of a territory, as are Russia and Khazaria. The Sarīr is the name of a kingdom, not of a city nor of people.

"The Khazars do not resemble the Turks. They are black-haired, and are of two kinds, one called the Qara-Khazars [Black Khazars], who are swarthy verging to deep black, as if they were a kind of Indians, and a white kind, who are strikingly handsome. The slaves found among the Khazars are idolaters. These permit the sale of their children and the enslavement of one another. As to the Jews and Christians among them, their religion condemns the enslavement of one another, like the Muslims. The Khazar country produces nothing which can be exported to other lands except isinglass. As to the slaves,[30] honey, wax, beaver- and other skins, they are imported to Khazaria. The dress of the Khazars and the surrounding nations is coats and tunics.[31] No clothing is [sc. produced] in the country. It is brought to them from the districts of Jurjān, Ṭabaristān, Armenia, Ādharbayjān, and the Greek empire.[32]

[27] Bahrām Chūbīn is mentioned as active on the Caucasus frontier under the Sassanids Anūshirwān and Hormuz.

[28] K alone has the last clause.

[29] I.e., apparently, apart from the Khazar capital.

[30] Text *al-zaybaq*, "quicksilver," but *al-raqīq* as in K is to be preferred, cf. De Goeje *in loco* (223).

[31] I.e., an outer and an inner garment.

[32] According to ibn-Faḍlān (§25) the Ghuzz Turks similarly got clothing from the lands of Islam south of the Oxus.

"As to their politics and system of government, their chief man is called Khaqan of the Khazars. He is greater than the king of the Khazars, except that it is the king of the Khazars who appoints him.[33] When they wish to appoint this Khaqan, they bring him and throttle him with a piece of silk till he is nearly strangled.[34] Then they say to him, How long do you wish to reign? He says, So and so many years. If he dies before then, well and good. If not, he is killed when he reaches the year in question.[35] The Khaqanate is only valid among them in a family of notables.[36] He enjoys neither the right of command nor of veto, but people do him honor and prostrate themselves when they enter his presence. No one except a few such as the king and those of his class [*ṭabaqah*] approaches him. When the king enters his presence, which happens only on a special occasion, he wallows in the dust, prostrating himself, and stands at a distance till he allows him to come near. When any serious eventuality befalls them, the Khaqan is brought out. None of the Turks and the other unbelievers, who are their neighbours, sees him but retires and does not fight with him, out of reverence for him. When he dies and is buried, no one passes his tomb without dismounting and prostrating himself, nor does he remount till he is at a distance from his tomb. Their obedience to their king[37] goes so far that when one of them is perhaps condemned to death and, being one of their great men, the king does not care to kill him openly, he commands him to kill himself, and he withdraws to his house and kills himself. The Khaqanate is in a group of notables who possess neither sovereignty nor riches. When the chief place comes to one of

[33] Ibn-Ḥawqal reverses the roles and makes the Khaqan install the Beg.

[34] Cf. a remarkable parallel in a Chinese account of the T'u-küeh (translation in St. Julien, *J. A.*, VI, iii [1864], 332).

[35] Cf. what ibn-Faḍlān says about this, below. Sir J. G. Frazer had an article on the subject, "The Killing of the Khazar Kings" (*Folklore*, XXVIII, 1917), to which Dr. H. G. Farmer kindly drew my attention.

[36] Cf. a few lines below. Does Iṣṭakhri merely repeat himself, or is this an indication that his account of the Khazar Khaqan is conflated?

[37] I.e., the Khaqan. Cf. ibn-Faḍlān's observation on the action of the Khaqan after a defeat.

them, they appoint him without regard to what his condition is. A reliable witness told me that he had seen in one of their markets a young man selling bread. They said that when their Khaqan died, there was none worthier of the Khaqanate than he, only he was a Muslim, and the Khaqanate is never given to any but a Jew. The throne and canopy [*qubbah*] of gold[38] which they have are never set up for any but the Khaqan. His tents when they go forth are above the tents of the king. His house in the town is higher than the house of the king.

"Burṭās is the name of a territory. The people have houses of wood and are scattered. The Bashkirs are of two kinds. The one is at the extremity of the Ghuzz country behind Bulghār. It is said that their total numbers amount to about 2,000 men,[39] in a strong position among woods where none can reach them. They obey the Bulgars. The other Bashkirs border on the Pechenegs, i.e., the Turkish Pechenegs[40] bordering on the Greeks. The language of the Bulgars is like that of the Khazars.[41] The Burṭās have a different language. Similarly, the language of the Russians is unlike those of the Khazars and the Burṭās.

"Bulghār is the name of a city. The people are Muslims, and in it is a cathedral mosque. Nearby is another city called

[38] The *qubbah* of gold seems rather to be connected with the tented car of the Khaqan (Chapter IV, n. 94) than with the golden tent of other chiefs (among the Uigurs of the Orkhon in 821, cf. Minorsky, "Tamīm," 279, 294-295, 303; among the Karayts in the time of Chingiz Khān, cf. Raverty, *Ṭabaqāt-i Nāṣiri*, 943 n.), though if it could be shown that the possession of a gold tent was a mark of paramountcy, the detail might serve to connect the Khazars with the Uigurs (cf. Chapter II). The Reply of Joseph mentions a "tabernacle" in religious use among the Khazars circa 960, but there is no precise reason for identifying this with Iṣṭakhri's "*qubbah* of gold."

[39] The same figure occurs in a story in Gardīzi (ed. Barthold, 85), according to which the ancestor of the Bashkirs was a Khazar noble, who at some unspecified time settled between the Khazars and the Kaymaks with 2,000 men.

[40] Bajanāk Atrāk, cf. Ḥudūd, §20.

[41] The language of the Bulgars is held to have been akin to Chuvash, e.g. Barthold, *E.I.*, art. Bulghār. Hence Iṣṭakhri appears to be correct in saying that it resembled the Khazar language, also akin to Chuvash, see below.

Suwār, in which also is a cathedral mosque. One who was preacher there told me that the number of people in these two cities amounts to about 10,000. They have buildings of wood in which they shelter in winter. In summer they spread abroad in tents. The preacher there told me that the night there is in summer so short that a man does not prepare to travel in it more than a league, while in winter the day is short and the night is long, so that a day in winter is like the nights of summer.

"The Russians are of three kinds. The king of those nearest to Bulghār lives in a city called Kuyābah [Kiev]. It is larger than Bulghār. Another kind, farther off than these, is called Ṣlāwīyah [Slavs], and there is a kind called Arthānīyah, whose king lives in Artha.[42] The people come to trade in Kiev. It is not recorded that any stranger has ever entered Artha, for they kill all strangers who set foot in their land. They descend by water to trade and say nothing of their affairs and merchandise. They let none accompany them or enter their land. From Artha are brought black sable-skins and lead. The fox-skins of Burṭās are brought from that country.[43] The Russians are a people who burn their dead. Girls are burned voluntarily with rich persons among them. Some shave the beard, others let it grow like a forelock. Their dress is the short coat. The dress of the Khazars, Bulgars, and Pechenegs is the full coat. These Russians trade as far as Khazaria,[44] the Greek empire and Great Bulgaria, which borders the Greek empire on the north. The last are very numerous. Their strength is so great that they

[42] The forms Arthānīyah, Artha are not certain. Cf. Minorsky, *Ḥudūd*, 434ff.

[43] Sentence added in K.

[44] Ibn-Khurdādhbih (154) has greater detail. "As to the route of the Russian merchants, who are a kind of Ṣaqālibah [generic name for the white-skinned races of eastern Europe], they bring beaver-skins and black fox-skins and swords from the most distant parts of the Ṣaqlab country to the sea of the Greeks [Black Sea], and the lord of the Greeks tithes them. If they travel by the Don, the river of the Ṣaqālibah, they pass by Khamlīj [Khamlīkh], the capital of the Khazars, whose lord likewise tithes them. Then they reach the sea of Jurjān [Caspian] and disembark on which of its coasts they will."

have levied a tribute on the neighboring Greeks. The people of Inner Bulgaria are Christians."

This very important account by Iṣṭakhri, written about 320/932,[45] presumably owes something to his predecessors, especially Balkhi, whose own work was composed in 308/920 or a little later,[46] but how much we are not in a position to say. It is, however, clear that it was extensively used, or rather taken over bodily, by Iṣṭakhri's successors. Thus ibn-Ḥawqal's account of Khazaria is practically Iṣṭakhri (somewhat differently in the two editions of ibn-Ḥawqal by De Goeje and Kramers).[47]

Yāqūt also drew extensively on Iṣṭakhri. This is not at first apparent, for Yāqūt's account of the Khazars is given on the authority of ibn-Faḍlān, one of the envoys of the Caliph Muqtadir to the Bulgars of the Volga in 310/922, and is introduced as what ibn-Faḍlān actually saw himself.[48] But the account as it stands contains obvious contradictions, which must appear to every reader. Thus it is stated, first, that the king of the Khazars is called in their language Y-l-k or Bāk[49] and later that his name is Khaqan. In consequence there has been doubt not simply as to ibn-Faḍlān's authorship of the whole account but, more seriously, whether on the basis of such a document any clarification of the Khazar problem was possible.

De Goeje seems first to have observed that the first part of Yāqūt's article on the Khazars was to be found in Iṣṭakhri, and he suggested that in spite of the attribution to ibn-Faḍlān, Iṣṭakhri was the author.[50] This was in fact the case, but there

45 Brockelmann, *G.A.L.*, I, 229, gives c. 340/951. De Goeje (*Z.D.M.G.*, 1871, 51) connected the publication of the work with that date, but it was, he thought, written between 318 and 321.

46 Barthold in *Ḥudūd*, 15.

47 Ibn-Ḥawqal, writing in 367/977, occasionally has new information, notably on the great Russian expedition which involved the destruction of the Khazar capital, but usually copies out Iṣṭakhri.

48 *Buldān*, II, 436.

49 The form Y-l-k may be a mistake, not a variant. Zeki Validi's remarks (*Ibn-Faḍlān*, 257) are not clear to me.

50 Cf. Wüstenfeld, *Mu'jam al-Buldān*, V, 173: "De Goeje macht mich darauf aufmerksam dass sich dieses Stück aus dem Reisebericht des Ibn

was no proof, so that Kmosko, writing in 1921, was justified in disregarding it.[51] Kmosko believed that ibn-Faḍlān had a good deal about the Khazars in common with Iṣṭakhri. There was the unmistakable fact that Yāqūt gave several pages on ibn-Faḍlān's authority which appeared also in De Goeje's edition of Iṣṭakhri. Kmosko accounted for this by the theory that they had a common source. Others had supposed that because ibn-Faḍlān wrote earlier, Iṣṭakhri might have adopted his account. Kmosko objected that on this view Iṣṭakhri had apparently substituted a much less vivid account of his own[52] for that of ibn-Faḍlān on the subject of the Khaqan (i.e., the last part of Yāqūt's article). As against Frähn and Geza Kuun, Kmosko was undoubtedly right in saying that Iṣṭakhri did not draw on ibn-Faḍlān, and he directed attention to the parallel accounts which we have of the Khaqan. But his own theory of a common source for ibn-Faḍlān and Iṣṭakhri (against which there was the a priori consideration that travelers like ibn-Faḍlān do not usually quote previous writers at length) has been disproved by the Meshed text of ibn-Faḍlān, published by Zeki Validi.[53] Here we see that ibn-Faḍlān has nothing in common with Iṣṭakhri. When ibn-Faḍlān comes to speak in detail about the Khazars, all that he says is to be found in the second part of Yāqūt's article. It is therefore clear that Yāqūt's notice is composite. The first part is Iṣṭakhri, though cited for some reason on ibn-Faḍlān's authority, but instead of continuing with Iṣṭakhri's account of the Khaqan, he avails himself of what ibn-Faḍlān really wrote. Naturally enough there are differences between the two accounts this conflated, but we can now make use of both, as independent sources.[54]

Fadhlân . . . auch bei Içṭachrí . . . findet, welchem er die Autorschaft vindiciren möchte, was mir noch zweifelhaft scheint."

[51] See his article "Die Quellen Iṣṭachri's in seinem Berichte über die Chasaren," *Kőrösi Csoma-Archivum*, I (1921), 141.

[52] The paragraph beginning "As to their politics" above. Cf. this with ibn-Faḍlān's account below.

[53] *Ibn Faḍlān's Reisebericht*, *A.K.M.*, Leipzig 1939.

[54] Professor H. Ritter writes (*Z.D.M.G.*, 1942, 126 n.): "Bekanntlich steht in Yāqūt vor diesem Abschnitte noch ein weiterer über die Ḫazaren,

Kmosko thought it possible to show further that the account of Khazaria in Iṣṭakhri consists of two parts originally separate, of which one, distinctly referring to the Judaism of the Khazars, goes back to about A.D. 800. If this can be made out, then of course the case for something like the traditional date of the conversion as A.D. 740 becomes very strong, and the alternative dating—soon after A.D. 863 (Marquart),[55] about 865 (Vernadsky)[56]—may safely be disregarded. Kmosko's arguments in detail are evidently vitiated by his mistaken view of what constituted ibn-Faḍlān's account of the Khazars. It remains to be seen if his theory of Iṣṭakhri's narrative as composite has anything in it, and whether some or all of it goes back to circa 800. It must be allowed that the suggestion that Iṣṭakhri's narrative (the complete account, that is, not the truncated form in Yāqūt) consists of two parts originally separate is attractive. The principal matters dealt with by Iṣṭakhri follow each other thus: the Khazars, especially with reference to the king (Bak, Beg)—the river Atil (Volga)—Samandar, Sarīr, Burṭās—the Khazars, especially with reference to the Khaqan—Burṭās, Bashkirs, Bulgars, Russians. Each of the components might thus begin with the Khazars and pass on to their neighbors, one giving a miscellaneous group of names, the other neighboring peoples to the north.[57] It is noticeable that the Burṭās are twice mentioned. There are other traces of repetition and contradiction, cf. what is said about the Khazar imports and the Khazar language. Towards the end Iṣṭakhri

---

den er gleichfalls Ibn Faḍlān zuschreibt, und der sich auch bei Iṣṭaḫri findet. Durch das Fehlen dieses Abschnittes in M [i.e., the Meshed MS. containing ibn-Faḍlān's *Riḥlah*] ist wohl endgültig bewiesen, dass dieser Abschnitt nicht aus Ibn Faḍlān stammt und dass Yāqūt ihn fälschlich und versehentlich Ibn Faḍlān zuschreibt." Ritter's caution (*wohl endgültig*) is formally justified. But the contradictions between the first and second parts of Yāqūt's notice are strictly incompatible with their being originally the work of one author.

[55] *Streifz.*, 23.

[56] *Ancient Russia* (1943), 351, citing his own article "The Date of the Conversion of the Khazars to Judaism," *Byzantion*, xv (1941), 76-86.

[57] Within this scheme there are perhaps traces of subdivisions, cf. nn. 23, 36.

mentions that the house of the Khaqan is higher than the Beg's, while earlier he has indicated that the castle of the king (Beg) is the principal landmark. These considerations are not entirely conclusive, but on the whole Kmosko seems to be right, and the narrative of Iṣṭakhri looks as if it has been put together in a systematic manner from more than one account.

As to the dating, Kmosko's conclusions appear more doubtful. He supposes that Iṣṭakhri in one place refers to a time when the Khazars had no mercenary troops, but only "a kind of militia, or better, a number of insurgents."[58] He is apparently thinking of the words: "The royal army consists of 12,000 men. When one dies another is put in his place. They have no regular pay, except a pittance which comes to them at long intervals. When there is war or any disturbance occurs, they assemble." Later, he argues, we know of a regular army of Muslims in Khazaria, from ibn-Rustah (?) and Mas'ūdi, from circa A.D. 800 when the Khazar army appears to have been reorganized. The theory that thereafter it consisted of Muslims who did not wish to be sent to fight their correligionists explains for Kmosko why, though the Caliphate was less powerful than formerly, after the Khazar invasions of 145/762 and 183/799 they did not again attack the Arabs (see below, Chapter VII). All this is very well, but there is no real evidence that the Khazar army was reorganized about A.D. 800. Mas'ūdi observes indeed that the king of the Khazars alone in these countries had a paid army, and says that the people called Arsīyah[59] who formed the royal army came to Khazaria "from the neighborhood of Khwārizm, long ago, after the appearance of Islam." The date of this can hardly be estimated. Ibn-Rustah says nothing explicit about Muslims in the Khazar army, and in any case his account, though no doubt referring to the first half of the 9th century (see below), can hardly be cited for a hypothetical reorganization of the Khazar army circa 800. Further, the words of Iṣṭakhri appear to indicate precisely a standing

[58] "Insurgenten," Kmosko, *ibid.*

[59] Cf. n. 21 and see also below, Chapter VII. The form is not certain.

army.[60] In general, we may say that the impression made by Iṣṭakhri's account of the Khazars, composite or not, is that it refers to a period not so long before his own time. Kmosko's view of the dating appears to be a particularly bold inference from the cessation of Khazar attacks on the Muslims after 800, the reason of which we do not know. The view may conceivably be right, but it can scarcely be used in support of a date prior to this for the conversion to Judaism.

If the impression made by Iṣṭakhri's account of the Khazars is that it is, so to speak, modern, the opposite is the case with what ibn-Rustah has to say on the subject. Yet there should not be more than thirty years between them, for ibn-Rustah compiled his encyclopedia, from which the account of the Khazars now to be given is taken, about 290/903, and Iṣṭakhri wrote circa 320/932. Ibn-Rustah's account[61] is quite short:

"Between the Pechenegs and the Khazars is a journey of 10 days through deserts and wooded country. There is no regular road or frequented paths between them and the Khazars. Their only route is through this wooded tangled country till they reach Khazaria. Khazaria is an extensive region, connected on one side to a great mountain [i.e., the Caucasus], the same as that which descends at its extremity to Ṭūlās[62] and Awghaz [Abkhāz]. This mountain extends to the region of Tiflis.

"They have a king who is called Īsha. The supreme king is Khazar Khaqan. He does not enjoy the obedience of the Khazars but has the name only. The power to command belongs to the Īsha, since in regard to control and the armies he is so placed that he does not have to care for anyone above him. Their supreme ruler is a Jew, and likewise the Īsha and those of the generals and the chief men who follow his way of thinking. The rest of them have a religion like the religion of the Turks.

60 So taken by Marquart, *Streifz.*, 4.
61 Ed. De Goeje, 139-140.
62 A compound with Ās, cf. Minorsky, *Ḥudūd*, 456.

"Their capital is Sārighshin and in it[63] [?] is another city called H-b ?-l-'(gh) or H(kh)-??-l-gh [? Khanbaligh]. The population remains during the winter in these two cities. When spring days come, they go out to the steppe and continue there till the approach of winter. In these two cities are Muslims, who possess mosques, imams, muezzins, and schools.

"Their king, the Īsha, levies a number of horsemen on the people of power and wealth among them, according to their possessions and the extent of their means of livelihood. They raid the Pechenegs every year. This Īsha takes charge of the departure himself and goes out on his expeditions with his men. They have a fine appearance. When they go out in any direction, they do so armed in full array, with banners, spears, and strong coats of mail. He rides forth with 10,000 horsemen, of whom some are regular paid troops and others have been levied on the rich. When he goes out in any direction, a kind of disk is prepared in his presence, fashioned like a drum. It is carried by a horseman who bears it before him [i.e., the Īsha]. He follows at the head of his army, who see the light of the disk. When they take booty, they collect it all in his camp. Then the Īsha chooses what he likes and takes it for himself. He leaves them the rest of the booty, to be divided among themselves."

There are some striking new points here. The subordinate king is said to be called Īsha, which is quite unlike Iṣṭakhri's Bak or Bāk. According to ibn-Rustah, the capital of Khazaria is neither al-Bayḍā' as in the Arab historians nor the Khazarān or Atil of the geographers (e.g. ibn-Ḥawqal), but Sārighshin, here mentioned with another town, perhaps Khanbaligh, Khambaligh (Khamlīj). Gardīzi, who wrote in Persian circa A.D. 1050, has an account[64] similar to ibn-Rustah. In this the subordinate king of the Khazars appears as Abshād. Gardīzi's names for the towns closely resemble those in ibn-Rustah, as do the forms given by Sharaf al-Zamān Marwazi, another

[63] Or "at it, near it."
[64] Ed. Barthold, 95ff.

writer of the 11th century, who has an abbreviated form in Arabic of the same general account.[65]

At first sight, there is nothing in common between Īsha or Abshād and Bak of the other tradition. The latter form is confirmed, as it seems, not only by ibn-Faḍlān, who gives Khaqan B-h for the subordinate king, and the Greek sources, where we find Peh, but presumably also by the later Turkish title Beg or Bey. Īsha and Abshād thus present a real difficulty. The original of which these words are evidently forms has been read in different ways, there being general agreement that the second syllable must be the title Shad, found elsewhere.[66] Zeki Validi has suggested that we should read Äbä-shad, where Äbä, Ebe, is ibn-Faḍlān's B-h, and presumably also the same as Iṣṭakhri's Bak.[67]

As to Sārighshin and Khanbaligh, it would appear that a double town is indicated, the later Khazarān-Atil. We may compare Buda-Pest, as perhaps showing a tendency to give separate names to settlements facing each other across a river. The transliteration here adopted is provisional. Sārighshin should be "Yellow (Town),"[68] the Arabic al-Bayḍā' "the White (City)," which certainly is applied, as we have seen, to the Khazar capital. Khanbaligh (Hab Baligh), according to Zajączkowski, means "the Whole Town."[69] It is probable that the word is the same as Khamlīj (or Khamlīkh), the Khazar capital according to ibn-Khurdādhbih,[70] or more exactly the eastern, commercial half of the town.[71] As to the identity of Sārighshin with Saqsīn we shall have something to say later.

Gardīzi's account of the Khazars contains some things which

[65] Ed. Minorsky, Royal Asiatic Society (Forlong Fund, XXII), 1942.

[66] Cf. Shath, son of Ziebel, and Chat-Khazar, above.

[67] *Ibn-Faḍlān*, 257. Other suggestions are Äl-shad (Marquart, *Streifz.*, 24), Ay-shad (Minorsky) and Alp-shad (Zajączkowski). Munkacsi had already suggested Äb-shad (*Finnisch-Ugrische Forschungen*, XII, 98-102, cited Zeki Validi, *ibid.*).

[68] Zajączkowski (cf. O. Pritsak, *Der Islam*, B. 29, 99) and similarly Marquart, *Streifz.*, 1 (Sarighshar) and Minorsky, *Ḥudūd*, 453. Pritsak (ib. 102) suggests "West Town."

[69] Cf. Pritsak, *op.cit.*, 99. [70] Cf. n. 44.

[71] Marquart, 203, cf. Minorsky, *Ḥudūd*, 454.

are not in ibn-Rustah. One of the additions gives interesting information, not found elsewhere, about the military arrangements of the Khazars. The general (*sālār*), by which perhaps the Abshād (Äbä-shad) or Beg is meant, gives orders that each of his men should carry with him what seems to be a sharp stake of a certain thickness or length, for constructing a palisade, further strengthened with shields, round the camp when on an expedition. He tells us also that the Khazars levied a small contribution from the Muslims in the two towns, and refers apparently to raids on the Burṭās, as to which ibn-Rustah is silent. In Khazaria, he says, are fields and gardens and abundance of good things. There is much honey, and good wax is brought from thence. Ibn-Rustah mentions nothing of this.

To return now to ibn-Rustah, there is general agreement that he is not the original author of the description of the Khazars and other northern peoples found in his book. It appears that this description goes back to Jayhāni, whose geographical work is now lost.[72] In Jayhāni's account, as reflected in ibn-Rustah, there are, however, unmistakable traces of a date much earlier than his own. Ibn-Faḍlān met Jayhāni in 309/921 on his way to visit the Bulgars on the Volga. But evidently quite a different order of dating is indicated for some of the contents of Jayhāni's book. It is not merely that isolated details, presumably from Jayhāni, such as that Britain is ruled by seven kings—a state of affairs which ceased to exist in 827 when the Heptarchy was dissolved—are found in ibn-Rustah and point to the first half of the 9th century,[73] but the situation of whole peoples is so represented as it existed at this time and not later, e.g. the Pechenegs.[74] It may be accepted with Barthold[75] that the main source of Jayhāni's account of the northern peoples was Muslim ibn-abi-Muslim al-Jarmi, who was alive in 231/846 and is known to have written about the Greeks and their neighbors,

[72] See Marquart, *Streifz.*, 24-27; Barthold, *E.I.*, art. Bulghār; Minorsky, *Ḥudūd*, xvii, and "A False Jayhānī," *B.S.O.A.S.*, 1949, xiii/1, 89-96.

[73] Marquart, *Streifz.*, 29.

[74] Marquart, *ibid.*, 160.

[75] *Loc.cit.*, cf. Marquart, *Streifz.*, 28.

including the Khazars.[76] Ibn-Khurdādhbih was familiar with al-Jarmi's work.[77] Jayhāni may have used him directly or through ibn-Khurdādhbih.[78]

That ibn-Rustah's account of the Khazars has traces of a date as early as the time of al-Jarmi is quite certain, even if it should later be found that the course of transmission has been different from what we have assumed. It is not simply that we find in ibn-Rustah the names Sārighshin and Khanbaligh, which in the 10th century, as we see from ibn-Ḥawqal, had passed out of use. Ibn-Faḍlān reports that in his time (310/922) the second king of the Khazars was called Khaqan B-h. But ibn-Rustah knows him as Īsha (Äbä-shad, Ebe-shad). This should refer to a period at least earlier than A.D. 833, when he was already called by his later title, as we see from the Greek account of the building of Sarkil.[79] How much farther back we have to set ibn-Rustah's account is not clear. Since his two towns correspond to the later Khazarān-Atil, it cannot in any case be earlier than the transference of the Khazar capital to the Volga. But as this important event is said to have taken place in the days of Salmān ibn-Rabī'ah[80] it is theoretically possible that ibn-Rustah's account envisages a time as early as 740, when the Khazars are said to have adopted Judaism.

It is objected, however, by Marquart that ibn-Rustah's account is not uniformly old, e.g., it says that in the two cities of Khazaria there are numerous Muslims with mosques, imams, muezzins, and schools.[81] But this cannot be shown to be an interpolation. So far from it being an anachronism to speak of Islam as already established in Khazaria in the first part of the 9th century, this is what we should be led from other sources to expect. Ibn-Khurdādhbih (circa 232/846) states that the direction for prayer (*qiblah*) of the Khazars is the Ka'bah at Meccah.[82] It seems certain that ibn-Khurdādhbih here refers to the Arsīyah already mentioned. These people were evidently

[76] Mas'ūdi, *Tanbīh*, 191.
[77] Ed. De Goeje, 105.
[78] Cf. Minorsky, *Ḥudūd*, xvi.
[79] See Chapter VII.
[80] Cf. above, Chapter III, n. 43.
[81] *Streifz.*, 27.
[82] Ed. De Goeje, 5.

numerous and later at least devoted to Islam. It is natural that they should already, e.g., before 833, have had the religious establishment indicated by ibn-Rustah.

It might be argued that the fact of the Khazar kings being Jews has been added by Jayhāni or another to an older account. But in this case it seems extremely likely that other "modern" traits would have been introduced. As this is not what we find, it would follow that ibn-Rustah's account of the Khazars is a unity. It is difficult to resist the conclusion that the Khazars or at least their kings and some of the principal men were Jews when this account was originally written, i.e., if we are right, not later than the first half of the 9th century.[83]

It is convenient to give here ibn-Faḍlān's account of the Khazars, noting that this does not purport to be the result of personal observation. What ibn-Faḍlān sets down, he heard from the Bulgars of the Volga, and perhaps partly also from the Khazar ibn-Bashtwa, with whom he traveled from Baghdad as far as Bukhara. In view of the unfriendly relations between the Khazar ruler and his nominal dependent, the Yaltawar (Elteber)[84] of the Bulgars, we can be quite sure that ibn-Faḍlān's informants were not prejudiced in the Khazars' favor, but the reverse. Subjective coloring seems discernible in more than one part of ibn-Faḍlān's account. This is so when he speaks of the domestic arrangements of the Khaqan, who is represented as having twenty-five wives and sixty concubines. The mere numbers, on the scale of a Solomon, suggest exaggeration. The harem of the Khaqan is, however, referred to a little after this time by Mas'ūdi.[85] We have also to allow that the mention of twenty-five wives "each the daughter of one of the kings who confront him" should bear some relation to what is said in one of the versions of Eldad ha-Dani (*flor.* end of 9th century A.D.), viz., that the Khaqan of the Khazars has twenty-five kings subordinate to him.[86] The situation has

[83] The remark of ibn al-Faqīh (circa 290/903) that "the Khazars are all Jews and have lately become so" (298) should go back through Jayhāni (cf. *Fihrist* 154, quoted Minorsky, *Ḥudūd* XVII) to al-Jarmi.

[84] Cf. Zeki Validi, *Ibn-Faḍlān*, 105.

[85] See below.

[86] For the narrative of Eldad ha-Dani, see Chapter VI.

a direct illustration in what ibn-Faḍlān's narrative tells us of how the Bulgar chief tried to save his daughter from the "king of the Khazars," and was no doubt described to ibn-Faḍlān in connection with this incident.[87] The difficulty, then, is not so much the number of the women as the fantastic setting. That each of them had a castle of her own, as is stated, is out of the question for the Khazar capital. As we find from other descriptions, there was a castle some distance from the Volga,[88] or alternatively, perhaps at a different period, on an island in the river,[89] where presumably both the Khaqan and the Beg had their quarters, or at most there were two royal buildings. So the Arabic sources. In the Hebrew Reply of Joseph, the queen with her women attendants and eunuchs lives apart from the camp. This in itself is quite probable. In the nature of the case, the Khaqan, like the Bulgar Almish, had a principal wife (Khatun),[90] though this is not indicated by ibn-Faḍlān, who appears to have been misinformed about the situation. The women had no doubt, not each a separate castle, but apartments or rather an apartment in the harem. This seems clear also from the mention of a single eunuch in attendance, and, although to say that this functionary conducts his charge to the king "more quickly than the flash of an eye" is fanciful exaggeration, it suggests that all the court lived within a short distance. The passage as a whole seems intended to represent the uxoriousness of the Jewish king in an invidious light, just as the description of punishments dealt out by the Khaqan to unsuccessful generals, when his active functions elsewhere and even in ibn-Faḍlān's account itself are represented as negligible or even nonexistent, is probably motivated by the desire to make him appear an arbitrary and cruel tyrant.

Apart from some incidental references to the Khazars in the course of his narrative which indicate the dislike and fear

[87] Ibn-Faḍlān, §78.

[88] Iṣṭakhri-ibn-Ḥawqal.

[89] Mas'ūdi (below); ibn-Sa'īd in abu-al-Fidā', ed. Reinaud and De Slane, 203 n.

[90] For the story of a Khatun of the Khazars, see Chapter VII.

felt for his Jewish masters by the Bulgar king,[91] ibn-Faḍlān's main account of the Khazars is as follows:

"As to the king of the Khazars whose name is Khāqān, he only appears every four months for recreation. He is called the Great Khaqan. His lieutenant is called Khāqān B-h. It is he who leads the armies and gives them their orders. He controls and manages state affairs, appears in public and goes on military expeditions. The neighboring kings obey him. He goes humbly in every day to the superior Khaqan, displaying deference and modesty. He never enters except barefoot, with a piece of wood in his hand. When he has greeted him, he lights the wood in his presence, and when it has finished burning, he sits with the king on his throne at his right hand. His place is taken by a man called K-nd-r Khāqān,[92] and his in turn by one called Jāwshygh-r.[93]

"The custom of the superior king is that he does not give audience to the people and does not speak with them, and no one enters his presence except those we have mentioned. Power to loose and to bind, punishments and the rule of the kingdom belong to his lieutenant, the Khaqan B-h.

"The custom of the superior king is that when he dies a great hall is built for him, containing twenty chambers. In each of these a grave is dug for him, and stones are broken till they become like powder, which is then sprinkled therein, and pitch is spread over that again. Under the building is a river.[94] The river is large and rapid. They bring the river over the grave[95] and say that it is in order that no devil or man,

[91] §§ 48, 78.

[92] Zeki Validi (*Ibn-Faḍlān*, 260) connects with the Magyar title Kündü, Künda, reading here for K-n-d-r, K-nda of which Kundājiq (see above) is a diminutive (*ibid.*, 135, n. 2). Zajączkowski (*Studies*, 33) suggests *köndür* "chief, judge."

[93] Cf. Chapter II, n. 33.

[94] The printed text of Yāqūt is here incomprehensible (*wa-taḥt al-dār w-al-nahr nahr kabīr yajri*). Frähn proposed *w-al-qabr* for *w-al-nahr* (*Khazars*, 608). The addition of *nahr* after *al-dār* in Zeki Validi's text restores the sense simply.

[95] The printed text has *wa-yaj'alūn al-qabr fawq dhālikā al-nahr* (they place the grave over that river), corrected in Zeki Validi's text.

no worm or creeping beast, may come to him. When he is buried the heads of those who buried him are struck off, so that it may not be known in which of the chambers is his tomb. His grave is called "Paradise," and they say, He has entered Paradise. All the chambers are spread with silk brocade interwoven with gold.

"The custom of the king of the Khazars is that he has twenty-five wives. Each of them is the daughter of one of the kings who confront him, taken freely or by force. He has also sixty slave-girls, concubines, all of superb beauty. Each of them, concubines as well as free-born ladies, is in a castle of her own. She has an alcove roofed with teak, and round each alcove is a pavilion. Each one of them has an attendant who acts as chamberlain. When the king wishes to embrace one of them, he sends to the attendant who is her chamberlain, and he brings her quicker than the flash of an eye. He sets her on the king's couch and stands at the door of the royal alcove. When the king has left her, the attendant takes her by the hand and goes away, nor does he thereafter quit her for a moment.

"When this great king rides out, all his army rides out with him. Between him and the troops of riders is a mile's distance. None of his subjects sees him without falling on his face, doing obeisance to him, nor does he raise his head till he has passed him.[96]

"The length of their rule is forty years. If the king exceeds it by a single day, the subjects and his courtiers kill him, saying, His reason has failed and his understanding is become disordered.[97]

[96] Cf. ibn-Faḍlān, §60. (The Yaltawar of the Bulgars rode out unaccompanied. His subjects stood up when he passed, taking off their caps, which they put under their arms.) The contrast between the free Bulgars and the abject Khazars is to some extent subjective, cf., however, what Iṣṭakhri says about prostration in Khazaria (mentioned thrice).

[97] Cf. also Mas'ūdi, below, Chapter VII. Saxo Grammaticus says that among the "Slavs," "by public statute of the ancients, the succession was appointed to the slayers of the kings" (translation of Elton, London 1894, 334).

"When he sends out a body of troops, they do not in any circumstances retreat. If they are defeated, every one who returns to him is killed. As to the army generals and his lieutenant [i.e., the Beg], when they are defeated he sends for them and their wives and children, and gives them in their presence to others, while they look on. He deals similarly with their horses, valuables, arms, and dwellings. Sometimes he cuts every one of them in two and crucifies them and sometimes he hangs them by the neck from trees. Sometimes, when he would treat them well, he makes them grooms.[98]

"The king of the Khazars has a great city on the river Atil, on both banks. On one bank are the Muslims, on the other the king and his companions. Over the Muslims is one of the king's pages called Kh-z,[99] who is a Muslim. The law-suits [*aḥkām*] of the Muslims living in the Khazar capital [*balad al-Khazar*] and those who pass back and forth to trade are referred to that Muslim page. None but he takes cognizance of their affairs or decides between the parties.[100]

"The Muslims in this city have a cathedral mosque, where they pray and appear on Fridays. It has a high minaret and several muezzins. When word reached the king of the Khazars in 310/922 that the Muslims had destroyed the synagogue which was in Dār al-Bābūnaj,[101] he gave orders to destroy the

[98] Iṣṭakhri and ibn-Faḍlān both mention the authority of the Khaqan in certain cases. Mas'ūdi has nothing of this.

[99] Possibly=Silk (*khazz*). Mas'ūdi, writing twenty years later than ibn-Faḍlān, speaks of a Muslim "vizier" in the Khazar capital, called Aḥmad ibn-Kūyah. These officials presumably had dealings with the respective informants.

[100] Iṣṭakhri implies that there were several Muslim judges, and this is distinctly stated by Mas'ūdi (two). The "vizier" mentioned in the preceding note is evidently different from the judges.

[101] Unidentified. As Zeki Validi says (*Ibn-Faḍlān*, 102, n. 4), Marquart's investigation of the passage (*Streifz.*, 4, 477-479) has led to no solution of what is meant by "Camomile House." But his own effort to connect the name with Spain (*Dār Adhālbūnaj*=the dwelling of Adalphuns, Alfonso) and the activities there of 'Umar ibn-Ḥafsūn is not convincing. Zeki Validi here translates *kanīsah* as "church," which in this context is not right. The Khazar Khaqan is of course represented as angry at the destruction by Muslims of a synagogue, presumably outside his own dominions. The suggestion of Brutzkus in *Encyclopedia*

minaret, and he killed the muezzins. He said, If I did not fear that not a synagogue would be left in the lands of Islam but would be destroyed, I should destroy the mosque.

"The Khazars and their king are all [*sic*] Jews.[102] The Ṣaqālibah [i.e., the Volga Bulgars, etc.] and all who live near them are subject to him. He addresses them as slaves and they serve him obediently. Some hold the opinion that Gog and Magog are the Khazars."[103]

The fact is striking that the mosques, imams, muezzins, and Muslim schools of Khazaria are mentioned by ibn-Rustah, while in ibn-Faḍlān's account only the Friday mosque and its muezzins appear. This does not mean either that the statement in ibn-Rustah is inaccurate, or that in ibn-Faḍlān's time Islam had suffered a setback in Khazaria. Ibn-Faḍlān is concerned to tell what happened to the principal mosque and leaves the others out of account, either because he had not heard particularly about them, or for some other reason. Twenty years later, the mosques of Khazaria are mentioned by Mas'ūdi.[104] There is no reason to suppose that only one existed when ibn-Faḍlān was on the Volga.

There is much that is interesting in ibn-Faḍlān's account, which, when all is said, yields to none of the Arabic sources on the Khazars in importance, though it has nothing specific about the conversion. We see clearly, as in Iṣṭakhri, that the Judaism of the kings and their circle existed side by side with institutions deriving from the heathen past. The double kingship has nothing to do with the acceptance of Judaism, nor was the Khaqan a figure in any way similar to a Jewish high-priest.[105]

Judaica art. Khazaren, that a town in the Caucasus with the name "Gate of Chungar" Bāb al-J-nj-r is open to various objections.

102 This is evidently exaggerated. Zeki Validi omits Yāqūt's *kulluhum* "all of them."

103 The last three sentences are regarded by Zeki Validi as an addition of Yāqūt.

104 See below, Chapter VII.

105 There have been various attempts to explain the title Khaqan from Hebrew *ḥākhām* "wise." Kasem Beg had a theory that it was connected with Hebrew *kōhēn*, "priest." Needless to say, such views are altogether unfounded. Cf. also Chapter VI, at n. 46.

The arrangements at his burial recall reports of the obsequies of Alaric (A.D. 410) and Attila (A.D. 453)[106] and connect him directly with Turkish antiquity.[107]

Evidently the Judaism of the Khaqan did not lead him to uproot old customs to which the populace was attached. The situation as we see it, not in ibn-Faḍlān alone, is undoubtedly to be connected with a number of facts which otherwise are difficult to account for: the impression of the Khazars as a pagan people gained in A.D. 780 by Abo of Tiflis, and again circa A.D. 860 by Constantine (Cyril); the absence of solid information about the Khazars from the headquarters of Jewry in Babylonia (Iraq), which apparently corresponds to a lack of interest in them and their doings; the stages in the rapprochement of the Khazars to Judaism according to the Hebrew "Khazar Correspondence." But of the fact of the Judaism of the Khazars, to the extent indicated, however much it fell short of complete Rabbinism, there is, in view of all the evidence, not the slightest doubt. Though it is not desirable to insist on a formal conversion taking place after a religious debate circa A.D. 740, as is stated by Jehudah ha-Levi—which remains on his authority and without specific confirmation from elsewhere—that Jewish influence began to be felt in Khazaria before the middle of the 8th century is distinctly more probable than that this was so only after A.D. 860. A rigorous demonstration that the leading Khazars became Jews at the earlier date is hardly possible, but in the face of the evidence as a whole this is undoubtedly the conclusion to which we seem to be led.

[106] Cf. Zeki Validi, *Ibn-Faḍlān*, 266.

[107] It may here be observed that the statement made by J. L. Rasmussen (*J.A.* I, v [1824], 305), that in the 6th century the Khazars fought a war with the Danish king Frode, seems difficult if not impossible to substantiate. Neither Jordanes nor Saxo Grammaticus mentions such an event, and it is only by the most fragile of hypotheses (from the possibility that the Khazars=the Akatzirs, who might have marched with the Huns) that one can bring the Khazars into relation with Frode, or rather with one of the rulers who are supposed to have borne that name.

CHAPTER VI

THE KHAZAR CONVERSION TO JUDAISM *ACCORDING TO THE HEBREW SOURCES*

THE ARABIC SOURCES offer no indication of the date of the conversion more precise than the statement of Masʿūdi, already quoted, that it took place in the Caliphate of Hārūn al-Rashīd, i.e., circa A.D. 800. In a work of Jehudah ha-Levi entitled *The Khazar* (*Khazari*) written originally in Arabic in A.D. 1140 and later translated into Hebrew by ibn-Tibbon under the title *Cosri* (*Kuzari*), the date 740 is given. Ha-Levi's work, as is well known, is a defense of Rabbinic Judaism, cast in the form of a dialogue which is represented as having taken place in Khazaria 400 years before the author's own time. In this dialogue the interlocutors are the Khazar king and others. Ha-Levi is not concerned to enlarge on the setting, his main interest being theological not historical, but he regards the conversion of the king to Judaism at this date as an accepted fact. The book *Cosri* (*Kuzari*) has at all times enjoyed high consideration that is not confined to Jewish circles. It was edited in the 17th century by the younger Buxtorf, and Herder, the German romantic, compared it favorably with the Platonic dialogues. In more modern times it has continued to be an object of study.

What little ha-Levi has to say about Khazaria and the Khazars is as follows: "Having often been asked what arguments and replies I had to offer to those philosophers who differ from us and to men of other religions (except the Christians), also to the heretics among us who deviate from the Jewish religion as it is commonly accepted, there occurred to my mind what I had heard of the reasonings and arguments of a certain scholar who was with the king of the Khazars, I mean him who accepted Judaism four hundred years ago. It is recorded and made known in the histories that a dream was several times repeated to him in which an angel spoke with him and told him that his intentions were acceptable to the Creator, but not his works. Yet he was very devout in the Khazar religion, taking part himself in the temple service and sacrifices with a sincere heart. While he was occupied with these works an angel appeared to him by night, saying, Your intentions are acceptable, but not your works. This caused him to enquire into the truth of faith and religion, so that finally he became a Jew, and with him many of the Khazars. Among the reasonings and arguments of the Jewish scholar were some in which his heart found rest and to which his understanding assented. I have thought it right to set down these things as they befell. The wise will understand.

"They relate that when the king of the Khazars had seen in his dream that his intentions but not his works were acceptable to the Creator and was commanded in his dream to seek the works which were acceptable, he enquired of a certain philosopher of the time about his faith."

A short dialogue with the "philosopher" then follows. Ha-Levi proceeds: "Afterwards the Khazar said to himself, I will ask a Christian and a Muslim. . . . So he sent for a wise man of the Christians."

There follows a dialogue with the Christian, and "afterwards," we are told, "he sent for a wise man of the Muslims." Their conversation is given as before. Finally a learned Jew is summoned, and after some discussion with the Jew the first part of the book ends. It should be noted that the speakers are introduced one after another. There is no general debate in which they all take part.

The second section of the *Kuzari* begins with the following *mise-en-scène*. "Afterwards, as is made known in the books of the Khazars, the Khazar revealed the secret of his dream to the general of his army. Now the dream had repeatedly told him to seek the work pleasing to God in the mountains of Warṣān [cf. Varach'an, Warathān]. So both of them, the king and the general, set out for the mountains, which are in a desert by the sea. They came by night to the cave where certain Jews rested all the Sabbath and, being seen by them, were admitted to their religion and circumcised there in the cave. Afterwards they returned to their own country. Though their hearts were inclined to the religion of the Jews, they concealed their faith till they had devised means to reveal their secret little by little to certain intimates. Finally they became numerous and avowed what they had not before disclosed. Thus prevailing over the rest of the Khazars, they induced them to become Jews. They sent to every land for learned men and books and studied the Law. It is also shown [i.e., apparently in the "books of the Khazars"] how they became prosperous, overcame their enemies, subdued territories, and had hidden treasures revealed to them. They increased, it is said, to hundreds of thousands, loved the Law, and wished for a sanctuary, so that they set up a tabernacle like that of Moses. They honored native Israelites and blessed their name. All this is related in their books. When the king had learned the Law and the Prophets, he took the scholar to be his teacher, asking him questions about the Jews. The first question was about the name and attributes ascribed to God." From this point the book proceeds by question and answer, the scholar replying to the king's enquiries.

On reading the passages just quoted, our first impression may well be that they are apocryphal. The crude supernaturalism does not indeed, by itself, invalidate a document of this period. But what is said of the Khazars throws doubt on the historical basis of the story. They are represented as having a place of worship in which prayers and sacrifices were offered, before accepting Judaism. This is not easily reconcilable with what we know of the heathen Turks, such as the Khazars undoubtedly were before conversion. Further, the presence with the king of the Khazars of a "philosopher," where we should expect a shamanist priest, is difficult. That the Khazar king and his general should have submitted to the rite of circumcision at the hands of obscure strangers seems incredible.

On the other hand, some details in the story speak more favorably for its objectivity. The prominence of the general side by side with the king is striking, in view of the Khaqan and Beg of Khazaria. The scene is set in the "mountains of Warṣān,"[1] said to be "in a desert near the sea." Warṣān should be Varach'an at the east end of the Caucasus,[2] identified with the northern Warathān[3]—conveniently near Khazaria, though not apparently at this time in Khazar territory, as the locality is presented by ha-Levi. The cave which he mentions has also to be noted. It appears to be referred to elsewhere. But, particularly, the precise dating of these events, which ha-Levi says took place "400 years ago," or as is given unequivocally in the course of the dialogue A.M. 4500, i.e., A.D. 740, seems to speak for the objectivity of the account. Though it is at present impossible to be sure where ha-Levi got this information, it would be hazardous to suppose that he simply invented it.

Rather, he had certain sources, to which he has given a free, literary treatment. He refers to the "histories" and the "books of the Khazars," though he does not say explicitly that he has used them. He may be writing from oral accounts, for in his own words "there occurred to my mind what I had heard of the reasonings and arguments of a certain scholar etc." We shall have something to say later about his possible oral sources. Meantime it may be noted that his insistence on the "books of the Khazars" appears to indicate at any rate a belief that such existed. We have the statement of the author of the Fihrist (circa 987) that the Khazars used the Hebrew script in their writing.[4] In the absolute nonexistence of Khazar documents in any other medium, we might suppose that if there were such

[1] The "river of Warshān" is apparently mentioned in the Reply of Joseph, at "20 parasangs" from the Khazar capital. Zeki Validi places it in the Volga delta (*Ibn-Faḍlān*, 157). Marquart's suggestion that here in the Reply "mountain of Warsān" is the original reading (*Streifz.*, 20) seems unlikely in view of L.V.

[2] For Varach'an, see Chapter III.

[3] Cf. Chapter IV, n. 90.

[4] Ed. Flügel, 20.

works as ha-Levi indicates, they were in Hebrew letters. On the other hand, according to the *Ta'rīkh-i Fakhr al-Dīn Mubārak Shāh*, written in 1206, "the Khazars have a script which is related to the script of the Russians [Rūs]. A group of Greeks [Rūm] who are near them write in this script and are called Greek Russians [Rūm-Rūs]. They write from left to right, and the letters are not joined to one another. They number twenty-one."[5] A contemporary of ha-Levi, Abraham ben-Daud, states that persons of Khazar extraction were in Toledo in his own time.[6] It is therefore not excluded that, as well as informants, "books of the Khazars" with information about the conversion to Judaism were available in Spain.[7]

In view of the undoubted existence of the so-called Khazar Correspondence in ha-Levi's time—it was in the hands of a Spanish rabbi forty or fifty years before the *Kuzari* was published[8]—the supposition that ha-Levi knew it is not unnatural. Whether this was so and to what extent he may have made use of it will be considered when we come to deal with the Correspondence, which purports to be an interchange of letters between Ḥasday ibn-Shaprut, a well-known Jewish personality in Spain, and Joseph, king of the Khazars, not later than 961, both texts being in Hebrew. It is enough to say here that the expression "books of the Khazars" is not applicable with any exactness to the Correspondence, and more especially that

[5] Ed. E. Denison Ross, London 1927, 46 (cited by R. N. Frye, "Notes to Islamic Sources on the Slavs and the Rūs," *Muslim World*, January 1950, 23).

[6] See the translation given below. It is not clear that the Khazar Jews seen by Abraham ben-Daud in Spain were descendants of the Khazar kings, as has repeatedly been said.

[7] The Yiddish printed book *Ma'aseh ha-Shem* by Simon Akiba Baer ben-Joseph (Bodleian Library, Opp. 8°, 1103 [1], fols. 29b-30b) has a curious story according to which the famous Abraham ben-Ezra marries the daughter of R. Judah (apparently R. Jehudah ha-Levi) in Khazaria. "Es war ein melek der hat geheissen Kuzari, der war ein grosser melumad, un einer heisst Rabbenu Judah, der war ein grosser Talmid hakham, un er lernet mit den melek Kuzari, un er war ihm maggid un war ein guter, frommer Jehudi. Nun war der Rabbi Judah stets bei den melek un er konnt nit ohn ihm leben, etc." This late Yiddish tale is of course quite unhistorical.

[8] Jehudah ben-Barzillay al-Barsalōni, see below.

important details given by ha-Levi are not in the letters, e.g., the visit to Warṣān and the date 740.

It is perhaps a question if the "histories" which he mentions are the same as the "books of the Khazars." We might naturally suppose that ha-Levi had knowledge of Mas'ūdi's lost account of the Judaizing of the Khazars,[9] which was written before 943-944 and appears to have been independent of the Khazar Correspondence. When he speaks of "histories," it might be to this or similar Arabic works that he refers. It is noticeable that in the passage quoted ha-Levi does not name the "scholar" in Khazaria, whose arguments he claims to give and who is elsewhere called Isaac Sangari. If he were dependent entirely on Mas'ūdi or other Arabic authors together with, perhaps, the Correspondence, he would presumably be ignorant of the name of Isaac Sangari. On the other hand, he gives one piece of information which he can scarcely have had from Mas'ūdi—the date 740 for the conversion. It is extremely unlikely that Mas'ūdi's lost account, whatever details it gave, contradicted his statement in the *Murūj al-Dhahab* that the Khazars became Jews in the Caliphate of Hārūn al-Rashīd. Unless this date is an arbitrary invention of ha-Levi, which seems improbable, he must have had it, it would seem, not from the Arabic tradition represented by Mas'ūdi, but from some Jewish, possibly Khazar source.[10]

[9] See Chapter V.

[10] The earliest Western authority for Khazar Judaism may antedate the earliest Jewish authority (cf. n. 44) by as much as a century. He is Christian Druthmar of Aquitaine (9th century), a Benedictine of Corvei in Westphalia, who wrote a commentary on St. Matthew's Gospel for the monks of a monastery in the Ardennes. Marquart (*Streifz.*, 23-24) supposed that this was written in 864 or shortly earlier. Druthmar was evidently a man of considerable independence of mind, cf. the remarks in his Preface (Migne, *Patrologia, Ser.* 2, t. 106): in this Commentary he proposes "plus historicum sensum sequi quam spiritalem: quia irrationabile mihi videtur, spiritalem intelligentiam in libro aliquo quaerere, et historicam penitus ignorare." On *Matthew* 24.14 (Migne, *ibid.*, col. 1456) he says: "Nescimus jam gentem sub coelo in qua Christiani non habeantur. Nam et in Gog et in Magog, quae sunt gentes Hunnorum, quae ab eis Gazari vocantur, jam una gens quae fortior erat ex his quas Alexander conduxerat, circumcisa est, et omnem Judaismum observat." This may have been written considerably before the year 864 suggested

One view of the Khazar setting of ha-Levi's book is ill-founded and has led to unfortunate results. The title-page of Buxtorf's edition of the *Cosri* (*Kuzari*) has the name R. Isaac Sangari as that of the Khazar king's principal interlocutor. Buxtorf appears to have got this from his own reading. The name Isaac Sangari is perhaps not attested before the 13th century, when he is mentioned by Nahmanides.[11] Shem Tob ibn-Shem Tob (*ob.* 1430) states that R. Isaac Sangari was "a scholar attached to the Khazar king, who became a Jew owing to him, many years ago in the country of Togarmah [the Turks], as is made known in certain writings. The fine responses of this rabbi, showing his great knowledge of the Law, the Kabbalah and all the other branches, existed in a disconnected form in Arabic. R. Jehudah ha-Levi, the Spanish poet, found them and composed a book in Arabic from them, just as they were, which was translated into Hebrew."[12] Ibn-Shem Tob was followed by R. Gedaliah (circa 1587), who stated, however, that the responses of Isaac Sangari were in the Khazar language.[13] What ibn-Shem Tob evidently means is that the substance of the scholar's replies to the Khazar king in ha-Levi's *Cosri* (*Kuzari*) was based on the responses of Isaac Sangari, who had formerly been active in Khazaria. But, waiving the difficulty of how these can be supposed to have existed to ha-Levi's hand in Arabic, much less in the Khazar language, as Gedaliah gratuitously stated, it is impossible to believe that the "reasonings and arguments" of the scholar, which now form the greater part of the *Kuzari*, a lengthy work, reached him from Isaac Sangari or anyone else. They were clearly composed ad hoc by ha-Levi from his knowledge of Rabbinic

---

by Marquart (800 has been given by an early editor of the commentary), but in view of the uncertainty of the exact date it can hardly be used in support of the Khazar conversion having taken place in the 8th century.

11 In a discourse before the king of Castile circa 1263 (ed. Jellinek with the title *Torat Adonai Temimah*, Vienna, 1872), cf. Strack, *Firkovitch und seine Entdeckungen*, Leipzig 1876, 24 n.

12 *Sepher ha-Emunoth*, quoted Buxtorf, Praef.; Strack, *ibid.*, 23 n.

13 *Ibid.*

Judaism, on the basis of something he had heard, as he himself says. There is no question here of direct oral transmission of a great number of actual responses. Nor is there anything in the *Kuzari* to suggest that the author had a collection of written responses before him. The "histories" and "books of the Khazars" can hardly by any ingenuity be taken in the sense of responses of a particular rabbi, and must refer to chronicles, etc., real or imaginary.

The view of ibn-Shem Tob was argued with great insistence by Firkovitch (19th century), who gave it a characteristic turn of his own. In a letter written at the beginning of his remarkable career, he expressed the view that the responses of R. Isaac Sangari came into the hands of Jehudah ha-Levi who, recognizing that they contradicted the teachings of Rabbinism, translated them into Arabic in an altered form.[14] Firkovitch was satisfied that Isaac Sangari was a Karaite, in accordance with his theory that the Karaites had left Palestine before the time of Christ and were in the Crimea earlier than the arrival of the Khazars.[15] His authority for this was not of course mere texts, but his own Karaite teacher, whom he names, and he clinches the matter by adding "and I agree with him."[16]

Firkovitch went much further than these assertions. He produced what he declared to be the epitaph of Isaac Sangari, which he claimed to have found in the Crimea, reading in Hebrew character "Isaac Sangari P-g."[17] The last letters suggested the Beg of Khazaria. This was of course rejected as unauthentic.[18] Another inscription reading simply "Sangarith"

[14] See a German version in Strack, *ibid.*, 16ff, also Harkavy, *Denkmäler*, 270ff.

[15] Cf. Strack, *ibid.*, 25-26. Firkovitch's view included that the Karaites were specially favored by the Khazars, perhaps with a passage of the Cosri (Kuzari) in mind (III, xxii). But it seems to be an anachronism to speak of Karaites so early as A.D. 740, and I know of no contemporary evidence that Karaites later were prominent in Khazaria.

[16] Strack, *ibid.*, 23.

[17] Cf. Harkavy, *Denkmäler*, 174 and facsimile (Plate 2).

[18] N. Slouschz in *Mélanges H. Derenbourg* speaks of Hebrew money found in Poland with the legend "Abraham Pech" (citing Harkavy, "Evrei-kazaki," *Russki Evrei*, 1880). An article by Lelewel discusses a

in rough Hebrew letters was also produced, with the claim that it was the epitaph of Sangari's wife. Apart from these spurious epitaphs, a number of Hebrew manuscripts, now in the Leningrad Public Library, but formerly in the possession of Firkovitch, contain dedications, etc., the text of which has been interfered with by him, *inter alia* one in which mention is made of David ben-Isaac Sangari.[19] All told, the interest which Firkovitch showed in Isaac Sangari has done nothing to throw light on who he may have been, but, on the contrary, by a natural enough association of ideas, has tended to make his existence more doubtful. It may indeed be said that the whole story of the conversion of the Khazars to Judaism has in the past been suspect in certain quarters, owing to the unscrupulous or rather frantic efforts[20] of Firkovitch to show that they were connected with his Karaites. It is unfortunate that Firkovitch should have acted as he did. His material has been canvassed by Harkavy and Strack[21] and by Chwolson.[22] An adequate survey of this and other relevant literature[23] would demand a special investigation. It seems that while Harkavy and Strack were certainly justified in drawing attention to various forgeries due to Firkovitch, the last word has not been said on the subject. A close examination of the documents in the light of modern criticism might afford additional information about the Khazars.

With regard to Isaac Sangari, it may be allowed that he can have been active in the Judaizing of the Khazars, as the Jewish tradition has it, with the *caveat* that he is not distinctly

---

range of coins to which the money referred to by Harkavy and Slouschz may belong ("Les bractéates juives de la Pologne," *Revue Numismatique*, 1860, 328ff).

[19] *J.A.*, VI, V (1865), 538.

[20] The aim of Firkovitch's contentions was to show that the Karaites were distinct from orthodox Jews and should not be discriminated against by the Christians, particularly the Czarist government.

[21] *Catalogue of the Leningrad Public Library*; Harkavy's *Altjüdische Denkmäler aus der Krim* (*M.R.A.*, 1876); and Strack's book already cited.

[22] *Corpus of Hebrew Inscriptions* (in Russian and German editions).

[23] See the short article by Neubauer and Munk in *J.A.*, 1865.

mentioned till much later. If genuine, the name might be explained from the town Sangarus or Sangara on the Asiatic coast of the Propontis.[24] Sangari would then be a Byzantine Jew, who may be supposed to have left Greek territory and passed to Khazaria, on the lines suggested by Mas'ūdi.

We now turn to the Khazar Correspondence which, as already said, consists of a letter sent apparently from Spain to Khazaria in the 10th century, and the reply of the Khazar king. The question of authenticity has been much debated. The Correspondence is central for the conversion of the Khazars to Judaism, of which its second part, the so-called Reply of King Joseph, offers detailed information. Obviously, if genuine, the Reply of Joseph has the nature of an official account of the event, from the authority best able to give the true facts. Sometimes indeed when the Khazar problem is spoken of, what is meant is principally whether the two Hebrew letters are to be regarded as historical or not. But the importance of the Khazar Correspondence can be exaggerated. By this time it is possible to reconstruct Khazar history in some detail without recourse to the letter of Ḥasday and Joseph. Even if both should prove spurious, the existence of the Khazars and the fact that at one time they were Jews are beyond suspicion, on the overwhelming testimony of many independent sources.

In what follows we shall not attempt a detailed criticism of the Correspondence, such as is now possible on the basis of Kokovtsov's excellent edition, which has been available in Russian since 1932.[25] But we shall indicate the contents of the two letters and of several associated documents, also in Hebrew, and some of the principal arguments which have been applied to these, and offer some considerations which seem to be of importance.

Until Kokovtsov's edition just referred to and even since then, at least in the West, in view of the inaccessibility of Russian books, the main source of our knowledge of the

[24] Cf. Marquart, *Streifz.*, 211.
[25] *Evreisko-khazarskaya perepiska v X veke*, Leningrad, 1932.

Khazar Correspondence has remained, it may be said, the text and Latin translation of the two letters, published by the younger Buxtorf as long ago as 1660. The letters were printed by Buxtorf, in his edition of the *Cosri* (*Kuzari*) already mentioned, from a Hebrew book entitled *Qōl Mebasser*, which had been sent to him by a friend. They were obviously regarded by Buxtorf with great suspicion. We underline the attitude of Buxtorf because other scholars before and since his time reacted similarly when the Khazar Correspondence was first brought to their notice. When Buxtorf first learned about the Khazars, he was inclined to connect their name with the Persian Khusraw (Chosroes).[26] This in itself shows that he was on very unfamiliar ground.

Buxtorf corrected his earlier impression of a connection between the Khazars and Khusraw,[27] but he proceeded to get into difficulties with the alleged sender of the letter to Khazaria, Ḥasday ibn-Shaprut. There is now plenty of information about this colorful personality, who rose to eminence in the Spain of ʿAbd-al-Raḥmān al-Nāṣir.[28] Of Jewish birth, his activities included the successful cure of a Christian prince and his reception in a spectacular manner at Cordova, patronage of several of the leading figures of the Jewish revival of letters in Spain, correspondence with the learned of Babylonia, and much else besides, which can be gathered from Arabic as well as Hebrew sources. Buxtorf had recourse to Ganz's *Zemah David*, a standard work of the time on Jewish chronology, and could only find references to Ḥasday Crescas and Shem Tob ben-Isaac Shaprut,[29] both belonging to the 14th century. Of the actual circumstances of Ḥasday ibn-Shaprut in the 10th he seems to have had no idea. Accordingly, when he found a mention of the Khazar Correspondence in Abraham ben-Daud,

[26] Buxtorf on *Cosri* (*Kuzari*), I, i, n. 6.

[27] Buxtorf, Praefat.

[28] See E. Lévi-Provençal, *Histoire de l'Espagne musulmane*, T. 1 (1944), 326ff; Grätz, *Geschichte der Juden*, ed. 3, v, 297ff, with the references there cited.

[29] Pointed out to me by Mr. J. L. Teicher.

who flourished in the 12th century, he suspected that the passage was interpolated. The account of Abraham ben-Daud is as follows:[30]

"You will find congregations of Israel spread abroad from the town of Sala at the extremity of the Maghrib, as far as Tahart at its commencement, the extremity of Africa [Ifrīqīyah, Tunis], in all Africa, Egypt, the country of the Sabaeans, Arabia, Babylonia, Elam, Persia, Dedan, the country of the Girgashites which is called Jurjān, Ṭabaristān, as far as Daylam and the river Itil [Atil], where live the Khazar peoples who became proselytes. Their king Joseph sent a letter to R. Ḥasday, the prince, bar Isaac ben[31]-Shaprut and informed him that he and all his people followed the Rabbanite faith. We have seen in Toledo some of their descendants, pupils of the wise, and they told us that the remnant of them followed the Rabbanite faith."

It is remarkable that Buxtorf was prepared to introduce the theory of interpolation to explain what he could not readily understand. Unaware of the historical Ḥasday ibn-Shaprut and misled by the references in *Zemah David*, which were to other people, he failed to see that this passage in Abraham ben-Daud is confirmation, so far as it goes, of the Khazar Correspondence. Buxtorf's services in making the letters generally accessible in the West are not to be minimized, but, great Hebraist as he was, his skepticism is demonstrably ill-founded. Our information by this time is much more extensive, for we now have sources which throw a flood of light on Khazaria. *Mutatis mutandis*, the case of Buxtorf deserves to be considered by those who would still cut the knot of an intricate problem by hasty recourse to a theory of interpolation.[32]

It may thus be said that the investigation of the Khazar Correspondence was unfavorably launched when Buxtorf took position to it in a negative sense. When more came to be

[30] *Sēpher ha-Qabbalah*, ed. Neubauer, *Mediaeval Jewish Chronicles* (*Anecdota Oxoniensia*, I), 78. The date of the work according to its editor (*ibid.*, xiii) is A.D. 1161.

[31] Text "ben." For juxtaposition of "bar" and "ben," see below.

[32] See especially "Le 'Glozel' khazare," H. Grégoire, *Byzantion*, XII (1937) 225-266.

known, there was still ground for uncertainty. Buxtorf gave some cursory data about his only source, the work *Qol Mebasser.* When this book was investigated closely, the yield of information was very slight. Its author, an otherwise unknown Jew called Isaac Aqrish, while on a voyage from Constantinople to Alexandria, as he tells us, in 1561-1562 and subsequently in Egypt, heard rumors of an independent Jewish kingdom, referring, it would seem, to the Falashas. In 1577 or later his findings on the subject were published in Constantinople in the book seen by Buxtorf.[33] Where Isaac Aqrish obtained the text of the Khazar Correspondence is unfortunately not mentioned. There is room for varying opinions on this important point. Mann says that he "evidently obtained his copy in Cairo."[34] It has been supposed that the two documents were from the Cairo Genizah. But nothing explicit is said in *Qol Mebasser*, and it may be that its author did not see the Correspondence until his return to Constantinople.

This is evidently unsatisfactory. But one is bound to dissent from the view that the Khazar Correspondence is not an integral part of *Qol Mebasser* and has been inserted later, with a reference to it interpolated in the introductory remarks of Aqrish in order to conceal the addition.

Aqrish reports that after his arrival in Cairo from Alexandria he visited a Jewish rabbi who was physician to the Turkish governor of Egypt under Sultan Sulaymān. The rabbi told Aqrish that a short time earlier he had seen the governor reading a letter from an Abyssinian prince Dōshdōmōr, who mentioned the help which he had recently received in war from a Jewish ruler. Aqrish goes on to describe the visit of another Abyssinian, unnamed, to Constantinople and gives the words of Sinān Pasha, vizir of the Sultan Murād, on the subject of the Jewish kingdom. Then he proceeds: "When I heard these words and saw a letter, which was sent to the king of the

[33] The Bodleian copies (Nos. 1074 and 1098) belong to different editions, both apparently undated. (1577 is the date of composition of the work.)

[34] *Texts and Studies*, I, 8.

Khazars and his reply, I decided to print them 'with an iron pen and lead' (*Job* 19, 24), to strengthen the people and in order that they should believe firmly that the Jews have a kingdom and dominion."[35] The context suggests that Aqrish saw the Correspondence in Constantinople rather than in Egypt. It was in any case in Constantinople that his book, as already said, was published.

In the passage just quoted, Landau,[36] following Grégoire, wants to excise the words "which was sent to the king of the Khazars and his reply" and supposes that the "letter" here mentioned had originally nothing to do with the Khazar Correspondence, but was in fact the letter of the Abyssinian prince Dōshdōmōr to the governor of Egypt. This seems to be demonstrably wrong: *a*, the matter of Dōshdōmōr's letter belongs to the visit of Aqrish to Egypt under Sultan Sulaymān (1520-1566). Aqrish has gone on to mention quite other things, the visit of another Abyssinian to Constantinople, and the remarks of Sinān Pasha under Murād (1574-1577). There is no reason why he should return to speak of Dōshdōmōr's letter. *b*, Aqrish had never seen Dōshdōmōr's letter but he saw the other. *c*, if Dōshdōmōr's letter were intended it should be referred to as "the letter," for it has already been mentioned. An interpolator might then conceivably have added the words "which was sent to the king of the Khazars and his reply" and the passage would read smoothly. But the text is "a letter" (*egereth*). This must be original, for an interpolator had no reason to alter "the letter" (*ha-egereth*) if Aqrish had written it. Clearly a second letter, not the Abyssinian Dōshdōmōr's, is intended by Aqrish.

I believe that these points are sufficient to dispose of the view that *Qol Mebasser* has been interpolated. Nothing conclusive has been urged in support of it. Landau says that Aqrish in Constantinople at the end of the 16th century must

[35] Following the text of *Qol Mebasser* in Kokovtsov.

[36] M. Landau, "The Present Position of the Khazar Problem," Zion, 1943, §1 (in Hebrew).

have known about the Khazars and been aware that their state had long ago ceased to exist. It looks as if he had never heard of them, though he knew the legend of the river Sambation. Aqrish gives the impression of having used the Correspondence in support of his contention that a Jewish kingdom existed in simple ignorance. The text as it stands confirms this. Apparently the name Ḥasday ibn-Shaprut has been omitted by Aqrish, in the passage quoted, as unfamiliar to him. An interpolator would surely have added it. It is altogether likely that he saw a copy of the Correspondence in Constantinople or elsewhere in the period 1574-1577 (reign of Murād) and shortly afterwards reproduced it in good faith.

So much for the possibility of interpolation in the work of Aqrish. If anyone thinks that the Khazar Correspondence was first composed in 1577 and published in *Qol Mebasser*, the onus of proof is certainly on him. He must show that a number of ancient manuscripts, which appear to contain references to the Correspondence, have all been interpolated since the end of the 16th century. This will prove a very difficult or rather an impossible task.

When we try to get behind the printed editions of *Qol Mebasser*, the results are not entirely satisfactory. The only known manuscript containing both the Letter of Ḥasday and the Reply of Joseph is in the library of Christ Church, Oxford.[37] This manuscript presents a remarkably close similarity to the printed text, as may be seen from Kokovtsov's edition and as I have personally checked. It is not easy to say what is the genetic connection between the two, but it is unlikely that the manuscript, as has several times been suggested, is actually a transcript of the printed text. Rather, as Kokovtsov says, the manuscript served directly or indirectly as a source of the printed text. But it has no claims to great antiquity.

Undated like the Christ Church manuscript is another in

[37] No. 193. Owing to the liberality of the Christ Church authorities I was able to consult this valuable MS. not only in the Bodleian but also in Glasgow University Library. Though collated once again by myself, the MS. yielded little or nothing which had escaped Kokovtsov.

the Leningrad Public Library,[38] which contains along with midrashic material a longer version of the Reply of Joseph than is found in the Christ Church manuscript and the printed text of Aqrish, but lacks the Letter of Ḥasday. Attention was directed to this manuscript by Harkavy, a most diligent student of Khazar antiquities, in 1874, and hailed by him as the undoubted original of the previously known version.[39] Unfortunately the Long Version of the Reply of Joseph passed to the Leningrad library via Firkovitch, who had apparently acquired it in Egypt in the sixties of last century.[40] This connection with Firkovitch did not predispose investigators to regard it as an undoubted relic of antiquity. It would appear, however, that in this case we need not immediately suspect a forgery. Chwolson, who had examined it, states that the whole manuscript is written in the same hand and there are no additions of any kind.[41] It is supposed to date from the 13th century.[42] Unless therefore this indication of date is completely wrong and Firkovitch is responsible for the whole—contrary to his usual method of fabrication, which was to make alterations and additions in authentic documents—we probably have to reckon with the Long Version as considerably older than the printed text of Aqrish. Harkavy, in spite of his very critical attitude to Firkovitch and his discoveries, had no hesitation in accepting it as the original of the Short Version in Aqrish, as already said. If the view of Harkavy, which for once coincides with Chwolson's, is not right, most people will agree with Kokovtsov's cautious statement[43] that as basis for both versions there is certainly the same original text, which is in general better preserved in the Long Version.

That the Khazar Correspondence is a forgery of the 16th century can scarcely be taken seriously in view of what has

38 MS. Heb. 157 of the 2nd Firkovitch Collection.

39 *Measeph Niddahim*, I, no. 8.

40 Chwolson, *Corpus*, German ed., St. Petersburg 1882, 143, n. 6.

41 *Ibid.*, 520 (quoted similarly by Kokovtsov from the Russian ed., 1884, 499).

42 *Ibid.*, 143 n. 6.

43 *Op.cit.*, Introduction.

been said, especially with regard to the plain references to it in works of much earlier date. We have already quoted one such from Abraham ben-Daud. This does not stand alone. Setting aside general references to the conversion of the Khazars in Jewish sources, such as we find frequently, at least from the 10th century,[44] we have what appears to be an authentic citation of the Reply of Joseph as early as the time of R. Jehudah ben-Barzillay of Barcelona, whose *Sepher ha-'Ittim* is dated between 1090 and 1105.[45]

R. Jehudah of Barcelona writes as follows: "We have seen in some MSS. the copy of a letter which King Joseph, son of Aaron, the Khazar priest [ha-Kohen, presumably for ha-Kagan, the Khaqan][46] wrote to R. Ḥasday bar Isaac. We do not know if the letter is genuine or not, and if it is a fact that the Khazars, who are Turks, became proselytes. It is not definite whether all that is written in the letter is fact and truth or not. There may be falsehoods written in it, or people may have added to it, or there may be error on the part of the scribe. . . . The reason why we need to write in this our book things which seem to be exaggerated is that we have found in the letter of this king Joseph to R. Ḥasday that R. Ḥasday had asked him of what family he was, the condition of the king, how his fathers had been gathered under the wings of the Presence [i.e., become Jews] and how great were his kingdom and dominion. He replied to him on every head, writing all the particulars in the letter."[47] There follows a part of the Reply of Joseph, agreeing in general with the Long Version and supporting the view of Kokovtsov that the Long Version preserves the original better than the Short Version.

It is pretty safe to allow that the Khazar Correspondence,

[44] The earliest Jewish reference to the Khazar conversion may be in the *Kitāb al-Riyāḍ wa-l-Ḥadā'iq of Qirqisani* (Brit. Mus. Or. 2492) circa 937, cited by Landau, "Present Position," Introd. But other references in Sa'adiah Gaon could be earlier (cf. Chapter VII, n. 273).

[45] S. Asaf, in *Jeshurun* XI, nos. 9-10 (cited Poliak, "Conversion," §3). Text in Kokovtsov.

[46] Cf. Poliak, "Conversion," §4.

[47] Following Kokovtsov's text.

the Letter of Ḥasday as well as the Reply of Joseph, existed already in the time of R. Jehudah of Barcelona. Kokovtsov says that R. Jehudah has not a word about the Letter of Ḥasday,[48] which is true, but its existence is certainly implied. Granting so much, the authenticity is still not certain. It is very striking that R. Jehudah himself expresses doubts about the Reply of Joseph. At first sight the fact that a skeptical view was thus early adopted may tend to confirm our suspicions. But it should be observed that the doubts of the rabbi are not precise and, as in the case of Buxtorf, may simply mean that he was not informed about the Khazars.

External evidence will take us little further than this, that the Correspondence seems to have existed in Spain in the 11th century. The question of authenticity will have to be decided, if possible, on internal grounds.

The Letter of Ḥasday begins with a poem (*piut*), which is remarkable for the acrostic given by the initial letters of the lines. This reads "I, Ḥasday bar Isaac bar Ezra bar Shaprut. Menahem ben-Saruq."[49] The latter name, given not quite perfectly in the text of *Qol Mebasser* but nearly enough, is that of the well-known literary man of the 10th century, whose connection with Ḥasday is undoubted, and it is plausible to suggest that the poem containing the acrostic and presumably what follows were written by him as Ḥasday's secretary. Obviously, the existence of the acrostic does not prove that the Letter of Ḥasday was written by Menahem ben-Saruq (though this has been said) and is therefore genuine, but from another angle this result can perhaps be reached. Landau has compared the extant works of Menahem with the Letter of Ḥasday, from the point of view of style, and has no doubt that it is his.[50] Another consideration is that the same *piut* exists in a manuscript of the Hebrew Bible examined independently by Har-

[48] *Op.cit.*, Introd.

[49] "Bar" as well as "ben," cf. above.

[50] "Present Position," §2, cf. his earlier *Beiträge zum Chazarenproblem*, Breslau 1938. Landau in his review (*Qiryath Sēpher*, XXI, 19ff) of Poliak's *Khazaria* takes him strongly to task for saying that the introduction only is in Menahem's style (cf. *Khazaria*, 21).

kavy and E. Deinard, where it is explicitly ascribed to Menahem.[51] This text of the poem appears to be independent of that in *Qol Mebasser*, though it is apparently of recent date.[52]

The poem appears to insist on the military glory of the Khazar ruler. After a number of lines devoted to good wishes for the success of his arms, there comes what looks like a reference to a particular victory:

Consider now, pillars of earth! Who has ever heard or seen the like?
That survivors should prevail over the mighty! They put them to flight and destroyed[?] a city and all that was in it.[53]
The strong arm of the Most High helped them and was their salvation.
This is the work of the Almighty and His recompense to the sinful kingdom.

Landau called attention to this passage, pointing out that the expression "the sinful kingdom" is regularly applied to Byzantium.[54] The point will be referred to again, when we come to discuss what is called the Cambridge Document.

The prose part of the Letter of Ḥasday, after compliments and generalities, proceeds to acquaint the Khazar king with the geographical situation of Spain, and the writer gives some information of the same kind about Khazaria, which, however, is quite obscure. Apparently he wishes to provide data by which his correspondent may fix the position of Spain with reference to Khazaria, and he has made use of Arabic geographical works for the purpose. The general tone of the Letter is, however, one of enquiry. The writer's knowledge of Khazaria, or perhaps of its importance, is represented as being of recent date. He states that two Spanish Jews, R. Jehudah bar Meir bar Nathan and R. Joseph Hagaris, have visited the country recently, but does not claim to have spoken with them. He sets out the natural wealth of Spain and speaks of himself

[51] Landau, *op.cit.*, §2.
[52] Cf. Kokovtsov, Introd.
[53] Or "delivered up" (?), cf. *Amos* 6, 8.
[54] *Op.cit.*, §4.

as in charge of incoming foreign trade. Among the foreigners who came to Spain were certain people who appear as "the merchant-envoys of Khurāsān.[55] These Khurasanians, if they were such, assured the writer of the Letter, as he tells us, that the Jewish kingdom of Khazaria existed, but he did not at first believe them.

Later, the writer of the Letter says, he heard an account of the Khazar Jews from the Byzantine envoys. This passage runs as follows: "I questioned them [i.e., the Byzantine envoys] about the matter [i.e., the report of the merchant-envoys of Khurāsān] and they replied to me that it was true, and that the name of the kingdom is Khazaria.[56] Between Constantinople and their country is a journey of 15 days by sea, but, said they, between us by land are many intervening peoples. The name of the ruling king is Joseph. Ships come to us from their land, bringing fish, skins [i.e., probably furs] and all kinds of merchandise. They are in alliance with us and honored by us. Between us and them are embassies and gifts. They are powerful and have a fortress for their raiding bands and armies which go forth at times."

Ḥasday, if he is in fact the sender of the Letter, here seems to tell us how he knew the name of his correspondent. In the heading of the Letter, conformably with this passage, Joseph is called "the king of the Khazars," whereas in the heading of the Reply he appears as "the Turkish [Togarmian] king." Obviously, however, these headings may be from the hand of an editor. There is no ground for certainty, even if the Reply is proved genuine, that "the Turkish king" was his official Hebrew style.

In the passage above quoted, Khazaria is said to be 15 days by sea from Constantinople. We may anticipate a little to mention that the Cambridge Document puts the distance at 9 days by sea. Possibly the writer of the Letter means the length of

[55] It is not clear why envoys from Khurāsān should visit the Cordovan court. See below.

[56] Text "al-Khazar." See below.

the journey to the Khazar capital on the Volga, while the other thinks of some point nearer Constantinople. The route by the Black Sea, Sea of Azov, and the Don-Volga passage, elsewhere called "the Khazarian way,"[57] must be intended in our passage and the "fortress" is doubtless Sarkil, built for the Khazars by Greek engineers in A.D. 833.[58]

It is probably nowhere else explicitly stated, as here, that the Khazars trade, in their own ships apparently, with Constantinople. Among the merchandise which they are said to bring, fish and apparently furs are specially mentioned. We know from Arabic sources that both articles were among the Khazar exports to the lands of Islam. The Khazar military power is again mentioned.

After what he had been told, Ḥasday, according to the Letter, decided to get in touch with the king of the Khazars, and by his own account had some difficulty in doing so. First, he sent a certain Mar Isaac bar Nathan to Constantinople with instructions to proceed from there to Khazaria. But his messenger was not encouraged by the Emperor, probably Constantine Porphyrogenitus, to continue his journey, and sometime later returned to Spain, without having visited the country of the Khazars. Then Ḥasday, still according to the Letter, considered the possibility of sending a message to Khazaria via Jerusalem, Mesopotamia, and Armenia. The arrival at Cordova of an embassy from "the king of the Gebalim, who are the Saqlāb"[59] altered his plans. With this embassy were a couple of Jews, Mar Saul and Mar Joseph, who, on hearing of Ḥasday's desire to make contact with the Khazars, offered their services as intermediaries. The suggestion was agreeable to Ḥasday, and we are to understand that the Letter actually reached its destination by their means, being finally put into the hands of the Khazar king, according to the Reply, by a certain R. Jacob or (L. V.) Isaac ben-Eliezer, a central European Jew.

[57] Cf. G. Vernadsky, *Ancient Russia*, Yale 1943, 350, citing the Slavic Vita Constantini.

[58] Chapter VII.

[59] Cf. Ṣaqālibah.

The Arabic author Maqqari[60] speaks of an embassy to Cordova from Huttu (Otto), king of the Ṣaqālibah, identified with the visit of John of Gorz, the envoy of the Emperor Otto I, in 953-955.[61] What nation is intended by the "Gebalim who are the Saqlāb" has not been finally determined.[62] Grégoire has advanced the view that the Gebalim are the Gauls,[63] which name the Hebrew may be said to represent (with pronunciation Gebhalim). It is very inviting to identify the Saqlāb with Maqqari's Ṣaqālibah, as subjects of the German Emperor, both forms apparently due to "Saxones." Ḥasday's Letter should thus allude at this point to the visit of John of Gorz. In any case, Mar Saul and Mar Joseph are said to have told Ḥasday that some years previously a Khazar Jew, or at least a former resident at the Khazar king's court, named Mar Amram had come to Spain,[64] but Ḥasday's enquiries for him had not proved successful. This should indicate that intercourse with Khazaria was rare.

Poliak's view that the Correspondence as a whole is not indeed a forgery, but a work of the 11th century (sc. *ante* R. Jehudah of Barcelona) composed in a conventional literary form to spread information about the Khazars among the Jews[65] is hardly tenable. If this is so, what is the point of mentioning half-a-dozen obscure names as those of men involved, one way or another, in Ḥasday's search for information? Why the Letter of Ḥasday at all, which, though considerably longer than the Reply of Joseph, has very little indeed about the Khazars, if the purpose of writing it and the Reply was, as Poliak supposes, simply to give a popular account of Khazaria? If the

[60] I, 235; ibn-Khaldūn, IV, 143.

[61] Cf. Lévi-Provençal, *op.cit.*, 383.

[62] Kokovtsov has a long discussion, *op.cit.*, 62, n. 3.

[63] In *Mélanges R. Dussaud*, 489. I owe the reference to Professor A. M. Honeyman.

[64] So apparently *bā ēlēnū*. Otherwise, "to the land of the Gebalim" (oratio recta).

[65] "Conversion," §3; cf. *Khazaria*, 19: the author of the Correspondence was alive in Spain in 1070-1080. Landau in his review, *loc.cit.*, rightly takes exception to this.

Letter is an introduction to the information about the Khazars in the Reply, it is certainly a very curious one—full of facts about Spain and the Umayyads which have nothing to do with Khazaria, and mentioning with great detail and, it must be allowed, considerable plausibility how it came to be written and despatched. A homilist or pamphleteer would surely have dispensed with all this and got down to the business of describing Khazaria with much less ado.

Poliak argues against the historicity of the Letter of Ḥasday on the ground that the sender had apparently never read the Arabic geographical and historical literature on the Khazars, and that this is unthinkable in a man in Ḥasday's position in 10th century Spain. The argument is not convincing. The sender of the Letter in fact gives us to understand that he has had recourse to books, presumably geographical works in Arabic, for the situation of Khazaria,[66] and he mentions certain details evidently based on these, e.g., correct statements of the latitude of Cordova and Constantinople. Poliak regards this as an inner contradiction within the Letter.[67]

Earlier than Poliak, Marquart had taken a similar line.[68] He thought that Ḥasday must have known about the Khazars, and refers in this connection to the Rādhānīyah, one of whose routes in their continuous journeying from West to East and back again was overland across Europe to "Khamlīj (Khamlīkh), the capital of the Khazars" and thence via the Caspian to Transoxiana and as far afield as China. According to ibn-Khurdādhbih (circa A.D. 846), who is the principal authority for the Rādhānīyah, they were Jews from Spain.[69] But in the Letter Ḥasday hears first of the existence of the Jewish king from the Khurasanians and the Byzantine envoys. Therefore, according to Marquart, it cannot be genuine. This again falls short of a demonstration. Conceivably the "merchant envoys of Khurāsān" and the Rādhānīyah were the same, regarded as Occidentals

[66] Cf. above. [67] "Conversion," §3. [68] *Streifz.*, 24.

[69] Ibn-Khurdādhbih, 153, has Rādhānīyah, which we have retained. Ibn-al-Faqīh, 270, has Rāhdānīyah, which may be from Persian (*rāhdān*, "knowing the way," cf. Marquart, *Streifz.*, 350).

(Spaniards) in the East, and Orientals in the West. In any case, the writer of the Letter repeatedly indicates that he knows something of Khazaria. His sources of information are not only books, but also traditions, apparently current in Spain.[70] If in one place he speaks of "the astonishment which filled me at the report of your kingdom, which had not reached us" the words should not be pressed too far. It would be hazardous to base a formal argument against the authenticity of the Letter on the alleged ignorance of its author in regard to the Khazars.

There is a very important passage in the Reply of Joseph which raises several questions and may be conveniently discussed here, in connection with the views of Poliak and Marquart just referred to. In the Short Version this reads: "What you have related of your country [i.e., Spain] and the genealogy of your king has already reached us. Already there have passed between our fathers letters of reciprocal civilities. This circumstance is preserved in our books [and] known to all the elders of our country, in all the East, as you have mentioned. We shall renew the old friendship between our fathers and make it an inheritance for our children." The words "in all the East, as you have mentioned" yield no plain meaning. We certainly find no reference to letters passing between Spain and Khazaria at an earlier date in our text of the Letter of Ḥasday.

It is clear that the Letter as we have it is not only corrupt in places but also incomplete. Landau has pointed out that in the Reply reference is made to an enquiry on the part of Ḥasday as to the possibility of a Khazar envoy coming to Cordova.[71] There is no trace of such an enquiry in our present text of the Letter. Did the Letter then contain originally some indication of previous contact between Spain and Khazaria? The answer seems to be that it did not. The same passage in the Long Version reads differently: "Already there have passed between our fathers letters and reciprocal civilities. This circumstance is preserved in our books [and] known to all the elders of our country. At all times we hear about your country and

[70] See below.

[71] "Present Position," §2.

the greatness of its king—may his Creator preserve him and God restore him to the kingdom of his fathers in the East, as you have mentioned. We shall renew the old friendship between our fathers and make it an inheritance for our children." This refers to the following passage in the Letter: "I shall tell my lord the king the name of the king who rules over us. His name is 'Abd-al-Raḥmān ibn-Muḥammad [ibn-'Abdullāh ibn-Muḥammad][72] ibn 'Abd-al-Raḥmān ibn-Ḥakam ibn-Hishām ibn-'Abd-al-Raḥmān. . . . 'Abd-al-Raḥmān, the 8th in line, was he who came to Spain when the Abbasids, their relations, who rule at present in Iraq, claimed to rule over them. . . . He was the son of Mu'āwiyah ibn-Hishām ibn-'Abd-al-Malik." Here the writer of the Letter has given the genealogy of the Spanish Umayyads and indicates that the Abbasids were usurpers. This is taken up in the Reply of Joseph, which expresses the polite wish that the Umayyads may be restored to the Caliphate in the East.

It is of course unthinkable that the Khazars were not perfectly well informed of the contemporary political scene among their old enemies, the Arabs. The Reply of Joseph, if an authentic document, must certainly have a correct notion of the rulers of the Muslim East. Yet this is far from clear in the passage of the Short Version just considered. The situation is saved, in this respect, by the Long Version, which clearly indicates that the writer of the Reply knew the relation between the Abbasids and the Umayyads.

What are we to say of the statement in the Reply that "already there have passed between our fathers letters and reciprocal civilities"? Would not the historical Ḥasday have known of previous contact between Spain and Khazaria? The answer must be that he almost certainly would. The Letter of Ḥasday indeed refers to one incident which probably comes under the rubric "previous contact with Khazaria," viz. the visit to Spain circa A.D. 880 of the Jewish traveler Eldad ha-Dani. Mention of the Danite comes immediately after a question

[72] The two names must be supplied.

about the Khazar spoken language. The point is evidently to ask the Khazar king if he knows anything about him.[73] Our versions of the Reply, however, afford no light on this.

Was Eldad really a Khazar? It seems at least possible. One fact about him which appears to stand out from a great deal of nonsense in the sources is that he insisted on speaking Hebrew. This may no doubt be explained in other ways, but the simplest reason perhaps is that he knew no Arabic. This is unthinkable if he were a Palestinian or African Jew, as has been suggested, but would be natural in a Khazar. Some of the Hebrew words which he used have been preserved in a letter of enquiry about him, directed by the Jews of Kairouan to Zemah Gaon in Babylonia.[74] Frankl was inclined to think these could be explained from the Greek, and consequently that Eldad was from a Greek-speaking country.[75] Grätz believed that he may have been an emissary of the Karaites,[76] and allows that he had visited Constantinople, where he supposes he heard about the Khazars on the Volga. As is well known, Eldad refers to Khazaria in his narrative, stating that Simeon and the half-tribe Manasseh lived there.[77] The Khazars, he says, were very numerous and took tribute from 28 kingdoms. Some of the Muslims were tributary to them. In view of the fantastic character of much of Eldad's narrative we cannot lay great stress on what is here said about the Khazars, but this certainly stands in some relation to other sources. We have already cited ibn-Faḍlān's remark about the 25 wives, each the daughter of a neighboring king, in the harem of the Khazar Khaqan. Some versions of Eldad give not 28 but 25 kingdoms as dependent on the Khazars. Again, the Reply mentions 9 + 15 + 13 nations as tributary to Joseph. There is some ground for thinking that the 9 nations form the home provinces of the country.[78] The remaining 15 + 13 correspond with Eldad's

[73] So Kokovtsov, *op.cit.*, 70, n. 1.

[74] See A. Neubauer in *J.Q.R.*, I (1889), 105.

[75] Cf. *ibid.*, 109.

[76] *Geschichte*, ed. 3, v, 239.

[77] See below.

[78] Cf. the quotation from Constantine Por., below.

figure. As to the location of Eldad's own tribe of Dan, he places it on the river Sambation. It is idle to pursue the question of whether the mysterious Sambation is to be connected with Sambatas,[79] which, according to Constantine Porphyrogenitus, was another name for Kiev, and so the Dnieper or possibly the Don.[80] In any case, Eldad ha-Dani may well have been a Khazar Jew, like others who came to Spain in the course of the centuries. But there is no hint of a Khazar embassy to Spain in our text of Ḥasday's Letter, nor could there have been originally, consistently with other things which are said.

The solution of the difficulty probably is that the writer of the Reply means to say that the Khazars had been in contact in past times, not with Umayyad Spain, but with the Umayyads in the East. A Khazar ambassador was certainly in the company of al-Faḍl ibn-Sahl, presumably in Baghdad, during the Caliphate of Ma'mūn[81] (A.D. 813-833). In the nature of the case there are likely to have been other earlier visits. Khazar relations with the Muslim East in earlier times are not most accurately to be described in the words of the writer of the Reply as "interchange of letters and civilities," but it would be natural to stress the pleasant side in reply to the Spanish minister. On the basis of this passage, Brutzkus seems to be right in saying that the Khazars had archives from which it was possible for them to draw information about the relation between them and the Umayyads in the 8th century.[82] It would be to the same records that the Reply elsewhere refers in speaking about the great Khazar expansion in the 7th century recorded in the

[79] De Admin. Imp., c.9. Cf. Minorsky, *Ḥudūd*, 431, n. 3, who mentions that a Russion investigator Lashchenko (*Kiev i Sambatas, Dokladi Akad., S.S.S.R.*, 1930) gives 22 different explanations of *Sambatas* (Slavonic, Scandinavian, Hungarian, etc.) and inclines to the Khazar origin of the name, as suggested by Brutzkus. Brutzkus would make Kiev and Sambat both Khazar names (*Enc. Jud.*, art. Chasaren).

[80] Cf. Marquart, *Streifz.*, 198.

[81] Ḥuṣri, *Zahr al-Ādāb*, I, 254.

[82] *Enc. Jud.*, art. Chasaren. Jehudah ha-Levi makes the Khazar king speak as if he were familiar with documents centuries old: "We find learned writings in the MSS. of their authors, [dating] from 500 years [back]"(*Kuzari*, I, 1).

Greek sources: "I have a written record that when my fathers were few, God gave them power, might, and valor, and they made war after war with many nations greater and mightier than they. With God's help they drove them out and inherited their land. Some of them they made tributary to this day. The land which I live in was formerly held by the W-n-nt-r. Our fathers the Khazars came and fought them, etc."[83] It is an interesting question, if the record was contemporary, in what language it was originally drawn up.

We are, however, diverging from our present business, which is to estimate the value of the Letter of Ḥasday as a historical source. After what has been said, that it was actually sent by the Spanish minister to Khazaria seems the safest conclusion. The date would be before A.D. 961, when 'Abd-al-Raḥmān ceased to reign, and perhaps after 954, taken as the year of the embassy recorded by Maqqari. Those who see in the Letter a reflection of the Messianic hopes of the Jews are perhaps right.[84] But Ḥasday evidently wanted a great deal more information besides the possible date of the end of the age, not all of which apparently he got. The Letter asks to what tribe Joseph belongs. There is no answer in the Reply, perhaps because he was not a Jew by descent and had no tribe. We have seen reason for the view that Khazar Judaism even in the 10th century was very imperfect. Hence perhaps there is no answer forthcoming on the part of Joseph to enquiries as to his method of procession to his place of worship, and as to whether war abrogates the Sabbath. It is plain that a Khazar king would not wish to give the number of his armed forces, though he was apparently requested by Ḥasday to do so. Unless there are important omissions in both versions of the Reply—which certainly cannot at present be proved—there is a marked absence of correspondence between questions of the Letter and answers given in the Reply. This should probably be regarded as an indication that the documents are what they purport to be and not a literary invention. Against the authenticity of the Letter

[83] Cf. Chapter III.

[84] Cf. Landau, *Beiträge, passim.*

of Ḥasday criticism has been unable to produce convincing proofs, so that provisionally it is to be accepted. As we see from the Latin *Life* (most conveniently in Migne's Patrologia, ser. 2, Vol. 137) c. 121, John of Gorz found Ḥasday (Hasdeu) occupying a trusted position at the court of ʿAbd-al-Raḥmān III, and actually fulfilling the kind of function which he claims for himself in the Letter. These facts strongly reinforce the conclusion already reached.

What of the Reply of Joseph? The Reply begins by referring to the principal contents of Ḥasday's Letter and recapitulating a number of his questions, which Joseph expresses himself as willing to answer in detail. After a short account of the early history of the Khazars in which the W-n-nt-r episode already cited takes a special place, Joseph proceeds to deal at considerable length with the Khazar conversion to Judaism under king Bulan. This in fact forms the main part of the Reply. Later, we are told, under Bulan's descendant (grandson?) Obadiah there was a reformation and (Rabbinic?) Judaism was introduced. Joseph then traces his own descent from Obadiah and gives a description of his country and capital. He refers to Ḥasday's question about the end of the age, which is answered in a somewhat noncommittal fashion, and finally expresses the hope that Ḥasday may come to Khazaria.

It is obvious that the genuineness of Ḥasday's Letter does not carry with it that of the Reply. Jost, a long time ago, accepting the Letter, found that the Reply contained Arabisms, and concluded that it must have been composed by an Arabic-speaking Jew in Spain.[85] More recently Steinschneider, while allowing the genuineness of the Letter of Ḥasday, characterized the Reply as a later fabrication.[86] What the grounds of this dictum may be he does not say. The position of Landau is that Ḥasday's Letter must be genuine because of the close similarity of its style to that of extant works of Menahem ben-Saruq, who

[85] *Geschichte*, Berlin 1826, VI, 365-366. Harkavy, who lists other Arabisms in the L.V. of the Reply (*Measeph Niddahim*, I, no. 10), rightly does not draw the conclusion that it must have been composed in Spain.

[86] *Geschichtsliteratur der Juden* (1905), 19.

evidently composed it for the minister. The Reply on the other hand may, he thinks, be genuine, but this is not demonstrable.[87]

One general consideration is that we have no independent testimony (apart from the Cambridge Document) that King Joseph was a historical person. This undoubtedly determines us to approach the Reply with somewhat greater hesitation than the Letter. Such evidence as the Muslim sources offer on the names of Khazar chiefs affords no support for the existence of a king in Khazaria with a Hebrew name. Further, it is not entirely clear whether Joseph is Khaqan or Beg. Not only does Ḥasday, in the *piut* already discussed, address him as a commander in war, but Joseph apparently refers to himself as "the mighty king, who has not been put to flight by armies, etc." and again says: "I live at the mouth of the river [i.e., Atil, Volga]. By the help of the Almighty, I guard the mouth of the river and do not suffer the Russians who come in their ships[88] to proceed by sea against the Arabs. . . . I fight with them, etc." This appears to be language more appropriate to the Beg than the Khaqan. Yet he is, as he tells us, descended from a long line of rulers, whereas the Beg's office was probably not hereditary. In one form of the text, that in the *Sēpher ha-'Ittim* of R. Jehudah of Barcelona, the title Kagan, Khaqan seems even to have been mentioned explicitly.

On the whole, it must be allowed that Joseph is the Khaqan. We have to suppose that the Khaqans of Khazaria had Hebrew "throne-names" in addition to their Turkish names. Possibly the Khaqan was at all times the titular commander of the armies (cf. the passage of ibn-Faḍlān, which gives us the information that he had power to replace unsuccessful commanders and even the Beg himself), though no doubt the conduct of operations was in the hands of the Beg, as the Muslim

[87] "Present Position," §3. Landau explicitly contradicts Poliak's statement ("Conversion," §3) that he (Landau) accepted as genuine both Letter and Reply. The view that Landau sponsored the authenticity of the Reply as well as the Letter has gained considerable currency and appears not only in Vernadsky's *Ancient Russia* (212), but also in Mrs. Chadwick's *Beginnings of Russian History* (41, citing Vernadsky).

[88] Cf. Chapters VII, IX.

sources tell us with practical unanimity. We know from them that the Khaqan occasionally rode out with the Khazar forces, even in time of war, so that when Joseph speaks of living with his captains and making excursions through the Khazar territory, he may envisage more than ceremonial occasions. That the Khaqan was prominent when winter-quarters were exchanged for the encampments of spring and summer seems very likely, and perhaps these important movements were brought into connection with the great Jewish festivals.[89]

The positive reasons against the authenticity of the Reply (in addition to the presence of Arabisms) have been listed by Landau as *1*, the sharp attacks on Islam contained in the Reply, unaccountable in a letter to a high official of a Muslim sovereign; *2*, the lack of Jewish and local color in the description of the Khazar state; *3*, omissions in the geographical description of Khazaria; and *4*, the improbable arguments used by the interlocutors in the religious debate, as recorded in the Reply.[90] Before examining these, it should be said that the two versions of the Reply stand or fall together. Though it is possible that the Long Version contains later additions—Kokovtsov has argued strongly that the eulogies, of which it has a number, may be such[91]—it is certain that, on the whole, it is nearer the original than the Short Version. A proof of this are the passages where the Short Version does no more than abridge the Long. Where, e.g., the Short Version simply refers to nine tributary nations on the Volga, fifteen towards the south and thirteen to the west, the Long Version gives their names in every case. We have already noticed a passage, incomprehensible in the Short Version, which becomes clear by the addition of some words in the other. Similar is the following in the Short Version: "From that day when our fathers were gathered under the wings of the Presence, He subdued before us all our enemies and humbled all the nations and tongues round about us. None

89 Reply (L.V.): "From the month of Nisan we go out. . . . I and my captains and servants set out. . . . At the end of the month Kisliw, in the days of the feast of Dedication, we return to the city."

90 "Present Position," §3.

91 *Op.cit.*, Introd.

has withstood us to this day. All of them pay me tribute *by the hands of* the kings of Edom and Ishmael [i.e., the Byzantine Emperors and the Caliphs]." It is nowhere else suggested and the fact is incredible that the Greek Emperor and the Caliph paid tribute to the Khazars as representatives of other nations—the plain meaning of the text. On the other hand, the Long Version has: "From the day that my fathers were gathered to this religion, the God of Israel subdued all their enemies and humbled every nation and tongue round about them, the kings of Edom, the kings of Ishmael and all the kings of the Gentiles. No man withstood them, and they were all tributary." This is less garbled than the Short Version and less objectionable. The suggestion that the Emperor and the Caliph paid tribute to the Khazars at all is somewhat disconcerting. But it appears as a mere rhetorical flourish in the Long Version. We know that a sum was promised and probably paid in ibn-Faḍlān's time by the Caliph Muqtadir to the Bulgars.[92] This money presumably passed across the Khaqan's frontiers without his knowledge, against his will. The purpose—to build a fortress for the Bulgar king—was certainly contrary to his interest. Other sums may have come from Baghdad, and from Byzantium at the time of the important Christian mission to Khazaria circa 860,[93] or after the military successes of the Khazars referred to in the Cambridge Document. Joseph uses a grandiloquent style about himself and his position elsewhere, as we have seen, and, recalling occasions when his powerful neighbors had found it expedient to send money into Khazaria, may have been ready to describe it as tribute. Or he may refer to the valuable presents such as were periodically sent to the northern nations from Byzantium, as tribute from the Emperor. Otherwise there is still the possibility of some remaining dislocation of the text in the Long Version which we are not in a position to set right.

Landau's first count has in view the hostile and inaccurate characterization of Islam put in the mouth of the Christian

[92] Ibn-Faḍlān, §§ 1, 48.

[93] See Chapter VII.

interlocutor in the course of the religious debate: "What is the religion of Ishmael, compared with that of Israel? They have no sabbaths and no sacred seasons, no commandments and no statutes. They eat every unclean thing, etc." It is difficult to see why these words can have no place in a genuine letter to Ḥasday. Written in Hebrew, the Reply was hardly likely to become common property in Spain and cause embarrassment to the recipient. Ḥasday himself was no Muslim and doubtless had no special tenderness for the religion of his master. The injurious statements are in any case represented as spoken not by Joseph, but long ago in the debate which preceded his ancestor's conversion.

As to Landau's second count, there is a good deal of Jewish color, if by that is meant reference to characteristic institutions of the Israelites. The Reply is written in Hebrew and in a Hebrew distinct from that of the Letter—a most important point, to which we shall return. After an attack on Ardabīl (for which we have the synchronism 112/730 in the Arabic sources)[94] the Reply tells that there was set up a tabernacle on the Biblical model (with ark, candlestick, etc.). We surely have the strongest Jewish color when the writer states that a generation or two after the conversion there was a reformation of religion under Obadiah, when synagogues and schools were built and the Khazars became familiar with Torah, Mishnah and Talmud and with the liturgy.[95] Joseph can produce a list of ancestors, all (except Bulan) with Hebrew names. He has been in touch with the Jew, ben-Eliezer. If on the other hand traits appear which are non-Jewish, notably the semi-nomadic life of the Khazar population, this is in accordance with what

[94] Cf. Chapter IV.

[95] For the period between Bulan and Obadiah it might be supposed that Karaism prevailed in Khazaria (circa 740-800), but this is probably too early ('Anan ben-David, usually spoken of as the founder of the Karaite movement, flourished circa 760). For the same period Poliak assumed a "religion of Abraham," distinct from Judaism ("Conversion," §§ 3-4, *Khazaria*, 141-143). This expression comes in the Reply without any unusual significance, as synonym for "religion of Israel."

we read elsewhere and is to be explained by the Turkish origin of the nation.

As to local color in the Reply, it is at least as evident as in the Letter of Ḥasday for Spain. One trait, the semi-nomadism of the Khazars, has just been noticed. What Joseph says about tribute-paying nations is well illustrated by the Russian Chronicle[96] and confirmed by Iṣṭakhri, whose statement about "regular payments assessed on the people of the different places" has already been quoted. Iṣṭakhri also confirms in a striking manner what Joseph relates of the exodus from the Khazar capital which took place in spring: "From the month Nisan we go out from the city, each man to his vineyard and to his field and to his tillage." There is one point in the Reply, which, according to Cassel,[97] is sufficient by itself to establish the truth of the whole document. This is the mention of "a certain one, their great general" (S.V.), or "a certain general among them" (L.V.) in the main part of the Reply (the conversion story) alongside the Khazar king. It certainly seems to be a reference to the Beg of Khazaria. Other points which may be noted are the statement that Joseph guards the Volga mouth and prevents the Russians coming downstream to the Caspian, and the threefold division of the Khazar capital (the measurements being raised to astronomical dimensions by the transmission).[98]

Thirdly, Landau refers to omissions in the geographical description of Khazaria. This point was stressed by Poliak, who argued that the geographical information in the Reply is what might be obtained by a traveler to the Khazar capital from Constantinople via the Crimea and overland from Tamatarkha (Taman), and suggested that the account of some such traveler was in fact made use of by whoever composed the Reply.[99] The absence of any definition of the Khazar frontier to the east appeared particularly significant to Poliak, since one of the requests in Ḥasday's Letter is for information about the cities "near to [Khazaria] in the direction of Khurāsān, Bardh-

[96] See Chapter VII.

[97] Quoted Kokovtsov, *op.cit.*, 76, n. 2.

[98] Cf. *ibid.*, 110, n. 38.

[99] "Conversion," §3; *Khazaria*, 21.

a'ah and Bāb al-Abwāb."[100] The apparent omission in the Reply may be accounted for by other reasons. In the direction of Khurāsān there were no important cities. What interest for a correspondent in Spain had the settlements of Ābaskūn[101] and Manqishlagh[102] on the east shore of the Caspian, with the exception of a fishing station, Dihistānān Sir,[103] north of Ābaskūn, perhaps the only places east of the Volga where there was a permanent population? The eastern marches of Khazaria were desert or at best poor grazing land, infested by semi-hostile tribesmen, still more barbarous than the Khazars themselves. More important than to list such names was to make clear that the Khazar frontier extended "towards Khwārizm as far as Jurjān [for Gurgānj?]," as the Reply (L.V.) does, in this agreeing with the Arab geographer Qudāmah.[104] Corroboration is forthcoming also in the narrative of ibn-Faḍlān, from which we see that the effective boundary between the Ghuzz nomads, who may have acknowledged Khazar supremacy, and the lands of Islam was the Oxus.

But why no information about Khwārizm, pursues Poliak, in view of the trade relations which existed between it and Khazaria? We simply do not know.[105]

The last of Landau's list of objections to the Reply has ref-

[100] Poliak here apparently assumes that Ḥasday's Letter is genuine.

[101] From Ābaskūn ships sailed across to Bāb al-Abwāb and northwest to the Volga mouth (Iṣṭakhri, 227, cf. 213). Mas'ūdi says that he himself sailed from Ābaskūn to Ṭabaristān (*Murūj*, I, 274).

[102] Manqishlagh lay on the Khazar frontier in the direction of Jurjān, according to Muqaddasi, 355 (Binqishlah there). It is identified by Barthold (*E.I.*, art. Mangishlak) with Siyāh Kūh, north of Abaskūn (Iṣṭakhri, 190, 219).

[103] Iṣṭakhri, 219. Minorsky (*Ḥudūd*, 193) would read Dihistānān-sar.

[104] *B.G.A.*, VI, 259.

[105] V. Altman ("Ancient Khorezmian Civilisation in the Light of the Latest Archaeological Discoveries [1937-1945]," *J.A.O.S.*, 67, 2, 1947) says that there are reasons to believe that Judaism "was brought to Khazaria in the 8th century through Khorezm," and that 8th century coins discovered by Sergei Tolstov's expedition "testify to the political unity of Khazaria and Khorezm in the middle of the 8th century." I do not know the grounds for these statements. Tolstov's article "In the Deserts of Khwarizm" (*Asiatic Review*, 40, 1944, 408-414) throws no light on the points mentioned by Altman.

erence to improbable arguments used by the interlocutors in the religious debate, as recorded therein. There is no a priori reason why the king must have given an accurate account of opinions which he did not share, in describing a theological debate held long before his time. It is obvious that the author of a fabricated "Reply of Joseph" might well have put appropriate observations in the mouth of his disputants. The words of the *qāḍi* who says of the Christians that they "bow down to the work of their own hands" seem to have clear reference to image worship. The trait seems authentic: image worship was already practiced in the 7th century and the beginning of the 8th.

As to the date of the conversion given in the Long Version of the Reply, it is there stated roundly that the event took place "340 years ago." The Reply, if genuine, must have followed Ḥasday's Letter, in which ʿAbd-al-Raḥmān al-Nāṣir of Spain is mentioned as still alive, at a comparatively short interval. At latest it must have been written in 961 or 962. On the reckoning of the Reply, the latest date for the conversion would accordingly be A.D. 621 or 622.[106] But obviously ten years before the Hegirah there could be no Muslim *qāḍi* in Khazaria or anywhere else, and the story of the debate as it stands in the Reply involves the Muslim *qāḍi* not incidentally but integrally. We must probably agree with Landau that the figure is a late addition of some copyist.[107]

It remains to adduce some new positive evidence in the matter. The following very simple test has not, I believe, hitherto

[106] Isidore of Seville (*Contra Iudaeos*, I, 8, quoted Grätz, V, 63, n. 3) writes: "Iudaei mentientes nescio quem regem ex genere Iudaeorum in extremis Orientis partibus regnum tenere." Cf. Harkavy, *R.E.J.*, V, 203. This was used by Harkavy in support of the date circa 620 for the Khazar conversion, Isidore's dates being 570-636. But all the other evidence is in favor of a later date. At the end of the 7th century the Khazars were still pagan; cf. Chapter IV (Alp Ilutver) and Chapter VII (the *tudun* of Cherson).

[107] Perhaps through an error the figure 340 has come down instead of 240. So Westberg, "K analizy vostochnikh istochnikov," *Z.M.N.P.*, 1908, 34 (cited Bury, *E.R.E.*, 408, n. 1).

been applied to the Khazar Correspondence.[108] In the Long Version of the Reply the classical Hebrew construction of *Waw* conversive with the Imperfect to express the past tense occurs not more than once or twice, as against nearly 100 instances where the past is expressed by the Perfect and simple *Waw*. On the other hand, in the Letter of Ḥasday the past tense is rendered nearly 50 times by *Waw* conversive and the Imperfect, and only 14 times by simple *Waw* and the Perfect. This is a radical difference of style, and on the face of it the Letter was written by a different hand. We may further adduce for comparison the Short Version of the Reply, which bears unmistakable traces of having been worked over and altered from the Long Version. In the Short Version the construction with *Waw* conversive is introduced whenever the redactor paraphrases the words of the Long Version, which he does frequently, and occasionally in other places. The process of substitution of the Imperfect with *Waw* conversive for simple *Waw* and the Perfect is quite plain and allows us to affirm with greater positiveness than Kokovtsov permitted himself that the Long Version is more original.[109] But the proportion of the two constructions in the Short Version and in the Letter is quite different, for in the Short Version, while *Waw* conversive with the Imperfect occurs 37 times, simple *Waw* with the Perfect registers itself no fewer than 50 times. These results may be tabulated:

	Waw Conversive with Imperfect	*Simple Waw with Perfect*
LETTER	48	14
REPLY (S.V.)	37	50
REPLY (L.V.)	1	95

Hence we may say positively that the Letter was not redacted by the same hand as the Short Version, as might have been suspected. We should therefore be entitled to compare it di-

[108] It was suggested by conversations with Dr. John Bowman, while we were together in Glasgow.

[109] See above.

rectly with the Long Version and, in view of the striking difference of usage, affirm a separate authorship.

The question of whether further conclusions are to be drawn from this result is to be approached with circumspection. It may be stated in general terms that nothing decisive appears to have been alleged against the factual contents of the Reply of Joseph in its more original form, the Long Version. The stylistic difference supports its authenticity. It is what might be expected in documents emanating from widely separated parts of the Jewish world, where also the level of culture was by no means the same. It is perhaps allowable here to record the impression, for what it is worth, that in general the language of the Reply is less artificial, more naïve,[110] than that of the Letter. There is nothing in the Reply corresponding to the elaborate *piut* with which the Spanish minister, or rather his secretary, begins to address Joseph. We may also draw attention to something more definite than impressions. The forms for the Arabic word *qāḍi* in the Long Version of the Reply are spelled with *Daleth* and have the Hebrew definite article: *qādi, ha-qādi.* In the Short Version, under Arabic influence, we find on the contrary *Tsaddi* with point and the Arabic definite article: *qāḍi, al-qāḍi.* Yet more striking is the fact that for the Khazars in the Letter of Ḥasday we have repeatedly the Arabicised al-Khazar, while in the Reply (L.V. and S.V.) the forms Kazar and Kazariim (without the Arabic article) alone occur. In the Reply the pass of Darial is Dar Ālān (the old Iranian name), while in the Letter of Ḥasday the pass of Darband is the Arabic Bāb al-Abwāb. The latter name also occurs in the Reply, but in the quaint form "Gate of Bāb al-Abwāb,"[111] which is tautological, implying ignorance of the meaning of the Arabic name. These look like real indications that the Reply originally was written in a non-Arabic-speaking environment.

It may at least be allowed that Poliak's theory of the Khazar Correspondence as a popular account of Khazaria, cast in the

[110] Similarly Landau, "Present Position," §3.
[111] Sha'ar Bāb al-Abwāb (L.V.).

conventional form of letters, which we have already suggested did not cover the facts, can now be ruled out, the difference between Letter and Reply going far beyond what might in this case be expected. But if the Letter and Reply are not by different hands, as they appear to be, an attempt had been made to give this impression. We cannot avoid this conclusion by bringing in the possibility of earlier redactions of the documents, for which there is no evidence. But who then can have fabricated them, presumably between the limits 961 and 1105, and for what purpose, are unanswerable questions. It is difficult not to admit that the Reply of Joseph is in the main authentic.

The authenticity of the Khazar Correspondence is also suggested by the mention of Ḥasday ibn-Shaprut in connection with Khazaria in a manuscript of ibn-Ḥawqal as early as A.D. 1086.[112] The passage runs: "Ḥasday ibn-Isḥāq thinks that this great long mountain [Caucasus] is connected with the mountains of Armenia and traverses the country of the Greeks, extending to Khazarān and the mountains of Armenia. He was well informed about these parts because he visited them and met their principal kings and leading men." The source and import of these words are alike obscure. In Ḥasday's Letter he expresses a desire to visit Khazaria, and in the Reply Joseph appears to welcome the idea. In any case, it appears that this is unexceptionable early evidence, independent, so far as can be seen, of the Hebrew tradition, for the interest of the Jewish statesman in Spain in the affairs of Khazaria.

The account of the Khazar conversion in the Reply of Joseph bears a general resemblance to that in the *Cosri* (*Kuzari*) of Jehudah ha-Levi. In both, the king of the Khazars has a dream in which an angel speaks to him. The general (?Beg) figures side by side with the king (Khaqan) in the two stories and in both a "tabernacle" is set up (called by the Reply *ōhel*, by the

[112] The notice appears on a map in MS. Serai 3346 dated 479/1086, used by Kramers as the basis of the 2nd edition of ibn-Ḥawqal, which see (193). Cf. Zeki Validi, "Völkerschaften," 50,n. 1.

Kuzari mishkan). The central episode in both accounts is a religious discussion.[113] There are also divergences. The *Kuzari* leaves the king unnamed. The Reply calls him Bulan. According to the Reply, Bulan, before the dream, has driven out the "sorcerers and idolators" (shamanists) from the land. According to the *Kuzari*, at this time he was very devout in the Khazar religion (shamanism). The course of the religious discussion is different in the two accounts, notably in the omission by the *Kuzari* of a general debate which according to the Reply concluded the proceedings. The *Kuzari* again disagrees with the Reply in making the erection of the "tabernacle" follow the discussion. Further, ha-Levi has nothing (possibly owing to the plan of the *Kuzari*) about the reform of religion which, according to the Reply, took place under a later king Obadiah. In view of the differences we cannot say roundly that Jehudah ha-Levi was acquainted with the Reply, but the probability seems to be that he was, and took such liberties with it as suited him. Certainly both the Reply and the *Kuzari* represent the same general form of the story.

Quite a different account of the conversion of the Khazars is given in the Cambridge Document, so-called from its pres-

[113] In view of the suggested connection between the Khazars and the Uigurs (Chapter II), an account in Juwayni (ed. Mirza Muḥammad, *G.M.S.*, I, 43ff) of the conversion of the Uigurs from shamanism to another religion is interesting. The parallels between this and what we read of the Khazar conversion from shamanism to Judaism are somewhat remarkable. In the Juwayni story the impulse to change is owing to a dream of the ruler Būqu Khān, and this dream appears also to his vizier. There follows a religious debate, at which the native representatives of the old religion and representatives of the new, summoned for the purpose, dispute, and the latter are successful. In Juwayni it seems fairly clear that Buddhism is intended as the new religion of the Uigurs. Marquart has shown (*Sitzungsberichte d. preuss. Akad.*, 1912, 486ff) that the basis of the story is the historical conversion of the Uigurs to Manichaeism under Būqu Khāqān shortly after A.D. 762 (*ibid.*, 487), and that Juwayni presumably got his information from the trilingual inscription of Qara-Balgasun, which reported the conversion (*ibid.*, 496-7). There is thus no possibility, in spite of the similarities, that one account is derived from the other. We must allow that the narratives refer to distinct historical events, and that where they resemble each other, this is due to coincidence, or rather to the presence of the same concepts in the minds of those who related the two occurrences.

ent location,[114] a fragment of rather less than 100 lines of Hebrew, dating perhaps from the 12th century, which belonged to the material from the Cairo Genizah and was first published by Schechter in 1912.[115] The Document is evidently part of a letter from someone unnamed, who speaks of Joseph, king of Khazaria, as a contemporary, to another anonymous person, who, like Joseph, is referred to by the writer as "my lord" and whose messengers have come to Constantinople by sea. It is natural to think of this other person as Ḥasday ibn-Shaprut, while the fact that the writer speaks of Khazaria as "our land," Joseph as "my lord," etc. suggests that he was a Khazar Jew. But what may be the relation of the Document to the Khazar Correspondence is not clear. Kokovtsov regarded the Document as formally an alternative answer to the Letter of Ḥasday, and found the circumstance suspicious.[116] The mutual silence between both parts of the Correspondence and the Cambridge Document is especially noteworthy. The Document appears to know that Ḥasday has already sent envoys to Constantinople, but not of either Letter or Reply. We may suppose therefore that it was written before the Correspondence, and that the envoys are Isaac bar Nathan and his company mentioned in Ḥasday's Letter. But why, then, does Joseph in his Reply not refer to a previous communication to Ḥasday from Khazaria? Similarly, we might expect that Ḥasday would refer to the Document, if he had received it. If the Document is later than the Correspondence, it might be expected to refer to Letter or Reply or both.

These difficulties can be got round by supposing that the Document was sent, not from Khazaria, but Constantinople,[117] perhaps when Isaac bar Nathan, Ḥasday's special envoy, unable to proceed farther, as is explained in the Letter, gave up his intention of traveling to Khazaria and returned to Cordova. This is very plausible, if it can be made out, with Dubnov,[118]

[114] T-S Loan 38 in Cambridge University Library.
[115] *J.Q.R.*, III (1912-1913), 181ff. [116] *Op.cit.*, Introd.
[117] Mann, *Texts and Studies*, I, 8, n. 11.
[118] *Weltgeschichte des jüdischen Volkes*, IV, 481.

that R. Jehudah of Barcelona mentions the Cambridge Document as well as the Khazar Correspondence in the following passage from his Sēpher ha-'Ittim, already referred to, where he says: "We have found a copy of another letter, which a Jew wrote in his own language in Constantinople from the kings [*sic*] of Constantinople and mentioning wars which occurred between the kings of Constantinople and king Aaron, likewise wars between the sons of the Gentile kings and king Joseph, son of king Aaron, and likewise that the Khazars had become proselytes and had kings who were proselytes. We have heard that the account of all this is in the books of the Arabs [and this is written in their books]." It has been argued that the language of a Jew in Constantinople should be Greek rather than Hebrew,[119] and further that, as the Cambridge Document represents the Khazar kings as Jewish from the first, not as becoming Jews, it cannot be the same as that seen by R. Jehudah.[120] But these are minor criticisms, and it may be that Dubnov's identification is right. The Cambridge Document certainly speaks of the Khazar conversion and gives a good deal of information about the wars of the Greeks and others with the Khazars in the time of Joseph and his immediate predecessors. If the document was written in Constantinople, it is readily understandable that neither Ḥasday nor Joseph should mention it. (Ḥasday may be presumed to have received it, when he wrote his Letter.)

But this does not solve other difficulties which the Cambridge Document presents. If the account of the conversion in the Reply is reliable, as it should be, what are we to say of the alternative version of that event in the Document? Here we are told that at an early date Jews arrived in Khazaria, apparently from Armenia, and merged with the native population. The Khazars at this time had no kings, but in time of war were commanded by elected generals. It happened that on one occasion a Jew (unnamed) became general. Later he came more directly under the influence of the Jewish religion. News of this reached

[119] Mann, *loc.cit.*

[120] Poliak, "Conversion," §3.

the kings of "Macedon" (the Greeks) and the Arabs, and envoys were sent to expostulate with him (?). Their representations apparently made an impression on other chiefs who remained unconverted, and it was resolved to hold a religious debate. When learned men of the three religions had met and debated without any satisfactory result being reached, the Khazar chiefs recommended that certain "books of the Law of Moses" should be brought out from a "cave in the valley of Tizul" and explained by the Jews. This was duly done, and in the sequel the Jews of Khazaria en masse repented of their previous indifference and carried the rest of the population with them to Judaism. Jews from "Baghdad, Khurāsān and the land of the Greeks" began to come to Khazaria. The Khaqanate was established. The name of the Jewish leader (so far anonymous) was changed to Sabriel, and he became the first king of the Khazars.

In this account the religious change under "Sabriel" is represented as a reformation carried through by certain Jews who have long been resident in Khazaria, as well as "Sabriel," his father-in-law, unnamed, and wife Seraḥ. There is a prima facie case for Schechter's suggestion that the conversion story in the Cambridge Document is an expansion of what we read in the Reply about religious activity under Obadiah, a descendant of Bulan. Schechter conjectured that the name Sabriel, seemingly unknown elsewhere, might be a corruption of Abdiel, Abdeel, itself an alternative form of Obadiah with similar meaning ("servant of El," for "servant of Jah"). But the ingenious suggestion has to be disallowed. We cannot assume that in the first part of the Document, now lost, there was an account of an earlier conversion. To assume with Schechter that Sabriel is Obadiah involves either that the debate under Bulan, which for some reason the Document says nothing about, was repeated later under Obadiah, or that the account of Bulan's activity and his successors to Obadiah in the Reply is a fiction. Both alternatives are cumbrous and improbable. We must therefore allow that Sabriel is Bulan under a Hebrew name.

Perhaps the most striking point in the account of the conversion in the Cambridge Document is what it says about an accompanying constitutional change. This is neither more nor less than the creation of the double kingship. It is explicitly stated that the Khaqanate now appeared. After the conversion "the men of the land appointed over them one of the wise men as judge. They call his name, in the tongue of Qazaria [Khazaria], Kagan [Khaqan]. Therefore the judges who arose after him are called by the name of Kagan to this day." The Document proceeds: "As to the great general of Qazaria, they turned his name into Sabriel and made him king over them." As Schechter said, this appears to refer to the office of Beg.[121]

The existence of a shadow king, as the Khaqan to a considerable extent appears to have been in the later period, at all events, might suggest the supersession of one dynasty by another, and Mas'ūdi evidently thought so.[122] It seems, however, among the Khazars to have been a feature connected with their nomadic past rather than an innovation.[123] In view of the later situation, it is conceivable that the Khaqan represented kings thrust aside by the Judaisers, whose leader established himself as a kind of "mayor of the palace" to the old dynasty. But this is not what the Document says. The Jewish general did not set aside the Khaqan in order to hold power as the first Beg of Khazaria, for there were no Khaqans till afterwards, according to this account. It is demonstrably wrong. There is no doubt of the existence of Khazar Khaqans in the first half of the 8th century, and Justinian II, for example, met one of them.[124] The only possible doubt is as to the existence at this time of the Beg, though he too is nearly certainly attested. The Cambridge Document, however, says that after the conversion the Khazars appointed a Khaqan as judge, subordinate, apparently, to Sabriel, who became king. This reverses the historical relationship, and as it stands is quite in-

[121] *Op.cit.*, 189.

[122] Cf. his remark quoted below, Chapter VII.

[123] Alföldi's view of the double kingship as derived originally from the system of independent command in the right and left wings of the horde is perhaps right, in his paper "La royauté double des Turcs" (*2me Congrès Turc d'Histoire*, Istanbul, 1937).

[124] See Chapter VII.

credible.[125] But there is yet more. According to the Document, the first Khaqan was one of the wise men, these presumably being the "wise men of Israel" mentioned just before. But that a Jewish rabbi was ever Khaqan of Khazaria, as seems to be said, is beyond the bounds of possibility. It is quite possible that Jewish judges were appointed after the conversion,[126] but of

[125] According to the Reply of Joseph the Khaqanate went back to the origins of the nation: "The son sits on the throne of his father. This is our custom and the custom of our fathers from the time that they were on the earth." We may here consider Zeki Validi's view (*Ibn-Faḍlān*, 270, 274) that the Khazar Khaqans belonged to a very ancient ruling family among the Turks called in the Chinese sources Asena (Achena, Ashihna, Assena) after an eponymous ancestor of that name (cf. St. Julien *J.A.*, VI, iii, 1864; Chavannes, *Documents*, *passim*). This family originally belonged to the Hiung-nu (Parker, *Thousand Years*, 129) and became the ruling group of the first Turkish empire (T'u-küeh, Kök Turks), providing Khaqans for both East and West Turks (Parker, *ibid*.; Marquart, *Streifz*., 46). Zeki Validi finds that the Qara-khānids (Īlek Khāns) and the family of Börchigin Qayat, to which the Mongol conqueror Chingiz Khān belonged, were branches of the Asena dynasty in later times. The principal basis for the view that the Khazar Khaqans were a branch of the same dynasty is a passage in *Ḥudūd al-'Ālam*, §50, according to which the king (Khaqan) of the Khazars is "one of the descendants of Ansa." This name, queried by Minorsky, is read Asna= Asena by Zeki Validi. The suggested new reading is very attractive. It is no objection that similar forms (Īsha, Abshād) are found in ibn-Rustah and Gardīzi for the second Khazar king (Beg). These forms have already found an explanation (Chapter V). Zeki Validi regards it as now certain that the ruling house among the Khazars was a branch of the Kök Turks, or rather that it and the ruling house among the Turks were independent branches of the same Asena family, on the ground that the Khazars had no close connection with the Kök Turks. Together with the Asena family there existed in Khazaria other racial groups who in central Asia were always closely connected with them, including doubtfully the Uigurs (*ibid*., 270-271).

This is of course the same line of thought as has been followed in Chapter II. It is somewhat remarkable that according to Bar Hebraeus (*Syriac Chronicle*, ed. Budge, 81v, col. 1=transl. 232) the wife of the Seljuk Malik Shāh was the daughter of "Ṭafrāgh, king of the Khazars." "Ṭafrāgh" is evidently Ṭamghāj ibn-Bughra, the Īlek Khan (*Ta'rīkh-i Guzīdah*, 444). Though not impossibly the Īlek Khans were of Uigur origin (cf. Barthold, *Zur Geschichte des Christentums in Mittel-Asien*, 1901, 47ff), this is by no means to say that they were Khazars. It is a question if Bar Hebraeus knew of a connection through the Asena with Khazaria. Marquart had already conjectured that the Asena provided the Khaqans of the Khazars (*Streifz*., 47).

[126] Jewish judges in Khazaria are mentioned by Iṣṭakhri and Mas'ūdi.

a constitutional change on the scale indicated at this time there can be no question. The Document gives the story of Bulan, from a different angle and under a Hebrew name. To say that he was of Jewish origin may be right, but it is more likely that he belonged to the Turkish house from which earlier Khaqans of Khazaria had sprung.[127] Whatever Bulan may mean,[128] the name is evidently Turkish. The misinformation about the Khaqanate could be explained by the impression which the writer of the Document had gathered of the later situation of the Khazar Khaqans and possible confusion of the title with the Hebrew word for "wise," *ḥākhām*. While the Cambridge Document is not to be impugned as unauthentic on the score of this garbled account of the conversion, one feels bound to regard its other data, e.g., the wars of the Khazars in the 9th and 10th centuries, of which it is almost the only testimony, with increased caution.

Poliak has attempted to defend from the Arabic sources what the Cambridge Document says about a political change accompanying the conversion. This must be judged a complete failure. His construction neither clears up the historical situation[129] nor offers the slightest ground for thinking that the Cambridge Document is here reliable.

[127] The Georgian Chronicle is said to give Bulkhan as the name of the Khazar commander in the raid of 112/730 (cf. Poliak, *Khazaria*, 141; Bury, *E.R.E.*, 406, n. 1, citing Westberg in *Z.M.N.P.*, 1908). Bulkhan is not reducible to any of the forms of the name Bārjīk, otherwise attested as the Khazar commander on this occasion (cf. Chapter IV, esp. n. 29). If Bulkhan is right and=Bulan, it seems preferable to admit that the Khaqan accompanied the expedition rather than that Bulan was simply the Beg.

[128] According to Brutzkus (*Enc. Jud.*, art. Chasaren) Bulan means "wise," but this is denied by Zajączkowski (*Culture*, §3). Poliak's remarks are not very helpful ("Conversion," §4; *Khazaria*, 141): Bulan is an Arabicized (*sic*) form of some such Turkish name as *balaban* "hawk"—otherwise it is "bear"—or *qaplan* "panther." Cf. the Khazar name rendered Bulkhan, Buljan, Bluch'an (previous note and Chapter VII). Also perhaps *ton Bōkhanon*, the name of the West Turkish commandant at Bosporus in 576 (Menander, 404).

[129] E.g., he treats the second part of Yāqūt's composite account of the Khazars (see previous Chapter) as a "pre-conversion source." It is in fact ibn-Faḍlān, as already given, written about 922.

If, then, the Cambridge Document has information which either cannot be checked by any sources or positively contradicts what we read elsewhere, can it be relied on in such cases? Dubnov[130] and also Landau[131] are evidently impressed by the historical facts which the Document appears to give on the relations of the Khazars with other peoples shortly before the correspondence. But how far can what it says be accepted? A good deal of the data cannot be checked in any way. For example, it speaks of a war with the Greeks under Benjamin, the grandfather of Joseph. Again, under Aaron, the father of Joseph, the Greek Emperor is said to have incited the Alans against the Khazars. Under Joseph himself the Russians are represented as attacking Tamatarkha,[132] at the instigation of the Emperor Romanus, and by way of reprisal the Khazars attack Greek territory, taking several towns and apparently assaulting the important center, Cherson.[133] All this seems to be in some disagreement with the account of Khazaria according to the Greek envoys in Ḥasday's Letter. Dubnov praises the objectivity of the Document, which, he says, does not introduce the supernatural element in speaking of the conversion. But it would be very desirable to test the objectivity with other information. It is true that Constantine Porphyrogenitus, writing in A.D. 947-950 visualizes conditions in which the Alans may be used against the Khazars.[134] But we should like to know that on a particular occasion about this time they were so used. In general, we scarcely read of war between the Khazars and Byzantines except in the Cambridge Document.

Various objections against the Document are raised by Kokovtsov. His main count is that it is dependent in style and content on Sēpher Josippon. This being so, he argues, the Cambridge Document must be a compilation, not an authentic letter.[135] The stylistic dependence alleged by Kokovtsov can hardly be said to be established.[136] As to the factual content, which Kokovtsov thinks has also been influenced by Josippon,

130 *Op.cit.*, IV, 480-481.
131 "Present Position," §4.
132 Kokovtsov, *op.cit.*, 118, n. 4.
133 See below.
134 Cf. the passage cited below.
135 *Op.cit.*, Introd.
136 Cf. Landau, "Present Position," §4.

the two instances he alleges scarcely prove the point. *1,* The writer of the Cambridge Document of course knows the later name Khazaria (he writes regularly Qazaria), but is concerned to tell his correspondent that the old name was Arqanus. This presumably goes back to Greek *'Urkanous.* Where the writer of the Document may have got it is a question. But it is not obvious that Josippon is the source. Bar Hebraeus in a notice of A.D. 1036 identifies Hyrcania with "the land of the Khazars,"[137] and if this is not proof of the validity of the statement in the Document, it at least opens possibilities other than that the writer of the Document simply borrowed his remark from Josippon.

2, Kokovtsov's other instance of presumed factual dependence on Josippon is the statement in the Document that "the name of the royal city is Qazar [Khazar]," which, thinks Kokovtsov, was borrowed from some lost version of the work. Undoubtedly the reference is to Khazarān, which as we have seen was the western half of the Khazar capital, where the king lived.[138] The Cambridge Document here gives authentic information.

Kokovtsov considers the identification of the Cambridge Document with the second letter seen by R. Jehudah of Barcelona, as already referred to, and finds it unproven. Some of the points he makes are not indisputable. He naturally also refers to what is said about the Khaqanate in the Document and characterizes it as fantastic.[139]

It may be observed that the use of *Waw* conversive with the Imperfect for the past tense is found in the Cambridge Document even more frequently than in the Letter of Ḥasday, and in this respect it is at the opposite pole from the Long Version of the Reply, thus:

	Waw Conversive with Imperfect	*Simple Waw with Perfect*
ḤASDAY'S LETTER	48	14
REPLY (L.V.)	1	95
CAMBRIDGE DOC.	57	8

[137] *Syriac Chronicle,* ed. Budge, fol. 69, col. 1=transl. 195.
[138] Cf. Chapter V, n. 10. [139] See above.

This result evidently confirms that the Cambridge Document and the Reply of Joseph are from a different source.

Let us see whether the Document contains verifiable historical material. It refers several times to the Alans. The famous pass and fortification of Dar-i Ālān (Darial) in the Caucasus figure constantly in the wars of the Khazars and the Arabs earlier, and though we do not gather from the Arabic sources that the Alans were at this period independent and ruled by their own king,[140] or that some of them were Jews, both these indications of the Document are in themselves quite credible. If we are to judge by what is said here in the Document and in Joseph's Reply, their independence was qualified and perhaps a matter of dispute.[141] On the situation in the 10th century we have the following passage, already referred to, from the *De Administrando Imperio* of Constantine Porphyrogenitus:[142]

"10. Concerning Khazaria, how war is to be made upon them and by whom. As the Ghuzz are able to make war on the Khazars, being near them, so likewise the ruler of Alania, because the Nine Climates of Khazaria are close to Alania, and the Alan can, if he wishes, raid them and cause great damage and distress to the Khazars from that quarter. For the whole livelihood and wealth of Khazaria consists of these Nine Climates.

"11. Concerning Fort Cherson and Fort Bosporus. As the ruler of Alania is not at peace with the Khazars,[143] but rather holds preferable the friendship of the Greek emperor, if the Khazars will not maintain friendship and peace, he can injure them greatly by blockading the roads and attacking them unexpectedly when they pass through to Sarkil, the Climates and Cherson. If the aforementioned ruler will take trouble to hinder them, Cherson and the Climates will enjoy profound

[140] This is implied perhaps in the accounts of Marwān's expedition in 119/737. The Alan capital Magas (distinct from the fortress in the Pass of Darial mentioned in Chapter IV) was destroyed in 1239 by the Mongols (cf. V. Minorsky, "Caucasica III," *B.S.O.A.S.*, 1952, xiv/2).

[141] The Reply (L.V.) indeed claims that "all the Alans" were tributary.

[142] Ed. Bonn, III, 80.

[143] Cf. n. 141.

peace. For if the Khazars fear an attack of the Alans and have no freedom of attacking Cherson and the Climates with an army, being unable to go to war with both at the same time, they will be compelled to keep peace."

In view of this passage it is perfectly credible when the Cambridge Document states that on one occasion in a previous reign the Emperor stirred up the Alans against the Khazars. But we do not read anywhere else that he actually did so.

So far as I know, the valley or plain of Tizul, where according to the Document there was a cave with books of the Jewish Law, has not yet been identified. It may be suggested that this name is the Greek *Tzour*, Arabic *Ṣūl*, for the Pass of Darband. Confirmation seems to be available in the other form of the conversion story, for according to the *Kuzari* the scene of the conversion was partly in a cave where certain Jews kept the Sabbath in the mountains of Warṣān. This should be the same locality, at the east end of the Caucasus.

As already said, we get no direct information elsewhere about the wars of the Khazars with the Greeks in the 10th century. The so-called Fragments of the Gothic Toparch,[144] a document written in Greek, apparently in the 10th century, seem to refer to the Khazars, without naming them, as the enemy to the north of the Crimea with whom the Gothic toparch is fighting. Brutzkus has suggested that there is an intimate connection between these Fragments, the Cambridge Document and the *piut* at the beginning of the Letter of Ḥasday.[145] This may well be. As already remarked, it is reasonable to suppose that the poem of Menahem ben-Saruq celebrated a definite victory of the Khazars in war, and presumably news of this had reached Spain in the Cambridge Document. If it was clear to the Khazar Joseph from the *piut* that Ḥasday already knew of his military success, it is possible, *pace*

[144] Westberg, *Die Fragmente des Toparca Goticus aus dem 10. Jahrhundert*, *M.R.A.*, 1902.

[145] *Pismo khazarskogo evreia*, Berlin, 1924 (cited Landau, "Present Position," §4).

Kokovtsov,[146] that he did not find it necessary to recall the recent victory in the Reply. We may go further than this. According to the Cambridge Document, after the attack by the Russians on the people of Tamatarkha at the instigation of Romanus, the Khazar "Pesah" (? Paseah) attacked Greek territory. This name appears to conceal the Beg of Khazaria (either for Peh, or even Pesah⟨Pe-sad⟨Pe-shad⟨Be-shad (Ebe-shad). The Hebrew words *Bu(o)lsh-tsi hu' Pesaḥ hmygr* are difficult. It is at least clear that the last word (translated doubtfully by Schechter as "the Reverer") is a *Pual* participle, written defectively and to be read *ha-meyuqqar*. We should no doubt render "Bulsh-tsi, who is the honored Beg." The Beg's function as supreme commander seems well indicated by the context. In the words of the Document: "He took three cities and very many hamlets besides. From there he marched against Shorsu(nu) and fought against it." Shorsunu is evidently Cherson.[147] If as seems likely the Document went on to say that Cherson was captured by the Khazars, we may suppose that it is the city referred to in the *piut* at the beginning of the Letter of Ḥasday.

There is another line along which it may be shown that the Cambridge Document appears to contain historical material. We have already mentioned that it presents a different account of the conversion and the events leading up to it from that in the Reply of Joseph, with which latter in the main the account in the *Cosri* (*Kuzari*) agrees. The Cambridge Document also does not, it seems, stand alone. As has been indicated, the Letter of Ḥasday contains traditions current in Spain, which are evidently quoted with the intention of finding out whether the Khazar king knows anything about them. Ḥasday asks his correspondent to inform him "concerning the root of the matter . . . how Israel came to be in that place [i.e., Khazaria]. Our fathers have told us that in the beginning of their[148] settlement the place was called Mount Seir, but my

[146] *Op.cit.*, Introd. [147] Kokovtsov, 119, n. 9.

[148] A print of the Khazar Correspondence, ed. A. Sipronі, Tel Aviv, n.d., has "your settlement."

lord knows that Mount Seir is far from the place where he lives. Our elders say that formerly it was called Mount Seir, but persecutions prevailed, and they went out from affliction to affliction, till they got possession of the land where they now dwell. Also the old men of the former generation who can be relied on have told us how on account of their faithlessness a persecution was decreed, and an army of Chaldaeans rose up in anger and wrath. They hid the books of the Law and the Holy Scriptures in a cave, and for this reason they prayed in the cave. On account of the books they taught their sons to pray in the cave morning and evening, till the times were lengthened and they forgot and no longer knew about the cave, why they were accustomed to pray therein. But they practiced the custom of their fathers without knowing why. After a long time there arose a man of Israel who was eager to know why. He entered the cave, found it full of books and brought them out from there. From that day they set themselves to learn the Law. Thus have our fathers told us, as the earlier generations heard, the one from the other. The whole matter is ancient." The last words seem to exclude the possibility that Ḥasday is simply rehearsing to Joseph some of the contents of the Document.

We may therefore see in Ḥasday's Letter, which claims to give a tradition current among the Jews in Spain, traces of the account of the conversion offered by the Cambridge Document, diverging in certain respects from what may be called the primary account in the Reply, e.g., the "man of Israel" who enters the cave bears a strong resemblance to Bulan-Sabriel as he appears in the Document. But if the Document contains existing tradition, it is an indication of authenticity. The Spanish tradition, so to call it, seems also to have left a trace in the *Kuzari*, viz. the visit to the cave.

The Document mentions historical characters, Oleg, the Russian chief, and Romanus Lecapenus, but these are introduced in such a way as to raise difficulties rather than solve them. In the case of Romanus there is some confirmation for what is represented as his persecution of the Jews in Mas'ūdi. An example of coincidence between the Document and other sources is afforded by the observation, "They say in our land that our fathers were of the tribe of Simeon, but we do not understand the truth of the matter." This undoubtedly corresponds to what is said in the narrative of Eldad ha-Dani about the tribe of Simeon and the half-tribe Manasseh being in the land of the Khazars.[149] In the version of Eldad's narrative given by Carmoly the Document finds a yet closer parallel, for there one reads: "The tribe of Simeon is in the land of the Khazars on the river Itil [Atil]. The name of their king is Ezekiel [*sic*]. They are innumerable and take tribute from twenty-five kingdoms. Many of the Arabs pay them tribute. The descendants of Simeon speak Hebrew, Khazar, and Arabic, and are occupied with the written and oral Law, with verbal tradition and logical deductions, etc."[150] This version of Eldad has been characterized as a forgery by Zunz[151] and Neubauer,[152] and there is no reason to dissent from their finding. The name of Ezekiel does not figure in the list of Khazar Khaqans in the Reply and is quite likely to be a figment.[153] In another work published by Carmoly and also regarded as a forgery, *Aqtan d'Mar Jacob*, we read that "When the Khazars adopted Judaism, Simeon joined them."[154] In view of Eldad's doubtful authority and the dubious character of the publications of Carmoly, these citations hardly strengthen the case for the authenticity, though it seems worthwhile to bring them together.

In general, the Document appears to contain historical fact. The presence of Jews from the East in Khazaria at an early date; the identity of Sabriel as the founder of Khazar Judaism

[149] D. H. Müller, *Die Recensionen und Versionen des Eldad had-Dani* (*D.K.A.W.*, 1892), cited Marquart, *Streifz.*, 198, n. 3.

[150] *Eldad ha-Dani*, Paris, 1838, end of *pereq g'*.

[151] *Gesammelte Schriften*, Berlin, 1875, I, 157-8.

[152] *J.Q.R.*, I, 114.

[153] A Khaqan Zacharias is mentioned in the short Life of Constantine, see below, Chapter VII. Steingass, *Persian Dictionary*, gives a Khazar king called Ilyās, without further information.

[154] Cited *J. E.*, art. Simeon.

with Bulan; the later wars of the Khazars (especially the campaign, apparently under the Beg, against the Greeks)—these are no doubt to be regarded as additions to our knowledge of the Khazars. On the other hand, the Document gives some information which is doubtful and some which is positively false, e.g., the account of the Khaqanate. Possibly many of the difficulties are due to the state of the text. Assuming that Schechter's dating of the manuscript is correct (12th century),[155] there would at all events have been plenty of time for corruption to take place. This may be the explanation of why the Cambridge Document, which has struck several critics as objective and historical, should also have given the opposite impression.

Before concluding this account of the Hebrew sources bearing on the Khazar conversion to Judaism, it is necessary to say something about certain fragments from the Genizah, which have been published by Mann.[156] The first is an incomplete letter addressed to a woman, sent, the editor thinks, by Ḥasday to the Empress Helena, wife of Constantine Porphyrogenitus. Ḥasday is indicated by the mention apparently of the writer's good intentions towards the Christians of Cordova. It is known that after Constantine got rid of Lecapenus, in 944, his wife was very active in the government. As this letter pleads for tolerance towards the Jews in Constantinople, it is reasonable to see in it another indication that the persecution of the Jews under Romanus was a fact. The second fragment is according to Mann the heading of a letter to Constantine, unnamed but eulogized in a way appropriate to that learned monarch. The writer mentions that a communication from his correspondent to the Caliph ʿAbd-al-Raḥmān has previously reached Spain. Presumably this letter too was written by Ḥasday. Landau, who suggests that both fragments are part of the same document, composed like the Letter of Ḥasday by Menahem ben-Saruq, takes Poliak strongly to task for arbitrarily supposing that the "Caliph ʿAbd-al-Raḥmān" is

155 *Op.cit.*, 184.

156 *Texts and Studies*, I, 21ff.

'Abd-al-Raḥmān I.[157] The test employed above (comparative frequency of *Waw* conversive and simple *Waw* with the Perfect for a past tense) can hardly be applied here owing to the fragmentary character of these Genizah documents. They did not originally belong, it seems, to the same manuscript as the Cambridge Document.[158] Yet there may have been some kind of collection of Ḥasday's correspondence in the Genizah at one time. The existence of the fragments certainly tends to confirm our impression that the Cambridge Document is not fraudulent.

We may tentatively put together the picture which seems to emerge, as follows. Sometime before 112/730, the leading Khazars may have come under the influence of Judaism. The indication of time in the Reply of Joseph (earlier than 961) is to be rejected, but possibly the Reply's "340 years ago" should be read as "240 years ago." This would give earlier than 721 for the first acceptance of Judaism by the Khazars. In 112/730 a successful Khazar attack on Ardabīl takes place, involving the defeat and death of Jarrāḥ ibn-'Abdullāh, the Arab general opposed to them. The situation is reversed in 119/737, when Marwān imposes Islam on a defeated Khaqan. Shortly after this the Arab armies withdraw, and the Khaqan accepts a modified Judaism, apparently after a religious debate, circa 740, the date given by ha-Levi in the *Kuzari*. Two generations later, circa 800,[159] a descendant of the Khaqan accepts Rabbinic Judaism. The part played by Byzantium in these transactions has scarcely been alluded to and will have to be considered in the course of the next chapter.

157 In his review of *Khazaria*, *loc.cit.*

158 Cambridge Document, 23 lines to a page; Mann's fragments, 25-26 lines to a page.

159 It will be remembered that this is approximately the date indicated for the conversion by the Arabic sources (Chapter V. *ad init.*).

CHAPTER VII

TWO HUNDRED YEARS OF KHAZAR HISTORY

IN DISCUSSING the Judaism of the Khazars we have been led to speak of events of the 10th century. We must now resume the chronological sequence from 119/737, when Marwān's expedition into Khazaria took place, as related at the end of Chapter IV, and even retrace our steps for some distance before that date.

As we have seen, there was contact between the Khazars and Greeks circa A.D. 627 under Heraclius. Thereafter the Byzantine writers appear to maintain silence in regard to the Khazars till the days of the second Justinian, son of Constantine IV. In 695, after a reign of ten years during which he had made himself intolerable to his subjects, Justinian II was deposed, mutilated, and banished to the Crimea.[1] It seems that he resided quietly in Cherson for some years,[2] and then caused great alarm by publicly declaring that he intended to recover his lost empire. Leaving Cherson for Doros (Daras), the capital of the Goths of the Crimea, he requested an interview with the Khazar Khaqan. The Khaqan received the ex-Emperor with great honor, listened to what he had to say, and gave him his own sister in marriage.[3] The Khazar appears to have been called Busir.[4] The name of his sister is given as Theodora. It is not to be inferred that she was a Christian before marriage. Rather, Theodora was a baptismal name,[5] dating from the time of her marriage or her husband's restoration, and chosen by

[1] Theophanes, ed. Bonn, 566; Nicephorus, ed. Bonn, 44.

[2] Perhaps till A.D. 704; cf. Bury, *Later Roman Empire*, II, 360.

[3] Theophanes, 571; Nicephorus, 46.

[4] *Bousēros* (cf. n. 12, below) or *Ibouziros* (Vernadsky, *Ancient Russia*, 251). Zajączkowski prefers Bazīr, and Pritsak compares the name of a 9th century Qara-khānid, Bazir Arslan Khan (*Der Islam*, XXIX, 99).

[5] As in the case of Eirene, wife of Constantine V, see below.

Justinian II because the queen of his famous namesake had been so called.[6] With the permission of the Khaqan, Justinian removed to Phanagoria,[7] now Taman, on the east shore of the strait of Kertch.

Meanwhile the Emperor, now Tiberius III, had heard of what was happening, and sent repeated messages to the Khaqan, offering him a large reward for Justinian alive or dead. The Khazar prepared to sacrifice his recently acquired ally. Under pretext of providing Justinian with a bodyguard, he dispatched a troop to Phanagoria. Instructions were at the same time given to his representative there, the Khazar Papatzes, and to Balgitzes,[8] governor of Bosporus across the strait, that the ex-Emperor was to be put out of the way. The plot was disclosed to Theodora by one of her brother's household and she informed her husband. Justinian requested to see Papatzes, with whom he had been on intimate terms, and, when they were alone together, contrived to strangle him with a cord. Later he disposed of Balgitzes in the same way. Having sent Theodora back to her brother,[9] he himself proceeded in a fishing-boat to Cherson, where a number of his friends joined him.

The further steps by which Justinian recovered his throne do not concern us here. Mas'ūdi gives a résumé of these and the following events, observing that Justinian did not like what he saw among the Khazars and turned for help to Terbel, king of the Bulgars.[10] When he was again securely established in Byzantium (A.D. 705), he sent a fleet to bring his wife from Khazaria. The Khaqan, evidently willing that the past should

[6] So Bury, *L.R.E.*, II, 358.

[7] Otherwise Tamatarkha (Constantine Por., *De Admin. Imp.*, c. 42), explained as "tarkhanate on the gulf" by A. Krymsky (cited Pritsak, *ibid.*); Tmutorokan or Tmutorakan (*Russian Chronicle*, c. 52, etc.); Samkarsh (ibn-al-Faqīh, 271, cf. Marquart, *Streifz.*, 163; Reply of Joseph, L. V.; Cambridge Document, cf. Chapter VI, n. 132). Cf. Theophanes, 545: *Phanagourian kai tous ekeise oikountas 'Ebraious.*

[8] This name is usually compared with Bulsh-tsi in the Cambridge Document. The latter Zajączkowski would read as Bulgi(Bolgi)tsi, Balgichi, in the sense of "governor" (quoted Pritsak, *ibid.*).

[9] Nicephorus (47) speaks of her father.

[10] *Tanbih*, 164.

be forgotten, wrote to the Emperor, criticizing him for not having been content to send two or three ships instead of the fleet (which had lost many ships on the voyage out by storms), as if he wished to recover his wife by force.[11] His letter also brought the news that a son had been born in Khazaria to the Emperor. Theodora and her infant son were escorted to the Greek capital by a certain Theophylact the chamberlain, and were duly crowned as Augusta and Augustus. The Khazar lady's statue was set up in Constantinople near her husband's, and it is said that the Khaqan himself often sat there when on a visit to the city.[12]

In the events which preceded Justinian's final fall, the Khazar Khaqan played an important, even decisive, part. The Emperor had retained a strong impression of the hostility with which he had been treated by the inhabitants of the Crimea. In 710 he sent a great armada to carry the 100,000 men who are said to have been embarked. The commanders of the expedition had orders to put to the sword the people of Cherson, Bosporus, and certain other places.[13] With them went two prominent men, the spatharius Elias and a certain Bardanes, who had been exiled by Tiberius III but recalled by Justinian. Elias was the Emperor's nominee for the governorship of Cherson, when it had been reduced. On the other hand, the presence of Bardanes with the expedition seems to have been a mark of Justinian's suspicion rather than special favor.[14]

This account in our authorities is not altogether satisfactory. The stated aims of the armament—to punish the inhabitants of cities in the Crimea and to set up a governor in Cherson—could, it seems, have been attained by a much smaller force.

[11] Theophanes, 575.

[12] So the anonymous *Parastaseis Suntomoi Khronikai* (dating from circa A.D. 750, according to Krumbacher) in Banduri, *Imperium Orientale*, Paris 1711, I, iii, 90=Codinus, ed. Bonn, 166ff. The Khaqan's name appears as *Bousērou Gliabarou*, the second part of which is rendered by Zajączkowski as Yalbars, Jilbar(s), (e.g., *Culture*, §4). Brutzkus is far wrong in saying that Busir-Gulawar was the name of the daughter of the Khaqan and means "Rose-gatherer" (*Enc. Jud.*, art. Chasaren).

[13] Theophanes, 578.

[14] Cf. Nicephorus, 50.

Was there a serious threat at this time from the Khaqan? We have noticed Khazar officials in Bosporus[15] as well as Phanagoria. In Cherson also there was a *tudun* as governor, representing the Khaqan.[16] This *tudun* had no doubt been sent to Cherson after Justinian had quitted the town, probably in 704. Otherwise, we may suppose, it would have been unnecessary for the ex-Emperor to proceed to Doros before making contact with the Khazars. There is evidence enough to say that the two most important cities in the Crimea were at least partially under Khazar control.[17] The reason for Justinian's great expedition may well have been to recover territory which was in danger of being lost to the empire or had actually passed into Khazar hands.

In any case, the consequences proved disastrous for Justinian. The Byzantine armament took Cherson without resistance. A number of the children were spared, as well as some of the principal men, including the Khazar governor (*tudun*). Others met a wretched end. What had been done or omitted proved not to be to Justinian's liking. Orders came that the expedition with their prisoners should immediately return to Byzantium. In spite of the late season—it was now October—the commanders had no choice but to obey. Setting sail, they ran into

[15] According to Bury (*L.R.E.*, II, 358, n. 1), Bosporus was conquered by the Khazars in the 6th century. This is too early. The passage which Bury had in mind (Menander, 404) says that Bosporus was attacked by the (West) Turks, cooperating with the Utigurs (*ibid.*, 399), circa 575. It has already been referred to in Chapter II.

[16] Theophanes, 578; Nicephorus, 51. *Tudun* is a title, not a proper name, as the editors, Classen and I. Bekker, and Bury (*L.R.E.*, II, 363-364) took it. Vasiliev (*Goths*, 85) mentions an attempted derivation from Chinese *tudunj*, "provincial commander," and suggests that the Khazars "may have assumed this title at that remote time when they were wandering as a nomadic tribe in Central Asia and were in contact with the Chinese." The *tudun* appears to have been a governor appointed by the Khazar central authority, distinct from the *elteber*, or semi-independent, hereditary prince, as among the Bulgars. But the system was evidently not uniform. According to ibn-Rustah (140) the Burdās or Burṭās were subject to the king of the Khazars and possessed a mounted force of 10,000 men. They had no chief (*ra'is*), i.e., neither *tudun* nor *elteber*, but in every locality one or two elders decided lawsuits.

[17] Cf. Bury, *L.R.E.*, II, 359.

a great storm, which wrecked many vessels and caused the loss of an estimated 73,000 lives. Justinian's reaction to this disaster indicates that his mind was unbalanced. He expressed only satisfaction at the news and made preparations to dispatch another armament,[18] to level Cherson to the ground. Yet he is to be acquitted of himself having supervised the torture of leading citizens of Cherson by burning or drowning.[19] This was done in the Crimea, and not necessarily by his orders.

When news of what they must expect reached the Crimea, the inhabitants determined to resist to the end. They made preparations for defense and sought help from the Khazars. Elias, governor of Cherson, and Bardanes declared against Justinian. This development was duly reported to Byzantium. Realizing perhaps, when it was too late, the seriousness of the situation, Justinian sent out a mission headed by two of the leading men in Byzantium, who were to restore the *status quo* as far as possible in Cherson and reinstate the survivors, some of whom, including the Khazar *tudun*, now accompanied them. The diplomats were also to make apologies to the Khaqan (evidently among other things for the removal of his *tudun* to Byzantium) and to return with Elias and Bardanes, against whom Justinian was now principally enraged. This was an impossible program to carry out. At Cherson they were refused a hearing. On the following day the principals were permitted to enter the city but were there put to the sword. A force of 300 soldiers had accompanied the envoys. These, with the former *tudun* of Cherson, were handed over to the Khazars and sent off together to the Khaqan. On the way the *tudun* died. The 300 Greek prisoners were at once slain in his honor, or rather as a sacrifice to accompany him on his last journey.[20]

[18] So Nicephorus. Theophanes appears to say that a fleet was actually sent.

[19] Bury (*L.R.E.*, II, 363) is surely wrong in saying so; cf. Nicephorus, 50-51. Certain important words appear to be omitted in the text of Theophanes.

[20] The practice is vouched for among the Scythians of Herodotus, Huns, etc.; cf. Zeki Validi, *Ibn-Faḍlān*, 138ff, 237.

Since they had murdered the ambassadors of Justinian, it was a logical step for the insurgents to elect one of themselves Emperor, and this they now did. Bardanes was chosen and assumed the title of Philippicus. When Justinian heard what had happened, he avenged himself in a shocking manner on the family of Elias at Byzantium and dispatched a fleet equipped with all the material for a mediaeval siege. Having reached Cherson, the Greek commander Maurus proceeded to reduce its defenses, and had overthrown two of the main towers when the arrival of Khazar reinforcements produced a lull in the fighting. Bardanes, or Philippicus as he should now be called, uncertain of the result, took advantage of the new situation to withdraw to the Khazar court. Maurus found himself no longer strong enough to force an issue. Afraid of returning unsuccessful to Justinian, he decided to acknowledge Philippicus as Emperor, and in this was followed by all his men. But the Khaqan refused to hand over his guest, though it was to his own countrymen who had already declared their allegiance, until they had taken a solemn engagement not to betray him, and further exacted from them a sum of money, by way of security or as a ransom for Philippicus. This was duly paid by the Greeks, and, no further difficulties being raised by the Khaqan, Philippicus was received by his new adherents. Before many months had passed, he was established in Byzantium, and Justinian and his son were dead.[21]

In the course of these events we see the Khaqan of the Khazars bulking large on the stage of the Crimea, if not dominating the situation. By abandoning Justinian he appears to have made the latter's downfall certain. Bardanes (Philippicus) could hardly have survived without Khazar support. It does not seem an exaggeration to say that at this juncture the Khaqan was able practically to give a new ruler to the Greek empire. The date was A.D. 711. The Khazars had emerged on the Black Sea not many decades earlier.[22] A few years after

[21] Cf. Theophanes, 583.

[22] Cf. Chapter III.

this they were ready to take the offensive against Islam (as already described).

It is interesting to notice that in 692, i.e., before his banishment and subsequent contact with the Khazars, Justinian II permitted the Trullan Synod to issue its decree for the "uprooting of Jewish perversity."[23] When Leo the Isaurian became Emperor, one of his measures, passed probably in 720,[24] was the compulsory conversion of all Jews to Christianity. These persecutions of the Jews of Byzantium are to be connected, as Mas'ūdi indicates,[25] with the adoption of Judaism by the Khazars. Sometime later, Leo the Isaurian married his son Constantine to a Khazar princess. The date is given as 732, i.e., a year or two following the great Khazar invasion of the lands of Islam recorded in the Hebrew and Arabic sources. The events are hardly unrelated.[26] That Constantine's bride was not originally a Christian goes without saying. Her name appears to have been Chichak.[27] She was baptized at the time of her marriage and renamed Eirene. We are told of her that "having learned the sacred letters, she became distinguished for piety."[28] The expression "sacred letters" should mean more than the Greek language, and possibly a knowledge of the Hebrew Bible is intended. If the princess is credited with a knowledge of Hebrew, it is attractive to think that she might have learned it in Khazaria. There is a description of her husband in the

[23] Bury, *L.R.E.*, II, 326-327, 388. [24] Bury, *op.cit.*, II, 431.

[25] Cf. Chapter V, *ad init.*

[26] Bury (*E.R.E.*, 407) observes that the Khazar princess who married Constantine V in 732 must have been the daughter or sister of the Khaqan defeated by Marwān, adding that "in this period there were circumstances tending to draw the Khazars in the opposite directions of Christ and Muhammad. And this is precisely the period to which the evidence of the Letter of Joseph seems to assign the conversion to Judaism" (Bury, *ibid.*). Cf. Chapter IV, *ad finem.*

[27] The scholiast on Constantine Por., *De Caerimoniis Aulae Byzantinae*, I, i (ed. Bonn, 22) explains the name *tzitzakion* for a certain kind of state garment as a Khazar word, apparently derived from the name of the Khazar Empress who introduced it. It is assumed, following Reiske (Constantine Por., ed. Bonn, II, 126-127) that the Khazar Empress was Eirene, mother of Leo the Khazar. The words of the text *tēs Khazarikos tēs augoustēs* might equally apply to Theodora; cf. above.

[28] Theophanes, ed. Bonn, 631.

12th century writer Zonaras which characterizes him as "neither Christian nor Hellene [i.e., pagan] nor Jew, but a mixture of impiety."[29] It seems possible that Zonaras thought of Constantine as a kind of Jew, with reference to his Khazar wife. These indications are tenuous, but perhaps they confirm the presence of Judaism among the Khazars at the time of the marriage of Constantine and Eirene. On the other hand, there is no evidence in the Arabic sources that the Khaqan was a Jew when in 737 he underwent religious instruction at the hands of two Muslim *faqīhs*.[30]

Constantine reigned from A.D. 740 (Constantine V) and having lost his wife about 747 remained a widower, as Bar Hebraeus mentions, for three years.[31] Eirene had borne her husband a son, who became Emperor as Leo IV, surnamed the Khazar after his mother (reigned 775-780). A passage in the *De Administrando Imperio* speaks of an Emperor Leo who "took a wife from Khazaria" and "contracted a marriage alliance with the Khaqan of the Khazars."[32] No Emperor Leo, so far as we know, married a Khazar princess. Nor is Leo the Isaurian acting for his son Constantine intended, but evidently Leo IV,[33] who in fact married an Athenian. It is remarkable that in this treatise the imperial author Porphyrogenitus appears to have confused the facts.[34] From the same passage we gather that a grant of robes of honor and certain wreaths or crowns was occasionally made to the Khazars, here described as one of the "unbelieving and unhonored Northern

29 Ed. Bonn. III, 265.

30 Cf. Chapter IV, *ad finem*.

31 *Syriac Chronicle*, transl. Budge, 113.

32 Ed. Bonn, 83, 87.

33 This seems certain from the words describing his death, *ibid.*, 84. Cf. Bury, *L.R.E.*, II, 479n.

34 Gibbon has a remark about "the marriage of Leo, or rather of his father, Constantine the Fourth, with the daughter of the king of the Chozars [Khazars]," in which perhaps he tacitly corrects Constantine (*Decline and Fall*, c. 53). Gibbon in general is not illuminating on these Khazar relationships, and in this case Constantine V should be named. Elsewhere he speaks of Constantine having "chosen a barbarian wife" (c. 48), which is scarcely likely, seeing that the bridegroom was a boy of 13 or so, and the match had obviously been arranged by his vigorous father (cf. Theoph., 614, 631).

races," by the Byzantine authorities. It would be natural if Leo IV, as well as making improper use of state garlands personally, as we are told he did,[35] wished to bestow them on his Khazar relations.

We may now pick up the thread of the narrative at the point where we abandoned it in Chapter IV. The second Arab-Khazar war had ended in the discomfiture of the Khaqan and, according to the Arabic sources, his forced conversion to Islam. The dissensions which vexed the Caliphate before and after the accession of Marwān ibn-Muḥammad enabled the Khazars to recover. In 134/751, when the Abbasids were establishing themselves in the distant province of Hind, the representative of the old order there, Manṣūr ibn-Jumhūr, was defeated and killed. His successor, unequal to the contest, fled with the harem and property of Manṣūr to Khazaria.[36] Clearly at this time the Khazar state was independent.

In 141/758 Yazīd ibn-Usayd al-Sulami governed Armenia for the Abbasid Manṣūr. A garrison was at this time established by him at the pass of Darial. Later instructions came from the Caliph, bidding his governor enter into a marriage alliance with the king of the Khazars.[37] It is reasonable to suppose that the Khazars were again felt to be dangerous, and this following events showed to be a fact.

Yazīd ibn-Usayd made ready to carry out his sovereign's wishes. We have an account of the magnificence of the cavalcade which brought the Khazar princess[38] south through the passes of the Caucasus. She was accompanied by *ṭarkhāns*[39] and numerous female attendants and slaves. Ten covered waggons—moving tents made of the finest silk, the floors of which were spread with sable furs—contained her suite. Twenty others carried the gold and silver vessels and other valuables

[35] *Ibid.*, 83.

[36] Ṭabari, III, 80.

[37] Ya'qūbi, II, 446; Balādhuri, 210. He was a son of Marwān's lieutenant in 737.

[38] According to Levond she was the daughter of the Khaqan (Vernadsky, *Anc. Russ.*, 288, citing Brosset, *Histoire de la Georgie*, I, 257, n. 1).

[39] Ṭabari, III, 647.

which made up the dowry of the Khazar lady.[40] The marriage was celebrated perhaps at Bardha'ah, where the princess later died at the birth of her son.[41] The child also died, and the Khazar attendants left for their own country, full of suspicions of the Muslims and persuaded, it is said, that their mistress had been treacherously killed. The Khaqan chose to regard what had happened as an occasion for war.[42]

Under a general whose name is given as Rās Ṭarkhān[43] the Khazars poured south.[44] The territories of Ḥaṣnīn (Ḥamzīn),

[40] Ibn-A'tham al-Kūfi, cited Zeki Validi, *Ibn-Faḍlān*, 120.

[41] Ṭabari, *loc.cit.*

[42] It is here assumed that what Ṭabari relates under A.H. 182 and 183 about a Khazar princess who goes as bride to the Barmecide Faḍl ibn-Yaḥya, then governor of Armenia, belongs properly to A.H. 145. Under A.H. 183 Ṭabari offers alternative reasons for the Khazar invasion which took place in that year. It looks as if his "daughter of the Khaqan" motivation is due to confusion with the events of 145. Cf. Marquart, *Streifz.*, 5 and n., 416.

[43] So Ya'qūbi, II, 446 (Ṭabari, III, 328, Astrakhān). Ya'qūbi calls him further "king of the Khazars" (*malik al-Khazar*). There is no variant Ḥalīs Ṭarkhān (cf. Chapter V, n. 21) in Ya'qūbi, in spite of Barthold (*E.I.*, art. Khazar) and Zeki Validi (*Ibn-Faḍlān*, 218 n.). Houtsma's text by a typographical slip offers two notes (*g*), and Ḥalīs is a variant for Ḥalbas, not for Rās, as these scholars assert. Houtsma's note on the passage reads simply: (*g*) Ita cod., calling attention to the reading Rās Ṭarkhān.—Ṭabari's Astarkhān, if original, perhaps means "Tarkhan of the Ās," (cf. Arṣīyah in Mas'ūdi), Ās Tarkhān (not Astār Khān, as in *E.I.*, art. Tiflis). There is more evidence for Ya'qūbi's form Rās Ṭarkhān, which Marquart thought he may have got from an Armenian source (*Streifz.*, 355, n. 2). Variants of the Armenian form are Tarkhan Rai and Razh Tarkhan (*Streifz.*, 5, n. 1 and 114). The latter is from Levond (ed. Shahnazarean, 163), who says that the Khaqan of the Khazars sent a great army under a general of that name, belonging to the horde of the Khatiriltber. Ya'qūbi would thus be wrong in calling Rās Ṭarkhān king of the Khazars, if by that the Khaqan is meant. Nor was he the Khazar Beg, if Khatiriltber includes the title *elteber*, as seems likely. (Zeki Validi explains Khatiriltber as a noble family among the Khazars, *Ibn-Faḍlān*, 106.) Ṭabari (*loc.cit.*) adds after the name Astarkhān "the Khwarizmian." This again suggests the Arsīyah, who are "from the neighborhood of Khwārizm" (Mas'ūdi). Vernadsky's observations on an assumed Rus (<Rās) Ṭarkhān (*Anc. Russ.*, 285ff) appear very hazardous.

[44] Ya'qūbi seems to put the event in A.H. 141, while Ṭabari gives A.H. 147 for the invasion under "Astarkhān the Khwarizmian." But Ṭabari (III, 318=ibn-al-Athīr, v, 212) gives a Khazar attack on Armenia via Bāb in A.H. 145, and this year is also given by Bar Hebraeus (*Syriac Chronicle*, transl. Budge, 114). Possibly the events now to be described lasted over several years. Yāqūt (Buldān, I, 439) gives no date.

Lakz, and the Alan country in the neighborhood of Darial were overwhelmed.[45] The invaders continued their passage into the lands of the Caliphate. The deputy of the governor was routed.[46] Yazīd ibn-Usayd himself avoided an encounter. Manṣūr on hearing the news dispatched a force of 20,000 from Syria and al-Jazīrah, which effected a junction with Yazīd ibn-Usayd. But the battle went against them, and they were obliged to retreat. The situation was now alarming. Regular troops not being available, the Caliph was forced to the extraordinary expedient of opening the gaols and releasing prisoners, to the number of 7,000, whom he armed and sent north. The army included masons and other artisans, and when the reinforcements arrived their first task was to construct a number of fortifications, which were speedily garrisoned and the Khazars in this way contained.[47] We hear of no other great battle. Shortly afterwards one of these fortresses which lay to the west (Kamkh) passed into the hands of the Greeks. Though attacked by the Caliph's brother during a whole summer (151/768), it was not retaken. This expedition is notable because Khazar troops formed part of the Muslim army.[48]

Mahdi succeeded Manṣūr as Caliph in 158/775. About 780 a young Arab of Baghdad, who afterwards enjoyed fame as St. Abo of Tiflis, visited the Khazar country in company of the Georgian prince Nerse. The saint's life was written in Georgian not very long after his death.[49] Though no doubt the product of cloistered ignorance rather than a firsthand relation of fact, this record may contain genuine reminiscences of the journey. According to its author, Nerse decided to leave his

[45] According to Bar Hebraeus (*loc.cit.*) the Khazars took captive 50,000 people. The *K. al-ʿUnwān* of al-Manbiji (Agapius of Mabbug) has the same figure (ed. Vasiliev, Paris 1909, II, 543, cited Kmosko, "Die Quellen Iṣṭachri's etc.," *Kőrösi Csoma-Archivum*, 1921).

[46] His name was Mūsa ibn-Ka'b (al-Manbiji, *loc.cit.*).

[47] Ya'qūbi, II, 447.

[48] Assemani, *Bibl. Orient.*, II, 113, citing Dionysius of Tel Mahre.

[49] See K. Schultze, *Das Martyrium des heiligen Abo von Tiflis, Texte u. Untersuchungen zur Geschichte der altchristlichen Literatur, Neue Folge,* 13, 1905.

country in consequence of the vexations of the Arabs. Sending his wife and children to neighboring Abkhazia, he withdrew at the head of 300 followers through the pass of Darial to Khazaria. No explanation of the visit is given, but it was doubtless to solicit armed help. It appears from the friendly manner in which he was received that Khazar policy was at this time independent of the Caliph and disposed to conciliate the Christians. Here, as in older accounts, Khazaria is styled the "Land of the North," and the Khaqan appears as the "King of the North." The legend connecting the Khazars with Gog and Magog recurs in this Georgian account. If the Khazars are here described as "wild men with hideous faces and the manners of wild beasts, eaters of blood,"[50] this too may be part of the tradition rather than what was actually observed by the travelers. Yet the Armenian author Moses of Kalankatuk speaks similarly of the "horrible multitude of Khazars with insolent, broad, lashless faces and long falling hair, like women."[51] A number of the towns and villages of Khazaria contained Christians, and we are probably to understand that in Khazaria Abo, for some time past an adherent of Christianity, was baptized "by reverend priests." In general, according to the writer, "the Khazars have no belief, but recognize only a creator God."[52] Nothing is said explicitly about the religion of the Khazar king.[53] It is not clear that the Georgian travelers ever reached the Khazar capital on the Volga. Some time after his arrival, Nerse asked leave of his host to depart to Abkhazia. The Khazar acceded and sent the party on its way with many gifts. They passed through "the land of the heathen, who believe in no God"[54] for three days and nights[55] before reaching their

[50] Schultze, 23.

[51] Quoted Marquart, *Streifz.*, 44, n. 4.

[52] Schultze, *ibid.*

[53] Zajączkowski draws attention to the interest shown at the Khazar court in Constantine's official post and status before assigning him his place at the royal table as an authentic trait, pointing to the existence of ancient Turkish traditions among the Khazars ("Culture," §4).

[54] Schultze, 24.

[55] Vasiliev (*Goths in the Crimea*, 99) says that the journey took three months.

destination. This detail of the distance to Abkhazia should be reliable. Perhaps the Georgians found the Khazar king at a camping ground far south of Atil.

Towards the end of the 8th century, in 786 or 787, the Goths of the Crimea were attacked by the Khazars. Doros,[56] their capital and chief fortress, was besieged and captured and a Khazar *tudun* installed.[57] Under their bishop John, the Goths rose against the intruders and at first met with some success. Eventually, however, the warlike bishop had to submit. While in prison he is said to have healed the child of the Khazar commandant.[58] The Khazars did not retain possession of Doros for long. A few years after this the town was in Greek hands.[59]

To turn again to the Muslim East, the Caliphate of Hārūn al-Rashīd–from 170/786–was marked by continual disturbances in Armenia. The Armenians had revolted on the death of Mahdi and remained unsubdued during the short reign of Hādi.[60] Under Hārūn al-Rashīd a succession of governors failed to establish peace. Beyond the frontier, the Khazars seem to have remained quiescent, not attempting to profit by the Caliph's difficulties. In 180/796 a new governor, Sa'īd ibn-Salm, was appointed.[61] For some time all went well. Then Sa'īd gave offence to the native aristocracy, and trouble began again. The

[56] Doros has usually been identified with the impressive site known as Mankup Qala (cf. Vasiliev, *Goths*, 47ff), but now the Russian archaeologists claim that Eski Kermen is mediaeval Doros (*op.cit.*, 51, 129 n.).

[57] *Op.cit.*, 91; cf. 106.

[58] The primary source is the Life of St. John of Gothia (in *Act. Boll.*). It has been published with a commentary by Vasilievsky, *Rus.-Vizant. Issledovaniya*, II.

[59] For a toparch of Gothia after A.D. 795 cf. Vasiliev, *op.cit.*, 105.

[60] Ya'qūbi, II, 515.

[61] Ṭabari, III, 648. Two alternative accounts of the sequel are offered by Ṭabari. The first seems properly to refer to an earlier incident, cf. n. 42. According to his second account, the Khazars are called in by a certain "ibn-al-Munajjim," apparently "the son of the astronomer," though Munajjim is also a personal name. It should probably be corrected to "ibn-al-Najm," see below. This second account has been followed. It is very unlikely that the loss of a daughter gave the Khazar Khaqan a pretext for war against the Caliphate on more than one occasion. The confusion may be due to similarity of name of the governors of Armenia in A.H. 145 (Yazīd ibn-Usayd) and 183 (Yazīd ibn-Mazyad).

commandant at Bāb was a certain Najm ibn-Hāshim.[62] The governor caused him to be executed and installed another officer in his place. His son threw off allegiance, killed Sa'īd's nominee[63] and wrote to the king of the Khazars for assistance against the Muslims.[64] The Khazar responded to the appeal and arrived at Bāb with a large army, put in one account as high as 100,000 men.[65] Overcoming all resistance, the invaders swept forward till they reached the river Kur (Cyrus). Here they halted, but not before Hārūn had been seriously alarmed. His first measures went awry, but for some reason the threat never fully materialized. After causing widespread devastation in which Christians, i.e., presumably Armenians, as well as Muslims suffered heavily, the Khazars retired with their prisoners. When some time had elapsed, Yazīd ibn-Mazyad al-Shaybāni, a former governor, arrived with full powers.[66] By then the Khazars had disappeared, and Armenia submitted quietly to his rule. The invaders had been in the country for seventy days. It was the last great Khazar exploit against the Arabs of which we have a record (183/799).

The Georgian Chronicle has a story[67] somewhat similar to the episode involving the daughter of the Khaqan and Yazīd ibn-Usayd, which we have assigned above to 145/762. According to the Chronicle, Juansher, the ruling prince of Georgia, had

62 Ya'qūbi, II, 518.

63 According to Weil (*Geschichte der Chalifen*, II, 158) one reason alleged by the historians (he cites ibn-al-Athīr, ibn-Khaldūn, and al-Yāfi'i) for the Khazar irruption circa A.H. 183 is that the Khaqan of the Khazars had been killed by an Arab who wished to avenge the death of his father. A possible source of this is the late writer al-Yāfi'i (his *Mir'āt al-Janān* composed circa 750/1349). Ibn-al-Athīr (VI, 54) and ibn-Khaldūn (III, 225) know nothing of any such fatality to a Khazar Khaqan. The mistake is noted by Vasiliev (*Goths*, 92).

64 Ṭabari, *loc.cit.*

65 So ibn-al-Jawzi, quoted by De Goeje in Ṭabari, *loc.cit.* Otherwise this was the number of Muslims stated to have been taken prisoner by the Khazars.

66 De Goeje (*Enc. Brit.* ed. XI, art. Caliphate) mentions also Khuzaymah ibn-Khāzim. In the text Ya'qūbi's account has been followed. The valor of Yazīd ibn-Mazyad against the Khazars was praised by the poets; cf. ibn-al-Athīr, VI, 55.

67 Cf. Marquart, *Streifz.*, 416ff.

a beautiful young sister. Her fame having reached the Khazar Khaqan, he sent an envoy with a proposal of marriage, promising in return to help the Georgians to resist the Arabs. The mother and brother of Juansher strongly disapproved, and the girl herself spoke scornfully of the Khazar. Three years passed, and the Khaqan sent his general Bluch'an into Georgia. Bluch'an (in the Armenian version of the story Buljan)[68] captured the castle of Juansher, taking him and his sister prisoners. As they were being escorted to Khazaria through the pass of Darial, the princess took poison. Bluch'an reached the Khaqan's court and told of the death of the prospective bride. The Khaqan requested to see the body and, enraged that it had not been brought to him, gave orders that his general should be punished by death. A rope was placed round his neck and the ends were given to two horsemen, who then rode apart, so that the head was torn from the trunk. After seven years' imprisonment, concludes the story, Juansher was permitted to return to his kingdom.

Marquart would connect the Khazar attack on Georgia under Bluch'an with the events of 183/799.[69] Certain points in the tale seem authentic. It is consistent with what we find elsewhere that the Khaqan should request the daughter of a neighboring ruler in marriage in a peremptory fashion, and that he should have absolute power of life and death over a general and even the Beg,[70] who may be intended in the story. On the other hand, the Khaqan is represented apparently as a heathen, not a Jew. The story can hardly be adduced, however, as evidence that the Khazar conversion had not yet taken place.

In the reign of the same Juansher, it appears that the Abkhazian prince Leo, son of a daughter of the Khazar king,[71] i.e. presumably the Khaqan, made himself independent of the Greeks with the help of the Khazars. This is one of the few occasions when we find them opposing the Emperor.

[68] Marquart, *ib.* 417, n. 2. For the name, cf. Bulan, Bulkhan (Chapter VI, n. 127).

[69] *Streifz.*, 417.

[70] Ibn-Faḍlān, Chapter V.

[71] Marquart, *Streifz.*, 422. Cf. Barthold, *E.I.*, art. Abkhāz.

In or about 218/833 the Khaqan and Beg of Khazaria[72] applied to Byzantium for help in building a fortress on the Don.[73] The Emperor Theophilus sent a naval squadron which proceeded via Cherson and the Sea of Azov to Khazar territory. Somewhere on the Don the Greeks built a fortress of brick, in Greek Aspron Hospition (Constantine Por.), or Leukon Oikema (Theophanes Con.), and called by the Russians Biela Viezha.[74] The Khazars themselves spoke of Sarkil.[75] All these names meant much the same, the White, or Yellow, House, or Castle. Sarkil can be explained in this sense from the Chuvash dialect of Turkish,[76] a fact which appears to provide a key to the statement of Iṣṭakhri-ibn-Ḥawqal, enigmatic in view of the Turkish affinities of the Khazars, that their language was different from Turkish.[77] For Chuvash is characterized by substitution of *l, i* and *r* for *sh, a* and *z* of the majority of Turkish dialects, e.g. Ottoman Turkish. A "Lir" Turkish dialect, to use the convenient expression, was no doubt incomprehensible, like Chuvash in modern times,[78] to "Shaz" Turkish speakers, and the remark that the Khazars did not speak Turkish is probably to be explained in this way. The language of the Volga Bulgars probably also belonged to the Lir Turkish group, and hence no doubt the Bulgar language is said by Iṣṭakhri-ibn-Ḥawqal to be like that of the Khazars.[79]

As to the purpose of the fortress, presumably it was intended for defense against an enemy coming from the west. Who this enemy may have been is not perfectly clear. The Pechenegs, suggested by one of the Greek sources which speak of the in-

[72] Constantine Por., *De Admin. Imp.*, c. 42; Theophanes Contin., 122.

[73] The exact site is doubtful. Vernadsky (*Anc. Russ.*, 305) places it on the left bank of the Don at the mouth of the Tsymla river. According to Marquart (*Streifz.*, 474), Sarkil lay at the mouth of the Don.

[74] Cf. Chapter IX.

[75] Reply of Joseph, L.V.: Sarkil (Sharkil).

[76] It can be explained similarly, according to Zajączkowski, from common, i.e., Shaz, Turkish (quoted Pritsak, *Der Islam*, XXIX, 99), see below.

[77] Cf. Chapter V.

[78] Barthold, *E.I.*, art. Bulghār.

[79] Cf. Chapter V.

cident, are not known to have passed west of the Don till sixty years later,[80] though earlier bands may be thought of.[81] Mas'ūdi, in a passage yet to be quoted, describing an expedition of Russians to the Caspian by way of the sea of Azov and the Don-Volga route in 301/913, mentions a Khazar strong point somewhere along their course, at which troops were regularly stationed against the Ghuzz.[82] This might be identified with Sarkil. It has also been thought that Sarkil was built against the Magyars.[83] Perhaps rather the enemies of the Khazars in this quarter were already (218/833) the Russians, whose strength at that time was presumably growing west and north of Khazaria.[84]

Sarkil doubtless remained a military post. It is named in the Reply of Joseph, but does not appear in the lists of Khazar towns given by Muqaddasi and *Ḥudūd al-ʿĀlam*,[85] nor elsewhere in the Muslim sources. For this reason alone Poliak's suggestion that Sarkil was the center of one of the four principalities into which, according to him, Khazaria was divided, is

[80] See below.

[81] I.e., "Turkish" Pechenegs. The "Turkish" Pechenegs living east of the Volga and west of the Ghuzz, till their emigration, are distinguished by *Ḥudūd al-ʿĀlam*, §§20, 47 from the "Khazarian" Pechenegs of the Caucasus, who had left their seats in Asia earlier, perhaps in company with the Ās. Cf. Zeki Validi, "Völkerschaften," 56-57.

[82] *Murūj*, II, 18ff.

[83] Marquart, *Streifz.*, 28, basing on ibn-Rustah's statement (143) that in earlier times the Khazars protected themselves with a ditch against the Magyars and other neighbouring peoples. Cf. Zeki Validi, "Völkerschaften," 51-52.

[84] So Vasiliev, *Goths*, 109ff; Vernadsky, *Anc. Russ.*, 304. But Bury (*E.R.E.*, 418) was earlier.

[85] Muqaddasi has a list of nine Khazar towns repeated in two places (51, 355): Atil, Bulghār, Samandar, Suwār, B-gh-nd, Q-yshw-y, al-Bayḍā', Khamlīj, Balanjar. For B-gh-nd cf. Bajkand, a flourishing town in the province of Saqsīn according to Aḥmad Ṭūsi (cited Zeki Validi, *Ibn-Faḍlān*, 205). Possibly Q-yshw-y represents or is represented by one of the Khazar place-names in the *Darband Nāmah*, e.g., K-ywān (Kasem Beg, 477). The remaining seven are more familiar. *Ḥudūd al-ʿĀlam* gives apparently ten Khazar towns (§50), of which at least five are otherwise known (Atil, Samandar, Khamlīkh or Khamlīj, Balanjar, Bayḍā'); cf. Minorsky's commentary.

unacceptable.[86] Still less was it the capital of Khazaria, as others have supposed.[87]

Several Arabic sources report a story which, if it does not afford a glimpse of the real Khazaria, at least presents the Khazars as seen by Arab eyes in the 9th century.[88] It is said to have been told in the company of al-Faḍl ibn-Sahl, the well-known vizier of al-Ma'mūn (813-833), by a Khazar ambassador.[89] On the occasion of a famine, the Khatun, sister of the Khazar king, by her wise advice caused the Khazars to submit themselves as a people to God's will, with the result of securing early relief from their predicament.[90] The words ascribed to the Khatun are sufficiently commonplace. It is significant, however, that in one version the Khazars have recourse first to "the door of the inferior king," apparently the Khatun's brother, and then to "the door of the superior king." The Khaqan and Beg are plainly indicated, and the trait seems authentic.[91] Al-Faḍl ibn-Sahl was one of the most powerful men in Islam, and it is natural that the Khazar ambassador should have visited him. On the other hand, we scarcely hear elsewhere of any Khazar mission to Baghdad. Nor is there any indication that Khazar women played an important part in affairs, though this would be natural enough, certainly in the case of ladies of the highest rank, among a Turkish people. In the story, after her successful intromission in politics the Khatun is apparently invested with the kingship. This detail at least seems pure fiction. Again, the content of the speech ascribed to the Khatun does not imply Khazar Judaism.

[86] Poliak ("Conversion," §2) does not attempt to prove that the Khazar empire was so divided and he has modified the view in Khazaria, 43-55, but cf. 218.

[87] E.g. Slouschz in *Mélanges H. Derenbourg*, 72, 76.

[88] Found in the *K. al-Mustajād min Fa'alāt al-Ajwād* of al-Tanūkhi (d. 384/994), ed. L. Paully, Stuttgart, 1939; the *Zahr al-Ādāb* of al-Ḥusri (d. after 413/1022; and the *Sirāj al-Mulūk* of al-Ṭarṭūshi (d. circa 520/1126). But the tale goes back to Jāḥiẓ (d. 255/869).

[89] The date is not later than 202/818, the year of al-Faḍl's death.

[90] *Zahr al-Ādāb*, ed. Zeki Mubarak, I, 254-255.

[91] *Sirāj al-Mulūk*, ed. Cairo 1306, 152, cited Zeki Validi, *Ibn-Faḍlān*, 264.

It is said that the Jews of Iraq entertained hopes that the Khazars would destroy the Caliphate.[92] How real the threat was at different times we have already seen. A certain light is thrown on the situation by the accounts of the fall of Afshīn.[93] This man, a Turk of Usrūshunah and one of the ablest of Mu'taṣim's generals, was disgraced and fell from power in 225/840. Shortly before his apprehension, it is said, he had planned to escape via Mosul and Armenia to Khazaria, whence he hoped to reach Turkestan and return to the lands of the Caliphate at the head of an army.[94] Clearly he entertained or at least was suspected of very grandiose schemes. He is said to have been in correspondence with the Greeks, and to have contemplated making use of the Khazars against the Muslims. When he was put on trial, the accusation was an unusual one. It was alleged that he was a Magian—an adherent, that is, of the proscribed religion of Zoroaster—and evidence was produced which at least gave color to the charge. This can have had nothing to do with the Khazars, for although one text describes them as Magians,[95] there is no corroboration that this faith ever flourished in their country.[96] The statement that the Khazars were Magians is on a par with others which make Zoroastrians of the Vikings who harried the coast of Spain, or the pagan Rūs. Vernadsky's suggestion that the original religion of the Khazars involved adoration of fire appears baseless.[97]

A reference in the Kitāb al-Aghānī[98] to a young Khazar page or slave who attracted the attention of the poet abu-Tammām (*ob.* perhaps in 231/846) raises the question of people of Khazar extraction living under the Caliphate. Undoubtedly there

[92] Harkavy in the *Kohut Memorial Volume*, 244—in Hebrew—citing the *Magid*, 1877.

[93] Cf. E. M. Wright, "Bābak of Badhdh and al-Afshīn during the years 816-841," *Muslim World*, 1948, 43-59.

[94] Ṭabari, III, 1305.

[95] Ṭabari, *Ikhtilāf al-Fuqahā'*, ed. Schacht, Leiden 1933, 200.

[96] Zeki Validi (*Ibn-Faḍlān*, 319, n. 1) suggests the possibility of Buddhists among the Khazars, but it is virtually certain that neither Buddhism nor Zoroastrianism ever influenced them to any extent.

[97] *Enciclopedia Italiana*, art. Chazari.

[98] xv, 107.

were such. Perhaps best known are Isḥāq ibn-Kundāj (or Kundājiq) al-Khazari, already referred to, and Takīn ibn-'Abdullāh al-Khazari, who was three times governor of Egypt[99] (*flor. circa* 920). Both were apparently soldiers of fortune who rose to power in the Caliph's service. 'Abdullāh ibn-Bashtwa al-Khazari, who has also been mentioned earlier, was perhaps a disaffected subject of the Khaqan. There were also people of humbler rank, like the 300 families who in 854 "left Khazaria because of their desire for Islam," and having arrived at Bab, were settled by the governor of Armenia and Adharbayjān in a northern town.[100] A number of traditionists are mentioned whose names suggest a Khazar origin.[101] Some of these doubtless were connected with the town of Darband-i Khazarān (Bāb) and hence used the *nisbah* al-Khazari, though of Arab or mixed origin, but others may well have been Khazars *pur sang*. We do not get the impression that Khazars in the lands of Islam were particularly numerous, but certainly they existed in various spheres of life.[102]

The Caliph al-Wāthiq (227/842-232/847) is said to have sent the learned Muḥammad ibn-Mūsa al-Khwārizmi at the beginning of his reign to "Ṭarkhān, king of the Khazars." If it is a fact that al-Khwārizmi visited Khazaria, very probably he did so for scientific purposes.[103] The notice is given only by Muqaddasi.[104] The visit of a certain Sallām the Interpreter to Khazaria[105] a little later is better authenticated. We are not here

[99] Cf. Zeki Validi, *Ibn-Faḍlān*, 109.

[100] Shamkūr (Balādhuri, 203); cf. Marquart, *Streifz.*, 412.

[101] Cf. Sam'āni, *Ansāb* (*G.M.S.*), fol. 198.

[102] For Khazars at Sāmarra, cf. Chapter VIII, n. 67.

[103] Cf. D. M. Dunlop, "Muḥammad ibn-Mūsā al-Khwārizmi," *J.R.A.S.*, 1943, 248-250.

[104] Ed. De Goeje, 362.

[105] Zeki Validi (*Ibn-Faḍlān*, 198, n.) used for Sallām's journey the complementary references in ibn-Khurdādhbih, Idrīsi, *Mujmal al-Tawārīkh* and Muqaddasi. To these may be added ibn-Rustah (149), Qazwīni (*Cosmography*, ed. Wüstenfeld, I, 128) and Nuwayri (I, 374, citing Idrīsi). Barbier de Meynard in his translation of ibn-Khurdādhbih (*J.A.*, 1865, 241, n. 1) says "Mukadessy ajoute ici un fait que je n'ai trouvé dans aucune autre version: Wathiq avait envoyé précédemment l'astronome Mohammed fils de Mouça, originaire du Khârezm, chez le Tharkhan, roi

concerned with the itinerary of Sallām's journey except as it relates to the Khazars, but something has to be said about the circumstances. Sallām dealt with the Caliph's Turkish correspondence and is credited with knowing thirty languages.[106] The account of his journey was given verbally to ibn-Khurdādhbih, from a written memoir prepared for the Caliph. According to this, Wāthiq, becoming alarmed to think that the "Wall of Gog and Magog" had been breached,[107] commissioned Sallām to proceed to it and investigate. Furnished with a letter from the Caliph to Isḥāq ibn-Ismā'īl ibn-Shu'ayb, the governor of Armenia,[108] Sallām started for the Caucasus and reaching Tiflis, met the governor and gave him Wāthiq's instructions. Isḥāq ibn-Shu'ayb sent the party on to the ruler of the Sarīr, with whom he was on good terms, and from the country of the Sarīr they successively reached the king of the Alans and the Fīlān Shāh. The latter wrote in the interests of the travelers to "Ṭarkhān, king of the Khazars." The information about Khazaria in Sallām's account is very meager. We are told that his party remained with the king only for a day and a night,[109] or for five days.[110] Ibn-Khurdādhbih gives the same name to the Khazar ruler as does Muqaddasi for a year or two earlier. But it is difficult to think that it is authentic. *Ṭarkhān* is a Turkish title rather than a proper name. We have met it several times already as the designation of subordinate officers. It would seem that in the account either "Ṭarkhān" has been substituted for something else,[111] or, if Ṭarkhān is right, another name has to be supplied before it, as in the combinations Hazār Ṭarkhān[112] and Rās Ṭarkhān.[113] Muqaddasi's use of the

---

des Khozars. *Ce voyageur se joignit à moi,* etc." (i.e., to Sallām). This is not what is said in Muqaddasi, ed. De Goeje, 362.

[106] Ibn-Rustah, 149; ibn-Khurdādhbih, 163.

[107] Cf. a tradition of Muḥammad's alarm for the same reason (Bukhāri, ed. Krehl, 60, 7) and similarly Qazwīni, *Cosmography*, II, 417.

[108] A governor of Armenia in Wāthiq's Caliphate is apparently referred to by Moses of Kalankatuk (III, 20, cited Marquart, *Streifz.*, 462) as "Khazr patgos."

[109] Ibn-Khurdādhbih, 163.

[110] Qazwīni, I, 128.

[111] Cf. "Khaqan, king of the Khazars," e.g., Ya'qūbi, II, 518.

[112] Cf. Chapter IV.

[113] See above.

same expression is hardly confirmation for its authenticity, for Muqaddasi (writing circa 375/985) doubtless makes use of what he found in his sources for Sallām's journey.[114]

There is no reason to suspect, in its main outline at least, what is said about Sallām's journey by his contemporary ibn-Khurdādhbih. The case is somewhat different for various stories which were later connected with Sallām's name and cited on his authority. One of these speaks of an "island of sheep," otherwise unknown, lying "between the Khazars and the Bulgars," which Sallām is said to have reached by ship.[115] Another mentions a kind of mermaid, seen by Sallām while in the company of the Khazar king.[116] Neither of these stories occurs in the account of ibn-Khurdādhbih.

A year or two before Wāthiq became Caliph, the overthrow of the powerful Uigur state (A.D. 840) brought about a revolution in Asia. It has been suggested that rumors of this reached the Caliph and caused him to send out the expedition just referred to.[117] In that case it is remarkable that Sallām was ordered to proceed to the Caucasus, not directly into central Asia. The journey was, however, conceived by the Caliph as to the "Wall of Gog and Magog." Gog and Magog and the wall built by dhū-al-Qarnayn (Alexander the Great) to contain them are of course mentioned in the Qur'ān.[118] The cryptic passage was at an early date explained to mean the Caucasus fortification (dating from pre-Islamic times) known as the Wall of Darband.[119] Hence doubtless Sallām was sent first to Wāthiq's governor in this quarter. There is a tradition in Ṭabari, already glanced at,[120] which, if known to Wāthiq, may have contributed to turn his thoughts to the Caucasus. According to this, the Persian governor of Darband, some time before the arrival of the Muslims, had sent out an expedition to Alexander's Dyke. The general ʿAbd-al-Raḥmān ibn-Rabīʿah is said to have been pres-

[114] Yet in *Ḥudūd al-ʿĀlam*, §50 we read that the king of the Khazars is called Ṭarkhān Khāqān.

[115] Qazwīni, *loc.cit.*

[116] *Ibid.*, cf. II, 418.

[117] Marquart, *Streifz.*, 90.

[118] Sur. 18, 91-97.

[119] Cf. Chapter I.

[120] In Chapter III.

ent when the leader of the Persian expedition returned exhausted after two years of travel. This man is represented as having reached the Dyke and is made to describe it in terms similar to the account of Sallām in ibn-Khurdādhbih.[121] It is impossible to be sure that Ṭabari's story is authentic, but evidently it was current about the time of Sallām's expedition.

Sallām's nationality is not clear. It is perhaps most natural to think of him as an Arab, but it is not excluded that he was a Khazar who had taken service with the Caliph. He may have been a Khazar Jew.[122] In any case, it would appear that after reaching Khazaria, he knew or was directed where to go to fulfill Wāthiq's commission. Mention is made of five guides—the comparatively large number apparently for a long journey—which the king of the Khazars assigned him.[123] The suggestion is that there was some knowledge of and interest in central Asia among the Khazars at the time. Unfortunately it is quite impossible to gather from Sallām's account how far Khazaria extended to the northeast.

We have already referred to the governor of Armenia and Adharbayjān who in 240/854 permitted a number of Khazar families to pass by way of Bāb al-Abwāb into the lands of

[121] Successive courses of bright and dark material (copper and iron) are the most prominent feature of both accounts, which of course may be influenced by the Qur'ān passage, in which iron and molten brass are mentioned. Sallām at any rate should be reporting something which he had seen. Perhaps Sallām came eventually, as Zeki Validi thinks (*Ibn-Faḍlān*, 196 n.) to the Iron Gate, Talka, north of Kulja in the Tien Shan. Marquart (*Streifz.*, 86) follows De Goeje (*De muur van Gog en Magog*, 87) in supposing that the Great Wall of China is meant. Count E. Zichy ("Le voyage de Sallâm l'interprète," *Kőrösi Csoma-Archivum*, I, 193ff) found that the Wall of Gog and Magog was some passage in the Urals, but this does not seem particularly likely. Yet a passage in the Chester Beatty MS. of Iṣṭakhri represents the Wall as "behind Arta (Artha)," a Russian province or people (cf. Chapter V). Another alleged visit to the Wall in the time of the Prophet is described by Damīrī, *Ḥayāt al-Ḥayawān*, ed. of Cairo, A.H. 1284, II, 478, s.v. Yājūj wa-Mājūj.

[122] The name Sallām was occasionally carried by Jews, e.g. Sallām ibn-abī-al-Ḥuqayq (Ya'qūbi, II, 51).

[123] Ibn-Khurdādhbih, 163. Zeki Validi ("Völkerschaften," 52) mentions a two months' journey from Khazaria to the Wall. Cf. ibn al-Faqīh, 298.

Islam. This was Bugha the elder.[124] He settled the immigrants on the old site of Shamkūr and renamed the place Mutawakkilīyah, in honor of the reigning Caliph. He is also said to have brought 3,000 families of Alans (Ās) through the pass of Darial,[125] these too perhaps subjects of the Khazar Khaqan. About the same time he attacked the Ṣanārīyah, a Christian group living in the mountains north of Tiflis.[126] Repulsing his first assault, they opened communication with the Khaqan, as well as with the Greek Emperor and the ruler of the Sḷavs.[127] There was no intervention, it seems, as a result of these *démarches*, but Bugha was soon recalled. In one account he is said to have come under suspicion of being himself in treasonable correspondence with the Khazars, who are described as his fellow-countrymen.[128]

About 833, as already mentioned, Khazar envoys visited Constantinople to solicit Greek help in building Sarkil. Later in the century an embassy from the Khaqan to the Emperor Michael III, perhaps in 860, brought a request of quite another kind, that persons might be sent them to explain Christianity.[129] The Patriarch Photius advised the Emperor to send to Khazaria a pupil and protégé of his, Constantine,[130] and this Michael agreed to do. Photius may have felt a direct and personal interest in Khazaria, for possibly he was himself of Khazar extraction. So, it seems, we might best explain the epithet "Khazar-face," applied to him once in anger by the Emperor.[131]

Constantine proceeded via the Crimea to Khazaria. He remained for a time in Cherson, studying the Khazar language,

124 Balādhuri, 203.
125 *Georgian Chronicle*, cited Marquart, *Streifz.*, 412.
126 Cf. Minorsky, *Ḥudūd*, 400ff.
127 Ya'qūbi, II, 598.
128 *Georgian Chronicle, ibid.*
129 Marquart, *Streifz.*, 13ff; Bury, *E.R.E.*, 486-487; Vernadsky, *Anc. Russ.*, 388. The work of Dvornik (*Les légendes de Constantin et de Méthode vues de Byzance*, *Byzantino-Slavica Supplementa*, I, Prague 1933) is frequently referred to by Zajączkowski, "Culture."
130 Often called Cyril, the Apostle of the Slavs.
131 Symeon Magister, ed. Bonn, 673.

or according to another account Hebrew and Samaritan[132] (?). Then by the Don-Volga route[133] he traveled to Atil, and down the Caspian coast, till he met the Khaqan,[134] possibly at Samandar.[135] A disputation was held,[136] represented as a victory for the Christian protagonist, but only 200 persons are reported to have been baptized. Though Constantine made a good impression on the Khazar chief, his mission was evidently not very successful. Some time later he returned to Constantinople.

The religious disputation took place in the presence of the Khaqan between Jews versed in Scripture on the one hand, and Constantine on the other. From this Zajączkowski[137] rightly concludes that in the middle of the 9th century the followers of Judaism were very important and even the decisive factor at the Khaqan's court, though he is careful to state, following Dvornik,[138] that there is no direct evidence here that the Khazars were already converted to Judaism. On the other hand, the accounts of Constantine's mission can hardly be used to show that the conversion to Judaism did not take place until a little later. The character of the Khazars as Judaized Turks has constantly to be kept in mind. This probably means that their Judaism—limited no doubt in any case to a comparatively small group—was always superficial. That they were liable to relapse to paganism may be implied by what is said in the Reply of Joseph about a reformation circa 800 under a new king. It is to be supposed that visitors like Abo from Baghdad and the highly cultured Constantine might get an unfavorable impression of the savage conditions of the country, but, even so, we have no direct record of what these two observers actually found in Khazaria. Their views on the Khazars and the record of their activities among them are simply what the

[132] Cf. Bury, *E.R.E.*, 394, n. 6.

[133] The so-called "Khazarian Way" (Vernadsky, *Anc. Russ.*, 350, citing the Slavic Vita Constantini).

[134] Marquart (*Streifz.*, 21) cites a short Vita Constantini in which the Khaqan is called Zacharias. There is no confirmation elsewhere.

[135] Vernadsky (350) affirms this positively.

[136] Or series of disputations. Cf. Bury, *E.R.E.*, 395, n. 2.

[137] "Culture," §4.

[138] Cf. n. 129.

biographers elected to write down. In face of the general accord of the Arabic and Hebrew traditions, especially since our investigation has throughout tended towards the rehabilitation of the latter, the negative testimony of the accounts of Abo and Constantine in regard to Khazar Judaism up to circa 861 seems of little weight.[139]

We must now discuss the important but embroiled question of relations between the Khazars and the Hungarians. Information on the subject is principally derived from a few chapters in the *De Administrando Imperio* of Constantine Porphyrogenitus. The imperial author says that 55 years earlier, i.e., in 893, assuming that his book was written in 948, the Khazars and the Ghuzz in alliance attacked the Pechenegs and drove them from their territory between the Volga and Ural rivers.[140] The date is confirmed approximately by the independent authority of Reginald of Prum, who gives 889 for the migration of the Pechenegs.[141] They passed into territory hitherto occupied by the "Turks," as the Hungarians are regularly called in the Greek sources. We may render "Magyars," though strictly this was the name of only one of their tribes. The Magyars in turn were forced to emigrate. It is the same process we have seen operating at an earlier period.

Constantine speaks as if the Magyars were obliged to withdraw before the Pechenegs twice,[142] first from Lebedia (so called after the Magyar chief or voevod Lebedias) to Atelkuzu, supposed to mean "[the country] between the rivers,"[143] and then from Atelkuzu to the region occupied by the Magyars in Constantine's time (and our own) on the middle Danube. While in Lebedia, as he further informs us, the Magyars for three years fought as allies of the Khazars, and the Khazar Khaqan gave Lebedias a noble Khazar lady as wife. She bore

139 Vernadsky and others place the final conversion of the Khazars to Judaism a few years after this.

140 *De Admin. Imp.*, c. 37.

141 *Reginonis Abbatis Prumiensis Chronicon*, cited Minorsky, *Ḥudūd*, 313, n. 2.

142 *De Admin. Imp.* c. 38.

143 Marquart, *Streifz.*, 33.

him no son. Soon after the Magyars had established themselves in Atelkuzu, the Khaqan summoned Lebedias to Chelandia (Kalancha) in the Crimea and offered to make him sole ruler (*archōn*) of his people under Khazar suzerainty. Lebedias proposed instead Almutzes,[144] whom failing his son Arpad. In the event Arpad was raised upon a shield in what Constantine calls the Khazar manner[145] and proclaimed, according to the text, *zakanos*, which perhaps is simply for Khaqan.[146] After some time the Pechenegs again attacked the Magyars and drove them westwards from Atelkuzu.

Various attempts have been made to explain the topography and chronology of the migrations of the Hungarians and to elucidate the relation with the Khazars which is involved. That this was at one time close there can be no doubt. Constantine tells us that before their migration into modern Hungary, the Magyars were joined by three tribes of people called Kabars[147] from Khazaria. It is not quite clear whether the form Kabar represents their original name or what they were called by the Magyars. They belonged to the defeated faction in a civil war and, escaping to Hungarian territory, had settled there in friendship with the inhabitants. The Kabars showed themselves more enterprising and warlike than the Hungarians, and obtained first place among their tribes. Constantine invites us to think of them as heading the migration into modern Hungary. So closely united were the two nations, or rather so influential did the Kabars become, that the Hungarians learned the language of the newcomers and had retained it up to Constantine's own time.[148] The singular fact that Khazar was

144 Or Salmutzes.

145 Constantine here (c. 38) perhaps accommodates the practice among Khazars and Kök Turks (cf. Chapter V, n. 34) to the classical elevation of the general on a shield.

146 For *zakanos* Vernadsky (*Anc. Russ.*, 214) compares the Slav word *zakon*, "law."

147 Others write "Kavars." Cf. "Cowari" in the *Chronicle of Salzburg* (cited Grégoire, "Le nom et l'origine des Hongrois," *Z.D.M.G.*, B. 91 [1937], 640).

148 *Op.cit.*, c. 39.

spoken in Hungary at least till the middle of the 10th century appears to be confirmed by vestiges of the "Lir" Turkish speech, presumably the idiom of the Khazar-speaking Kabars, which are said to be discernible still in Magyar.[149]

It has to be borne in mind that the Khazar empire in the west in the 9th century covered a wide area and included a number of tributary groups. Thus we read in the Russian Chronicle[150] that at one time the Polians, south of the middle Dnieper, were attacked by the Khazars in the wooded, hilly country along the river and obliged to pay the tribute of a sword per hearth. The Chronicle says that these swords were two-edged, and that when the fact came to the knowledge of the Khazar ruler and his elders,[151] they were alarmed, for the swords of the Khazars had but a single edge. The story refers presumably to the period before A.D. 859,[152] in which year, also according to the Chronicle, the Polians, Severians and Viatichians paid the Khazars an ermine or sable skin for each household.[153] The Khazar occupation of Kiev is undoubted. According to the Russian Chronicle, the inhabitants of this town paid tribute to the Khazars before 862.[154] Sometime later the Russian Oleg established himself there,[155] and hence no doubt, as no longer a Khazar possession, Kiev does not appear in the Reply. But the Khazars left traces of their presence which were long in disappearing.[156] Of the peoples mentioned, at least the Via-

[149] Cf. Z. Gombocz, *Die bulgarisch-türkischen Lehnwörter in der ungarischen Sprache*, *M.S.F.-Ou.*, XXX, 1912. Recently the position has been contested by J. Benzing, "Die angeblichen bolgar-türkischen Lehnwörter im Ungarischen," *Z.D.M.G.*, B. 98 (1944), 24-27.

[150] C. 12.

[151] A council of elders among the Khazars does not seem to be mentioned elsewhere. The expression "elders of our country" in the Reply of Joseph appears to have only a general significance. Yet cf. Chapters IV, n. 112; VII, n. 16, *ad fin.*

[152] Vernadsky (*Anc. Russ.*, 332) thinks that the Khazars first appeared at Kiev about 840.

[153] *Russian Chronicle*, c. 14.

[154] *Ibid.*, c. 15.

[155] *Ibid.*, c. 18.

[156] According to the "Notary of King Bela" (13th century) the men of Kiev were conquered by the Magyars under their voevod Olom (Vernadsky, *Anc. Russ.*, 332). Olom is apparently the same as Almush

tichians seem to have remained subject to the Khaqan till 965, when Sviatoslav was told by them that they gave the Khazars a piece of money per plough.[157]

About the migration of the Magyars into Hungary, in the circumstances indicated, at the end of the 9th century there is general agreement. It is their earlier history which has been the subject of debate. Marquart supposed that though they had previously given the Khazars trouble (as evidenced by an obscure remark of ibn-Rustah that the Khazars at one time had made a wall or ditch to defend themselves from the Magyars)[158] they were checked by the building of Sarkil and lost their power to injure their neighbors. Situated west of the Don, the Magyars were brought into dependence on the Khazar Khaqan. In 862 they are mentioned in a chronicle as appearing on the Danube and even in German territory.[159] Once before, circa 839, they are spoken of on the Danube.[160] The interval 840-860 corresponds, says Marquart, to the time when they were allied with the Khazars and engaged in the Khaqan's wars.[161] Thus Constantine should have said twenty, not three years, for the length of time during which the Magyars, while in Lebedia, belonged to the Khazar empire. Then, circa 860, they were thrust by the Pechenegs west of the Dnieper into Atelkuzu, extending from the Dnieper as far as the Sereth. This was a severe blow for the Khazars, and explains why it was easy for the Russians to establish themselves in Kiev. The Khaqan was unwilling to give up his empire in the west without a struggle.[162] He

---

(Almish, see n. 170 below) and *Almoutzes* in Constantine Por. The palace of Almush seems to be spoken of in the *Russian Chron.*, c. 18, as on a hill near Kiev. The situation of the cathedral of St. Elias in Kiev is also connected in the *Chronicle*, c. 27, with the Khazars. The legend of the founding of Kiev (c. 15) mentions a certain Khoriv, i.e., perhaps Horeb, with reference to the Khazar Jews (cf. Vernadsky, *Anc. Russ.*, 333). A further indication of their connection with Kiev is or was the so-called Gate of the Khazars (N. Slouschz, in *Mélanges H. Derenbourg*, 79).

[157] *Chronicle*, c. 32.

[158] Cf. n. 83, above.

[159] Marquart, *Streifz.*, 33, citing Hincmar of Rheims, *Mon. Germ. Scr.*, I, 50.

[160] *Streifz.*, 30.

[161] Cf. n. 156.

[162] *Streifz.*, 34.

was no longer afraid of the Magyars and wished to strengthen them against the Pechenegs and Russians. So, shortly after their establishment in Atelkuzu, he sent for Lebedias and offered him the kingship of the Magyars.

Bury's view is in principle the same.[163] The Magyars were displaced from their seats in Lebedia, the country between the Don and the Dnieper, by the Pechenegs, advancing from the Volga. They passed into Atelkuzu between the Dnieper and the lower reaches of the Pruth and the Sereth, and the first use they made of their new position was to invade central Europe in 862, as already indicated. Bury argues that the migration of the Magyars from Lebedia must have taken place before 862 but after 860, when Constantine is reported to have met raiding Magyars on his way from the Crimea to Khazaria.[164] This shows, according to Bury, that at that date they were still in their old habitat, Lebedia. Constantine Porphyrogenitus says that while in Lebedia they fought in the Khazar wars for three years, but this, in the view of Bury, as well as Marquart, is too short a time. Bury adopts Westberg's correction of 3 to 33, and assuming that the Magyars were in Lebedia for 33 years, fixes their arrival there, doubtfully from the Caucasus region, in 822-826.[165]

Further, Bury follows Constantine in saying that Lebedias married a noble Khazar lady before the migration to Atelkuzu and shortly after that event was approached by the Khaqan, who offered to make him ruler of all seven tribes of the Hungarians. Arpad was chosen, and thus the Khazars instituted kingship among the Magyars. Bury remarks that it is difficult to see why the Khazar government should have taken the initiative.[166] He proposes to connect the innovation with the arrival of the Kabars from Khazaria, who, as we have seen, rapidly took a leading place in the councils of the Magyars. Bury does not take into account the idea (Marquart) that the migration of the Magyars to Atelkuzu increased the danger to

[163] *E.R.E.*, 423ff.
[164] See above.
[165] *E.R.E.*, 491.
[166] *Ibid.*, 426.

the Khazars from the Russians and that it was this which determined the appointment of a Hungarian king subordinate to himself by the Khaqan, nor does he allow Marquart's suggestion that the new line of kings descended from Arpad were Khazars (Kabars).[167]

Another account of these obscure transactions is given by Grégoire, who finds that the Magyars were defeated and displaced by the Pechenegs once only, circa 894-897.[168] Their previous home between the Dnieper and the Sereth was called alternatively Lebedia and Atelkuzu. Constantine's chapter 38 appears to speak of successive migrations. In fact, it contains two distinct accounts of the same event. It is unnecessary therefore to look for an earlier habitat of the Magyars, or to attempt to find a date for their migration from Lebedia to Atelkuzu, which is a figment. When the Magyars are said to have been allied with the Khazars for three years in Lebedia/Atelkuzu this, according to Grégoire, is a misreading of *t'* as *treis*. But *t'* means 300. The Magyars were 300 years in Khazar alliance and fought with them, as Constantine says, "in all their wars."

It is thus easily explained how the Magyars could raid central Europe in 839 and again in 862. Earlier than this, we scarcely hear of them, but it does not follow that they were not in approximately the same region under Khazar suzerainty for a long time, as Grégoire says. On the other hand, the Dnieper-Sereth territory as the Magyar habitat during the whole period seems too far to the west. Vernadsky, who on the basis of toponymical and archaeological evidence accepts that the Magyars were in south Russia for long, thinks that they were centered in different areas at different times.[169] He points out that they are likely to have come in from the Caucasus area soon after the expulsion of the Bulgars (Onogundurs) by the Khazars in

[167] *Streifz.*, 52 and n. The suggestion does not seem right. Marquart elsewhere (*Str.*, 497) cites Simon de Keza, II, i, 19, according to which Almus (sic), father of Arpad, was "de genere Turul."

[168] H. Grégoire, "Le nom et l'origine des Hongrois," *Z.D.M.G.*, B. 91 (1937), 633.

[169] Vernadsky, *Anc. Russ.*, 240-242.

the 7th century, and therefore regards the time-note "300 years" as approximate only. He does not doubt that the restoration of that figure is right.[170]

We have now to consider Constantine's remarks in chapter 38 of his work already referred to, to the effect that when the Pechenegs defeated the Magyars and invaded their country, a section of the latter went off towards Persia and that these preserved the old name of the Magyars "Sabarti-asphali," by which previously all had been known. There should be some connection between the Sabarti (Savarti) and the Sāwardīyah who circa 765 sacked Shamkūr, south of the Caucasus.[171] Yet we read of the departure of the former towards Persia only after a defeat by the Pechenegs, apparently towards the end of the 9th century. Is Grégoire's view then to be modified in the sense that though the Pechenegs, as he says, defeated the Magyars once only, circa 896, the latter were earlier defeated, split in two and obliged to leave their territory by some other people?[172] Strictly speaking, according to Constantine, the people who defeated the Magyars and induced the departure of a

170 The relation between Magyars and Bulgars must at one time have been close. Even as late as Constantine Por. (10th cent.) one of the Hungarian tribes retained the name *Koutourgermat-ou* which, however it is to be explained (cf. Minorsky, *Ḥud.*, 319), is presumably the same as Kutrigur, etc., which appear among the Bulgars (Chapter III). Magyar and Bashkir (Bashgird) are in some sense interchangeable names (e.g., Marquart, *Streifz.*, 68). Németh's view mentioned by Minorsky (*Ḥudūd*, 318) is that the latter were originally a Hungarian tribe which migrated northwards from the Caucasus (see below), and according to Moravcsik (Minorsky, *ibid.*) this took place at the same time as the Onogundurs were driven westward (cf. Chapter III). In ibn-Faḍlān's time (310/922) the native Bulgar ruler on the Volga was called apparently Almish, which should be the same name as Almutzes the Magyar. Though the Turkish origin of the Magyars is contested (cf. J. Szinnyei, *Die Herkunft der Ungarn*, 1923), differentiation may largely consist in this, that the main body of the Bulgars withdrew themselves from Khazar influences at a much earlier period than the Magyars, there being at least 200 years between the westward movements of the two peoples.

171 Balādhuri, 203; cf. Mas'ūdi, *Murūj*, II, 75: Siyāwardīyah. This event took place "in the days when Yazīd ibn-Usayd [cf. above] had left Armenia."

172 Vernadsky (*Anc. Russ.*, 271) in effect answers this question by fixing on the Norsemen, but what he says is not convincing. Cf. Grégoire, *op.cit.*, 635.

section of them to the east were the so-called Kangars, the bravest of the Pecheneg tribes.[173] Grégoire has identified the Kangars with the Khazar tribes called Kabars, giving plausible reasons for this paradox.[174] Was it then after a defeat by the Kabars, circa 760, that the "Sabarti-asphali" went off "towards Persia"? It is attractive to think that the "insurrection" (*apostasia*) of the Kabars which forced them to withdraw from Khazaria, as Constantine tells us, had something to do with the conversion of the ruling section of the Khazars to Judaism circa 740. But unless the defeat of the Magyars was much later than 760, the Arpad who "a short time afterwards"[175] became first king of the Magyars could not possibly have had grandsons who were alive in the time of Constantine, circa 950. As to the fact that two grandsons of Arpad were alive at that date there is no reasonable doubt.[176] The events then of which Constantine is speaking are hardly to be connected with the raid of the Sāwardīyah in 760 or so. This merely confirms the presence of Magyars in or near the Caucasus at the time[177] and is independent of any defeat of their kinsmen in the Russian steppes. The movement of the same people "towards Persia" of which Constantine speaks took place later. It appears to be unrecorded in the Muslim sources.

As to the kingship among the Magyars, Grégoire finds that the reason for Arpad's appointment was not what is suggested by chapter 38 of the *De Administrando Imperio*—either that the Khazar wife of Lebedias had no son, or that Lebedias for some private motive, e.g., magnanimity, was unwilling to act. Rather, Lebedias was set aside because of his failure against Symeon the Bulgar, when invited by the Emperor Leo VI to attack him.[178] Against this, it is distinctly mentioned by Constantine that the Liuntis (not Lebedias) who led the unsuccess-

[173] *De Admin. Imp.*, c. 37. [174] *Op.cit.*, 638.

[175] *De Admin. Imp.*, c. 38.

[176] They are named *De Admin. Imp.*, c. 40.

[177] The Magyars appear to be mentioned in the Caucasus region by *Ḥudūd al-ʿĀlam*, §22 (written 372/982).

[178] *Op.cit.*, 635-636.

ful expedition against Symeon was the son of Arpad, and the relationship is not doubted by Bury.[179] It seems likely also that Lebedias was no longer leader of the Magyars at the time of the expedition (895). Granting that the final expulsion of the Magyars from Atelkuzu was in 896, as Grégoire says, the Pechenegs, if Reginald of Prum is to be relied on,[180] had already appeared in 889. A suitable time for direct Khazar intervention (we assume that the Kabars had joined the Magyars at an indefinite period earlier) would be after the first Pecheneg assault, not later than 890 or 891. The suggestion therefore is that from that date Arpad, not Lebedias, was in control. We thus have certain reservations in accepting what Grégoire says, but on the main issue—that Constantine is speaking of one great historical migration of the Magyars, not two—his view seems undoubtedly to be right.

We may now give some important extracts from Mas'ūdi's principal surviving work, the *Murūj al-Dhahab* (Meadows of Gold), to which reference has been frequent in the foregoing Chapters. This book was begun in 332/943 and completed in 336/947.[181] Mas'ūdi thus can tell of the Russian expedition into the Caspian at the beginning of the 4th century of the Hijrah, but knows nothing of a later disastrous attack on the Khazar capital.[182]

Paris ed., II, *7-14.* i) "The people of Bāb al-Abwāb suffer injury from a kingdom called Khaydhān.[183] This nation forms part of the Khazar empire,[184] the capital of which used to be a

[179] *De Admin. Imp.* c. 40; *E.R.E.*, 490.

[180] Cf. n. 141 above.

[181] Brockelmann, *G.A.L.*, I, 145. For the date 332/943 cf. Chapter V, ad init.

[182] Cf. Chapter IX.

[183] Not Jīdān as the Paris ed. has; cf. Chapter IV, n. 28. According to Mas'ūdi (*Murūj*, II, 39), Khaydhān was the most dangerous (*sharr*) of the Caucasus kingdoms, but had not been able to subdue certain independent Arabs who had lived between it and Bāb al-Abwāb since the conquest. The king of Khaydhān, though a Muslim and claiming Arab descent, had the title S-l-yfan which seems to be Turkish (?Khazar). Minorsky (*Ḥudūd*, 449, n. 4) compares the title Se-li-fa in the Chinese sources, citing Chavannes, *Documents*.

[184] The same phrase (*dākhilah fī jumlah mulk al-Khazar*) is used below

city 8 days[185] from the city of Bāb, called Samandar,[186] which at the present time is inhabited by a Khazar population. The fact is it was conquered in early times by Sulaymān ibn-Rabīʻah al-Bāhili,[187] and the king removed thence to the city of Atil,[188] between which and the former is seven days' journey.[189] It is in Atil that the king of the Khazars now lives. The city is in three parts, separated by a great river which comes down from the higher parts of the lands of the Turks. A branch goes out from it to the territory of the Bulgars and falls into the sea of Maeotis.[190] The city is on both banks. In the middle of the river is an island containing the king's palace.[191] His castle is on the edge of this island.[192] There is a bridge of ships to one of the banks. In this city are Muslims, Christians, Jews and pagans. . . .[193]

"As to the pagans in his territory they are of several kinds, including the Ṣaqālibah[194] and the Rūs, who live on one of the two banks of this city. They burn their dead with their horses,

---

of the Burṭās. Here the Paris ed. has *mulūk* for *mulk*, but the correct reading is in Bodleian MS. Marsh 243 (cf. Chapter V, n. 1).

185 According to Iṣṭakhri (219) it was only four days from Bāb to Samandar, which, if Samandar is Qizlar on the Terek (Chapter V, n. 26), seems more plausible.

186 In the *Tanbīh* (62) Masʻūdi states that Balanjar was the Khazar capital. Yāqūt (*Buldān*, s.v. Samandar) gives the same information as here, citing al-Azhari, i.e., abu-Manṣūr Muḥammad ibn-Aḥmad, ob. 370/980 (Brockelmann, *G.A.L.*, I, 129), while Naṣīr al-Dīn al-Ṭūsi (J. Greaves, *Binae Tabulae*, 13) agrees with the *Tanbīh* that Balanjar was the capital. Cf. Chapter III, n. 40.

187 There seems to be nothing in the sources about any attack on Samandar by Salmān ibn-Rabīʻah, for whose exploits see Chapter III.

188 The Paris ed. has Āmul for Atil, in error, throughout.

189 So Iṣṭakhri, 219. Elsewhere (227) he has eight days between Atil and Samandar.

190 The "branch" is the Don.

191 Masʻūdi agrees with the Reply of Joseph that the king of the Khazars (Khaqan) lived on an island.

192 It is not clear whether a second building is meant.

193 A reference to the Khazars as Jews follows here. It has already been given at the beginning of Chapter V.

194 Zeki Validi (*Ibn-Faḍlān*, 295-331) seems to have shown that "Ṣaqālibah" is not simply an equivalent for Slavs, but applies also to Turco-Finnish, Finnish, and even Germanic peoples. Cf. Chapter VI. Ṣaqālibah apparently for Saxones.

arms, and personal adornments. When a man dies his wife is burned alive with him, though if the wife dies, the man is not burned. If one of them dies unwed, he is given a wife after death. The women desire to be burned, in order themselves to enter paradise along with (their husbands).[195] This is also the practice of the Indians, as we have mentioned previously, except that the woman among the Indians is not burned with her husband unless she chooses.

"The predominating element in this country are the Muslims, because they form the royal army.[196] They are known in this country as Arsīyah,[197] and are immigrants from the neighborhood of Khwārizm. Long ago, after the appearance of Islam, there was war and pestilence in their territory, and they repaired to the Khazar king. They are strong and courageous, and the Khazar king relies on them in his wars. They have continued to reside in his country on certain conditions, one being the open profession of their religion, with permission for mosques and the call to prayer. Further the vizierate must belong to them.[198] At present the vizier is one of them, Aḥmad ibn-Kūyah.[199] When the king of the Khazars is at war with the Muslims, they have a separate place in his army and do not fight the people of their own faith. They fight with him against all the unbelievers. At such times about 7,000[200] of them ride with the king, archers with breast-plates, helmets, and coats of mail. Some also are lancers, equipped and armed like the Muslims. They also have Muslim judges (*quḍāt*). The custom in

[195] An eyewitness account of a ceremony which took place after the death of a Russian chief in (Volga) Bulgar territory is given by ibn-Faḍlān (§§87-92).

[196] Cf. the similar phrase in Iṣṭakhri (Chapter V), and below.

[197] The Paris ed. has the variants Lārsīyah (Lārisīyah), Arsīyah (Arisīyah), Arīsīyah, etc. It is natural to compare Ās, Āṣ, the usual later name for the Alans (from the time of the Mongol invasions, but also as early as the 9th cent., Marquart, *Str.*, 172). Cf. Chapter V, n. 21, *ad finem.*

[198] Mas'ūdi probably exaggerates here. See below.

[199] Or "Gūyah," "Guwaih," "Kuwaih."

[200] Cf. the figures in Iṣṭakhri and ibn-Rustah given in Chapter V, and on the other hand the much larger numbers in time of war, reported by the Muslim historians.

the Khazar capital is to have seven judges.[201] Of these two are for the Muslims, two for the Khazars judging according to the Torah, two for those among them who are Christians judging according to the Gospel,[202] and one for the Ṣaqālibah, Rūs and other pagans judging according to pagan law, i.e., on theoretical principles.[203] When a serious case is brought up, of which they have no knowledge, they come before the Muslim judges and plead there, obeying what the law of Islam lays down.[204]

"None of the kings of the East in this quarter has a regularly provisioned army except the king of the Khazars. All the Muslims in those parts are known by the names of these people, the Arsīyah, and the Rūs and Ṣaqālibah, whom we have mentioned as pagans. They are the army and servitors of the king.[205] In his city are many[206] Muslims, merchants and craftsmen, besides the Arsīyah, who have come to his country because of his justice and the security which he offers. They have a cathedral mosque and a minaret which rises above the royal castle, and other mosques there besides, with schools where the children learn the Qur'ān. If the Muslims and Christians there are agreed, the king cannot cope with them.[207]

"Mas'ūdi says: What we have said does not refer to the king of the Khazars, we mean the Khaqan. The fact is that in Khazaria there is a Khaqan, whose custom it is to be in the power of another king and in his house. The Khaqan is in the interior of a castle, able neither to ride forth nor to appear to the nobles

[201] Cf. Iṣṭakhri, *ibid.* According to *Ḥudūd al-'Ālam*, §50, "This king has in this town [Atil] seven judges [not "governors"] belonging to seven different creeds." The word used (*ḥākim*) reflects Iṣṭakhri (*ḥukkām*) rather than Mas'ūdi (*quḍāt*).

[202] A misconception. Some ecclesiastical code may be intended, like the "Livre Timonnier" in Russia (Platonov, *Russie Chrétienne*, 521).

[203] The words used are *qaḍāya 'aqlīyah.* Cf. ibn-Faḍlān (§20) of the Ghuzz: *la yadīnūn li'llāh bi-dīn wa-la yarji'ūn ila 'aql*, "they do not worship God, nor do they have recourse to reason."

[204] This is not confirmed by the case mentioned by ibn-Ḥawqal, see below.

[205] I have followed the text—not the rendering—of the Paris ed. with some hesitation, adopting *wa-hum* (K) for *hum.*

[206] The Bodleian MS. (n. 184) adds *kathīr.*

[207] Cf. below in the next citation from Mas'ūdi.

or commons, nor to go out from his lodging,[208] where he is with his women, neither ordering nor forbidding, nor managing affairs of state. Yet the sovereignty of the Khazars is not secured to their king save by the Khaqan being with him in the capital and in his castle. When Khazaria suffers from dearth or any calamity befalls their country or war with some other nation or any emergency, the commons and the nobles hasten to the king of the Khazars,[209] saying, We have drawn a bad omen from this Khaqan and his reign, and have augured ill of him, so kill him, or hand him over to us to kill. Sometimes he hands him over to them, and they kill him.[210] Sometimes he undertakes this himself. But sometimes he shows him mercy and protects him, as guilty of no crime or sin. This is the custom of the Khazars at present. I do not know if it originated in ancient or modern times. The dignity of this Khaqan belongs to a family among their chief men, in whom I suppose the kingship originally resided,[211] but God knows best.

"The Khazars have boats,[212] in which passengers embark with merchandise on a river above the city, which flows into its river from the country higher up. It is called Burṭās, and on its banks are Turkish nations of settled habits, forming part of

[208] This is either due to exaggeration or refers to the custom in later times. Iṣṭakhri, however, as well as the Reply of Joseph indicates that the Khaqan took part in military activities.

[209] Cf. what appears to be an instance of this above, when the "Khatun of the Khazars" allays a popular outcry.

[210] The Khaqan in certain circumstances might also dispose of the life of the Beg, according to ibn-Faḍlān (Chapter V).

[211] Zeki Validi speaks of the double kingship at some length (Ibn-Faḍlān, 292-295, also 257 and 272), as an institution among the Qara-Khānids and Avars and paralleled among non-Turkish peoples by the Shogun beside the Mikado in mediaeval Japan. The parallel between the Khazar Khaqan and the Mikado was likewise drawn by Schechter (*J.Q.R.*, III, 189). The double kingship at Sparta naturally also occurs to mind. Recently Alföldi's theory that the double kingship among nomadic peoples corresponds to leadership of the two wings of the horde, involving division of the tribes (cf. O. Pritsak, "Karachanidische Streitfragen," Oriens, III, 2 [1950], 211), has won wide acceptance. Cf. Chapter VI, n. 123.

[212] *Zawāriq*, pl. of *zauraq*. These cannot have been very small boats, for certain troublesome Hanbalites were conveyed from Baghdad as far as 'Umān in a *zauraq* in A.H. 321 (ibn-al-Athīr, VIII, 86). See below.

the Khazar empire. Their holdings stretch uninterruptedly between Khazaria and the Bulgars. This river comes from the neighborhood of the land of the Bulgars, and ships pass on it between the Bulgars and the Khazars."

Paris ed., II, *18-23.* ii) "The Rūs form several nations of different kinds, among them a sort called Lūdh'ānīyah,[213] who are the most numerous. They pass with merchandise to the countries of Spain, Rome, Constantinople, and Khazaria. Some time after A.H. 300(=A.D. 912-913) there came about 500 ships, manned each by 100 persons, and entered the strait of Nīṭas[214] which is connected with the river[215] of the Khazars. Men in the service of the Khazar king are posted there with strong defenses,[216] blocking the approach of anyone who comes from the sea and from that direction by land where a branch[217] from the river of the Khazars connects with the sea of Nīṭas. The fact is that nomads of the Turkish Ghuzz come to that region and winter there. Often the water which connects the Khazar river with the strait of Nīṭas is frozen, and the Ghuzz cross over with their horses. It is a great water, but does not give way under them, owing to the extent to which it is frozen. Thus they pass into Khazaria.[218] Often the king of the Khazars

[213] So Bodl. MS. The Paris ed. has al-Lūdh'ānah, rendered "Lithuanians." Marquart, who always reads al-Lūdhghānah (*Streifz.*, 342-353), discussed possible explanations of the word, which comes again in Mas'ūdi (*Tanbīh*, 141) as al-Kūdhkānah (De Goeje, *in loc.* suggested for the latter al-Kūdhlānah, comparing Gotland). Marquart wanted to find a connection with al-Rādhānīyah or al-Rāhdānīyah (cf. Chapter VI, n. 69). But Minorsky seems right in identifying the difficult word with al-Urdmānīyūn, the Norsemen (*E.I.*, art. Rūs). The Leiden MS. 537a (cf. Marquart, *Streifz.*, 330 ff.) has here Lūdhā'īyah.—Elsewhere in this section I have once or twice followed its readings.

[214] I.e., of Kertch.

[215] So read, not "sea of the Khazars," as both the Bodleian MS. and Paris ed. show (*nahr al-Khazar* for *baḥr al-Khazar*). Mas'ūdi elsewhere (*Murūj*, I, 273) is concerned to show that there is no connection between the Black Sea (*Nīṭas*) and the Caspian (*baḥr al-Khazar*).

[216] Tamatarkha rather than Sarkil seems to be meant.

[217] The singular is required. Cf. "that branch of water" below.

[218] Mas'ūdi appears to say that the Khazar garrison was exposed to attack from the land side by the Ghuzz before they reached Khazar territory. This is possible if a Don fortress is meant. Cf. Marquart, *Streifz.*, 341.

goes out against them, when the men he has posted there are unable to hold them. He prevents them from crossing the ice and drives them from his kingdom. In summer it is not possible for the Turks to cross.

"When the ships of the Rūs came to the Khazars posted at the mouth of the strait, they sent a letter to the Khazar king, requesting to be allowed to pass through his country and descend his river, and so enter the sea of the Khazars, which is the sea of Jurjān, Ṭabaristān and other places belonging to the barbarians, as we have mentioned, on condition that they should give him half of what they might take in booty from the peoples of the sea-coast. He granted them permission, and they entered the strait,[219] reached the river mouth,[220] and began ascending that branch of water till they reached the river of the Khazars. They descended it to the city of Atil, and passing through, came out on the estuary of the river, where it joins the Khazar sea. From the estuary to the city of Atil the river is very large and its waters abundant.

"The ships of the Rūs spread throughout the sea. Their raiding parties were directed against Jīl,[221] Daylam, Ṭabaristān, Ābaskūn on the coast of Jurjān, the naphtha country and the neighborhood of Ādharbayjān. The fact is that from the city of Ardabīl in Ādharbayjān to the sea is about three days. The Rūs shed blood, destroyed the women and children, took booty, and raided and burned in all directions. The nations round the sea were greatly alarmed, because they had not been accustomed in time past to any enemy making his way to them there, for only merchant-ships and fishing vessels used to pass therein.[222] The Rūs fought with the people of Jīl, Daylam and the coast of Jurjān and some of the inhabitants of Bardha'ah, Arrān, al-Baylaqān and Ādharbayjān,[223] and also with an officer

219 Marquart suggested that the Russians had sailed down the Dnieper and round the Crimea (*Streifz.*, 335).

220 Sc. of the Don.

221 Or Jīlān.

222 There had been Russian expeditions to the Caspian previously.

223 Some of these names are read only in the Cairo print of A.H. 1303 (in the margin of ibn-al-Athīr).

of ibn-abi-al-Sāj[224] and came to the naphtha coast in the country of Shirwān, which is known as Baku. When the Rūs withdrew from the coasts of the sea, they took shelter in islands near the source of the naphtha, a few miles from it. Now the king of Shirwān at the time was ʿAli ibn-al-Haytham.[225] The people made preparations and embarking in small boats and merchant-ships, passed over to the islands. But the Rūs turned on them, and thousands of the Muslims were killed or drowned. The Rūs continued many months in this sea, as we have described, and none of the natives who border it were able to reach them. People armed themselves against them and were on the alert for them, since the sea is populous, with many nations living on its shores.

"When they had gained enough booty and were tired of what they were about, they started for the mouth of the Khazar river, informing the king of the Khazars, and conveying to him rich booty, according to the conditions which he had fixed with them. (The king of the Khazars does not possess ships, nor are his men experienced in handling them.[226] If it were not for this, there would be great harm done to the Muslims by him.) The Arsīyah and other Muslims who were in Khazaria learned of the situation of the Rūs, and said to the king of the Khazars, Leave us to deal with these people. They have raided the lands of the Muslims, our brothers, and have shed blood and enslaved women and children. And he could not gainsay them. So he sent to the Rūs, informing them of the determination of the Muslims to fight them. The Muslims assembled and went forth to find them, proceeding downstream.[227] When the two armies came within sight of each other, the Rūs disembarked

[224] Abu-al-Qāsim Yūsuf ibn-abi al-Sāj, d. 315/928 (Zambaur, 179).

[225] He was later killed in a war against the Khazars (Minorsky, *Ḥudūd*, 406, citing Aḥmad ibn-Luṭfullah Münejjim-Bashi, *Ṣaḥā'if al-Akhbār*, iii, 174, a Turkish abridged translation [Istanbul, 1285/1868] of his Arabic *Jāmiʿ al-Duwal*, which though late [the author died in 1113/1702] uses a *Ta'rīkh Bāb al-Abwāb* of the 10th or 11th century).

[226] This should mean that there was no navy in Khazaria. Cf. Chapter VIII.

[227] I.e., on land.

and drew up in order of battle against the Muslims, with whom were a number of the Christians living in Atil, so that they were about 15,000 men, with horses and equipment. The fighting continued for three days. God helped the Muslims against them. The Rūs were put to the sword. Some were killed and others were drowned. About 5,000 of them escaped, and re-embarking on their ships, reached the other bank in the neighborhood of the Burṭās. Here they left their ships and kept to the land. Some of them were killed by the Burṭās. Others who had reached the Bulgars (who are Muslims) were killed by them. Of those slain by the Muslims on the banks of the Khazar river there were counted about 30,000.[228] There has been no repetition on the part of the Rūs of what we have described since that year."[229]

Paris ed., II, *58ff.* iii) "We say that near Khazaria and Alania, to the westward, there lie four Turkish nations, who trace their descent originally from a common ancestor. They are both nomad and settled, and are difficult of approach and very courageous. Each of them has a king. The extent of each kingdom is several days' journey. A portion of their territory touches the sea of Nīṭas. Their raids extend to the lands of Rome and almost as far as Spain. They have the mastery over all other nations in these parts. Between them and the king of the Khazars is a truce, and so with the ruler of the Alans. The region where they live is contiguous with Khazaria. The first of these nations is called Bajna [?], next to which is the second, called Bajghird [Bashkir].[230] Next to the latter is a nation called Bajnāk [Pecheneg], which is the most warlike of these nations, and next again another called Nūkardah[231] [?]. Their kings are nomads.

228 Of the original number of Russians (50,000), 35,000 are thus accounted for.

229 Mas'ūdi knows nothing of later Russian expeditions in 943 and 965, for which see Chapter IX.

230 Presumably the Magyars are here meant, cf. n. 170.

231 Perhaps for the Lombards, cf. Anqīrdah (ibn-'Abd al-Barr, *K. al-Qaṣd wa-l-Amam*, Cairo, A.H. 1350, 28), Ankubardīyīn (ibn-Rustah, 128), but Marquart pertinently asks what the Lombards have to do with the Pechenegs and Magyars (*Str.*, 66).

"After A.H. 320, or in that year,[232] they were at war with the Greeks. The Greeks possess on the frontier of their territory, near these four tribes which I have mentioned, a large Greek city called Walandar.[233] It has a large population, and is strongly situated between the mountains and the sea. The inhabitants held off the nations which we have just mentioned, and the Turks were unable to reach Greek territory, owing to the obstacles presented by the mountains, the sea and the inhabitants of the town.

"Now there was war among these four tribes, arising out of some difference among themselves in regard to a Muslim merchant from Ardabīl. He had been the guest of one of them, and the people of another nation had wronged him. Hence they were divided.[234] The Greeks of Walandar raided their homes while they were absent, took captive many children and drove away the cattle. News of this reached them while engaged in their war. They came together and rendered each other the price of blood. Then they moved in a body against the city of Walandar with about 60,000 horsemen. This was without any mustering or levy. If there had been such, they would have amounted to about 100,000 horsemen. When news of them reached Romanus, the present Greek Emperor, it being now A.H. 332, he despatched against them 12,000 horsemen, who had been converted to Christianity. These were armed with lances in the Arab fashion. They were supported by 50,000 Greeks. They advanced to the city of Walandar in eight days and encamping behind it, confronted the enemy. Though the Turks had killed many of the people of Walandar, yet its inhabitants resisted thanks to their wall, till these reinforcements reached them. When the four kings learned of the arrival of the newly-converted Christians and the Greeks, they sent to

[232] Ibn-al-Athīr, who follows Mas'ūdi, gives 322/934, and according to Georgius Monachus in 934 the Magyars overran Thrace and came as far as Constantinople (both cited by Marquart, *Streifz.*, 64).

[233] See below.

[234] The presence of merchants from the lands of Islam in east and central Europe is confirmed elsewhere, see below (ibn-Ḥawqal) and Chapter VIII.

their own lands and collected the Muslim merchants among them, who had come to their country from Khazaria, Bāb, Alania and elsewhere, and also those in the four nations who had been converted to Islam. These have no intercourse with the others except in war against the unbelievers. When the two armies were drawn up for battle, the new converts to Christianity appeared in front of the Greeks. The merchants who were in the foremost ranks of the Turks went out to them and invited them to become Muslims, declaring that if they adopted the faith of the Turks, they would escort them from their own country to the territory of Islam. They refused, however, and the two sides closed with one another." Mas'ūdi then relates the success of the Turks, their capture of Walandar and appearance in the neighborhood of Constantinople, before going farther afield in search of booty.

The contents of the first and second of these extracts are discussed fairly fully in other chapters. Here something has to be said about the third. This deals principally with an attack on "Walandar" circa 320/932 by four Turkish tribes. In the *Tanbīh*[235] Mas'ūdi says that the town of Walandar lay on the extreme eastern frontier of the Byzantine empire and gave its name to the Turkish nomads in the vicinity, who were known collectively as al-Walandarīyah and comprised the same four tribes as in the passage from the *Murūj al-Dhahab* just quoted. We are apparently to understand that after their capture of Walandar, as related in the sequel to that passage, they were known by its name. It is quite plain from both passages that Mas'ūdi thinks of the Turkish tribesmen as operating on the European side of the Bosporus and indeed far into central Europe. While there is some ground for thinking that the name Walandar is to be connected W-n-nd-r, W-b-nd-r, W-n-nt-r,[236] etc. in the Caucasus region, it seems impossible that the military operations described by Mas'ūdi took place there.[237]

235 Ed. De Goeje, 180.

236 Cf. Chapter III.

237 Zeki Validi ("Völkerschaften," 48ff) makes the "large Greek city called Walandar" into a mountain-fortress in Abkhazia.

Grégoire's suggestion that Walandar is Adrianople[238] (captured by the Bulgars in 923) fits well with the detail that the Greeks advanced to meet the Turks for eight days (? from Constantinople) and with the fact that large numbers are said to have been engaged. There is, however, agreement that the passage is embroiled. One remark may be added. It is mentioned elsewhere that some of the Imperial guard from Constantinople fell into the hands of Symeon the Bulgar, shortly before the Magyar expedition against him of which we have spoken. Among the guardsmen were Khazars, as had for a considerable time been usual.[239] Symeon is said to have sent them back to the capital with their noses cut off.[240] The savage action receives an explanation if he, or rather some of his officers, regarded the Khazars in Greek service as traitors. This would no doubt have been the case if Symeon actually had Khazars fighting in his armies, as may be implied by Mas'ūdi's story.

Ibn-Ḥawqal's narrative, as has already been said,[241] follows Iṣṭakhri's very closely, usually almost verbatim. A very interesting addition in ibn-Ḥawqal is the following story, inserted after Iṣṭakhri's account of the Khazar judges.[242]

"Frequently things occur in the decisions of the king of the Khazars which sound like a fairy-tale. Such, for example, is what al-Mu'taḍid related, when he had been mentioned in his presence and the speaker referred to him scornfully. Not so, said the Caliph. It is related of the Prophet that he said, God Whose name is great makes no man ruler of a people, without aiding him by a kind of guidance, even if he is an unbeliever. A good instance of this is that there was a certain man belonging to Khazarān,[243] who had a son, skilled in trading and experienced in buying and selling. He sent him to Inner Bulgaria and kept him supplied with merchandise. Then, after he had sent his son away, he adopted one of his slaves, brought him

[238] *Op.cit.*, 642.
[239] See below.
[240] Cf. Marquart, *Streifz.*, 521.
[241] Cf. Chapter V.
[242] Ibn-Ḥawqal, ed. De Goeje, 279ff; ibn-Ḥawqal, ed. Kramers, 391ff.
[243] The western half of the double town is intended, see below.

up and educated him. His intelligence was good in what was suggested to him in the way of business, so that the merchant called him his son, owing to his nearness to him through dutifulness and ability. The real son continued long abroad, while the slave remained in the service of his father, until the man died. Application was made by the son for supplies, not knowing that his father was dead. The slave, however, took what was sent him, without sending equivalent merchandise in return. The son wrote asking him to send supplies to the usual amount. The answer of the slave was a summons to return home, that the account might be settled for the goods which he held, and that he [i.e., the slave] might recover from him his father's property. This was enough to bring the real son back to his father's house in Khazarān, and the two of them began to dispute and argue the case with proofs. But when one of them had produced what he reckoned adequate proof, the other advanced objections which held him up.

"The dispute between them lasted a whole year. The quarrel, having gone on so long, became very involved, so that the matter ended in a deadlock. The king then undertook to try the case between the parties and, having assembled all the judges[244] and the people of the city, held a court. The contestants repeated their claims from the beginning of the dispute. The king could see no advantage for either, owing to the equality of the proofs in his sight. So he said to the son, 'Do you really know your father's grave?' 'I have been told of it,' he replied, 'but I did not see his interment, to be sure of it.' Then he asked the slave who made the claim, 'Do you know your father's grave?' 'Yes,' said he, 'I had charge of his burial.' Then the king said, 'Away, the two of you, and bring me a bone, if you find any.' The slave went to the grave, removed a bone and brought it to him. Then he said to the slave who claimed to be the merchant's son, 'Bleed yourself,' which he did, and the king gave orders that his blood should be cast upon the bone. But the blood went from it and adhered to no part of it. Next

244 Who had presumably heard the preliminaries.

the son was bled, and his blood was cast upon the bone and adhered to it. Then the king punished the slave severely and handed over him and his wealth to the son."[245]

It is clear that we have here to do with a very primitive order of ideas. As in similar cases, if this does not correspond to the stage of intellectual development actually reached by the Khazars up to the time of al-Muʿtaḍid (reigned 279/892-289/902), it evidently represents what their neighbors thought about them. Assuming that the story has a basis of truth, it tends to strengthen the impression that the superiority which the Arabs appear to have felt as a more cultured nation than the Khazars was justified. It provides also a further indication that the Khazar state was far from being administered on the lines laid down by Rabbinism. For Rabbinism the decision of a legal issue by any such method as is here ascribed to the Khazar king is out of the question.

The authenticity of some of the details at all events is doubtful. Al-Muʿtaḍid must have had the story, if it be his, at second hand. The direct participation of the king in legal proceedings, however natural in itself, is in contradiction to Iṣṭakhri's statement, actually incorporated in ibn-Ḥawqal's own account. On the other hand, in the development of the dispute the existence of judges is perhaps implied and they are said to be present—along with the townspeople—at the final trial. There is no confirmation for Masʿūdi's remark that in difficult decisions the Muslim judges were consulted and the law of Islam was followed.[246] It is of course possible that in exceptional circumstances the king (?Beg) took charge. The principal actors live in Khazarān, i.e., presumably the aristocratic western bank of the double town.[247] We cannot, however, infer that they were

[245] The point of the story should be that the *soi-disant* son alone is willing to desecrate his father's grave.

[246] Quoted above.

[247] It seems possible that the name Khazarān, as the king's residence, was sometimes applied to the Khazar capital as a whole, cf. Chapter V, n. 16. On the other hand, Khazarān occurs, apparently as a Persian plural form in -ān, for the people (Chapter I, n. 61), i.e., equivalent to al-Khazar.

Jews, for according to Iṣṭakhri not all the Muslims lived on the eastern bank, though mostly they did. The son is sent to Inner Bulgaria, i.e., probably, the territory on the Danube, present-day Bulgaria.[248] We seem already to have learned from Mas'ūdi that there were Muslim merchants on the northern frontier of the Byzantine empire.

This story of ibn-Ḥawqal seems to find an echo in the *Tuḥfat al-Albāb* of abu-Ḥāmid al-Andalusi,[249] who there speaks of his eldest son as living in Bashghird (cf. Bajghird) and says that he was there himself in 545/1150.[250] Abu-Ḥāmid's work is described as a modest account of a journey.[251] It is, however, difficult to reconcile such an estimate with some of the contents, e.g., the statement that in Bashghird there are 78 cities, each as great and prosperous as Baghdad or Iṣfahān.[252] Even if Bashghird is here Hungary, as Ferrand suggested, the exaggeration is excessive. Abu-Ḥāmid in the *Tuḥfah* claims to have traveled extensively in the lands north of the Caliphate. He had "passed from Sakhsīn [Saqsīn] in the country of the Khazars and Turks to the Khwārizm Shāh[253] three times"[254] and been "near Rome,"[255] of which he has given a description. But abu-Ḥāmid's travels may have taken him no farther than the cities of Syria and Iraq—though indeed even these were a long way from his reputed birthplace in Granada. The *Tuḥfat al-Albāb* certainly gives the impression of being to a considerable extent a collection of miscellaneous information and sensational reports gathered from earlier writers and perhaps partly invented. His son in Bashghird, whether this is Hungary, the Bashkir country in Russia[256] or somewhere else, may like his journey there be pure fiction.[257] However this may be, Mar-

[248] Marquart, *Streifz.*, 517.
[249] Ed. Ferrand in *J.A.*, 1925.
[250] Ferrand, 194-195.
[251] Brockelmann, *G.A.L.*, Sup. I, 878.
[252] Ferrand, 195.
[253] Or rather this is here a place-name. Cf. Chapter IX, n. 59.
[254] Ferrand, 87.
[255] *Ibid.*, 195.
[256] Brockelmann, *loc.cit.*
[257] A full investigation of all the books bearing his name is needed before the status of abu-Ḥāmid can become perfectly clear. A work on him is promised by Professor E. García Gómez of Madrid.

quart's suggestion that the Reply of Joseph is dependent on the *Tuḥfat al-Albāb* cannot be accepted.[258] As the book was written in 557/1162,[259] it was obviously not the source of the Reply, which as we have seen was already known in the first years of the 12th century at latest.

The Khazars in the service of Byzantium, mutilated by the Bulgar Symeon, have already been mentioned. Khazar guards in the Greek capital are spoken of at least as early as ibn-Rustah. They are represented as stationed at one of the gates of the Imperial palace, holding bows in their hands.[260] At a later period the Emperor Constantine refers to Khazar guards repeatedly. With the men of Farghānah they formed a small *corps d'élite*,[261] paying a considerable sum for the privilege of enrolment.[262] The collocation of Khazars and men of Farghānah is interesting. It is met with also at Sāmarra.[263] To the Feast of the Nativity, Constantine tells us, the Khazars of the guard were invited along with their comrades from Farghānah and elsewhere.[264] At this ceremony, as again at the Easter celebrations,[265] the Bulgars had precedence over the Khazars.[266] It seems extremely unlikely that the Khazars in the Emperor's service practiced Judaism.

We may close this chapter with some particulars about the Khazars in relation to the headquarters of Jewry in Iraq, or Babylon, as the Hebrew writers still affected to call it. In the Reply of Joseph it is stated in regard to the "end of the portents," i.e., the expected appearance of the Messiah, that the Khazars "look towards the Lord our God and towards the wise

[258] *Streifz.*, 10.

[259] Brockelmann, *loc.cit.*

[260] Ibn-Rustah, 120.

[261] *De Caer. Aul. Byz.*, ed. Bonn, 693.

[262] Bury (*E.R.E.*, 228, n. 5) calculated that a Khazar of the guards had paid £302.8.0 to be admitted.

[263] Cf. Chapter VIII, n. 67.

[264] *Op.cit.*, 749.

[265] *Ibid.*, 772.

[266] Ibn-Rustah (124) gives an extraordinary description of the state procession of the Emperor to the church of San Sophia, according to which he is accompanied by 10,000 (!) Turkish and Khazar pages, wearing gilt breast-plates and carrying gilt spears and shields. Cf. Marquart, *Streifz.*, 219.

men of Israel, the academies of Jerusalem and Babylon."[267] But it is difficult to show that Khazaria fell within the sphere of authority of the Prince of the Captivity. The Jewish traveler Benjamin of Tudela (circa 1170) found Khazars both at Constantinople and at Alexandria.[268] He is silent about Khazaria as such, presumably an indication that the kingdom no longer existed, especially if, as Adler thought,[269] one reason for his journey was to find an asylum for the Jews. When he speaks of "all the land of the Turks (Togarmim)" with Alania and Jurjān as subject to the jurisdiction of the Prince of the Captivity, this only doubtfully includes reference to the Khazar Jews.

On the other hand, R. Petahiah[270] (circa 1185) is said to have seen at Baghdad ambassadors from some northern people, called Meshech or Magog, who had become Jews and been in communication with the Head of the Academy. They welcomed poor scholars to teach their children Torah and Talmud.[271] It is by no means clear that the Khazars are meant, though both Meshech[272] and Magog have Khazar associations. R. Petahiah mentions Khazaria distinctly, and has nothing more to say of it than that he passed through the country in eight days and heard the wailing of women and the barking of dogs. There is evidence in the Hebrew sources that the Khazars were known in Iraq. The famous Sa'adiah Gaon (892-942) was certainly aware of their existence and mentions them more than once.[273] The expression "Hiram, king of Tyre" he explains not as a proper name, but as a title "like Caliph for the ruler of the

267 Kokovtsov (Introduction) notes that the academy at Sura continued to function till circa A.D. 943-953. Thereafter there was only one Babylonian academy, which is the situation represented in the Reply of Joseph (S.V.).

268 Cf. Chapter VIII, n. 64.

269 Benjamin of Tudela, ed. Adler, Introduction, xii.

270 Ed. Benisch, London, 1856, 46ff.

271 Scholars going from Egypt are specially mentioned.

272 For Meshech=Saqsīn, cf. Chapter IX. Petahiah also speaks of the country of Kedar, E. of the Dnieper. Perhaps in both cases there is a more or less arbitrary use of Biblical names, cf. Sepharad=Spain.

273 Cf. Harkavy, *Kohut Memorial Volume*, 244ff.

Arabs and Khaqan for the king of the Khazars."[274] Commenting on a Biblical verse[275] Sa'adiah notices a custom told him of the Khazar kings. In Khazaria, when a man executes an order, he does not tell the king that it has been carried out till he receives another. Again in one of his responses the Gaon mentions a certain Isaac bar Abraham, who has apparently gone from Iraq to Khazaria and settled there. In a passage from the Karaite Japhet ibn-'Ali of Basrah (*flor.* 950-980) the word *mamzēr*, translated "bastard," is significantly explained by the Khazars "who became Jews."[276] In another Karaite author, Jacob ben-Reuben (11th century) the Khazar conversion to Judaism is mentioned, and they are said to form "a single nation, who do not bear the yoke of exile, but are great warriors paying no tribute to the Gentiles."[277] Further, W. Bacher[278] thought that he had found a reference to the conversion of the Khazar king in the midrashic work *Tanna d'Bē Elijah* (*Elijah Rabbah*), circa 974.[279]

The yield of Hebrew passages is small, and none of these passages tells us explicitly that the Khazars came under the jurisdiction of the central Jewish organization. They are represented as remote from the centers of Judaism, little known, and the object of conjecture rather than observation or informed opinion. It was scarcely physical remoteness alone that determined the attitude of the Jewish authorities, as mirrored in the literary works at our disposal. The reason for official neglect of the Khazars was, at least in part, their imperfect adherence to the practice of Judaism.

274 Harkavy mentions that he has seen a reference to the Khazar Khaqan in Bīrūni (*op.cit.*, 245). I do not know what passage he refers to.

275 *Exodus*, 19.9.

276 At the time of the Exile, adds the author. He means that it happened a long time ago.

277 Both these references are taken from the same article by Harkavy.

278 *R.E.J.*, xx (1889), 144-146.

279 It is remarkable that Druthmar, the earliest Latin authority for the Judaism of the Khazars (Chapter VI, n. 10), antedates all these references by many years.

CHAPTER VIII

CAUSES OF THE DECLINE OF THE KHAZARS

IT IS PLAIN that at one time the Khazars were more powerful than any of their neighbors except the Byzantine Greeks and the Arabs of the Caliphate, yet national groups, such as the Bulgars and the Georgians, which suffered at their hands or were actually included in the Khazar empire, are still in existence, while the Khazars themselves have long since passed away, or at most are represented by vestigial communities in the Crimea, the Caucasus, and perhaps elsewhere.[1] To consider the reasons for the decline of a people is always interesting. In the case of the Khazars the process was so complete as to merit our special attention. Do the sources belonging to the period when their state flourished suggest any inherent causes of weakness?

It has been usual for those who have studied the history of the Khazars to stress that while the religion of the ruling class was Judaism, so that Khazaria during the highest stage of its development, the 9th and 10th centuries of our era, may fairly be called a Jewish state, other religions were extensively practiced. The Muslims especially, as forming an important part of the army, must have wielded considerable political power. The mixed character of the state in this respect has been pointed

[1] A "Khazar" community at Chufut Qala near Bakhchi-sarai in the Crimea last century is mentioned by Munk (*J.A.*, VI, v [1865], 544). Zajączkowski's view that the Karaites are modern representatives of the Khazars has already been referred to. The Karachais are usually spoken of as the Caucasus group having most affinities to the Khazars (e.g., Zajączkowski, "Culture," §6, quoting A. Samoyelovitch, *The Question of the Successors of the Khazars and their Culture*—in Russian [*Evreiskaya Starina*, XI, Leningrad 1924]). For the "Mountain Jews" of the Caucasus, cf. Marquart, *Streifz.*, 285. George Sava (*Valley of Forgotten People*, Faber and Faber, 1941) describes a visit to the Mountain Jews, but cannot be relied on for details.

to as a favorable feature, connected with the Judaism of its rulers, whose policy, it is conjectured, involved full liberty of religion for all. We may note in passing that the degree of civilization reached by the Khazars may easily be exaggerated.[2] It is by no means clear that the idea of religious toleration ever presented itself to them, or could have done so. Granting, however, that there was *de facto* toleration of various creeds to a greater extent than in contemporary Christian or even Muslim states—the situation rather resembling that in countries ruled by the Mongols later—we may enquire whether this lack of uniformity of faith was not a serious source of weakness. It seems trifling to suggest that the Judaism of the Khazars in itself led to a decline of the national vigor.[3] There may be more in the view that the cosmopolitan character imparted to the state by Jewish leadership endangered its survival and in the end proved disastrous.

Historically, however, the situation among the Khazars appears to have been the result of causes with which their Judaism—never in any case highly developed—had nothing to do. The parallel of the Mongol state already suggested holds. In the normal course of their expansion and consolidation as a political power, groups of varying religious allegiance came under the control of the Khazars from an early date. For the presence of Christians and Muslims in Khazaria, presumably in large numbers, Khazar Judaism does not seem in any way accountable. Nor can it be said that this was in the long run fatal. The downfall of Khazaria, as we shall see, was not the result of defeats inflicted by Byzantium or the Caliphate. There is no question of a wholesale defection to the enemy of one of the non-Jewish groups. Rather we have to take the religious

[2] H. Rosenthal in *J.E.* says: "The Chazars enjoyed all the privileges of civilised nations, a well-constituted and tolerant government, a flourishing trade and a well-disciplined standing army. In a time when fanaticism, ignorance, and anarchy reigned in western Europe, the kingdom of the Chazars could boast of its just and broadminded administration" (art. Chazars). Even Munk (*loc.cit.*) writes: "les lois des Khazares proclamaient une liberté de conscience illimitée."

[3] Marquart, *Streifz.*, 27, cf. 5.

differences among the Khazar population along with racial differences. Together these undoubtedly gave a highly diversified pattern to the Khazar empire. Nomads of the steppes, townsmen of the capital and the other cities (each no doubt with special characteristics), cultivators and hunters from the western provinces, Turks, Jews, and Arabs, as well as men of Slav and Finnish or kindred race—all were represented in Khazaria. This conglomeration of peoples and creeds is to be thought of as presided over by an aristocracy, whom we may call the White Khazars,[4] consisting of a relatively small number of partially Judaized Turks. It was apparently they who held together the various countries and provinces, which for the rest remained under native rulers. When this picture is examined, it turns out to be not unlike what we find in other empires. The diversity of population in the territory controlled by the Khazars was no doubt very great, scarcely to be matched indeed among contemporary states, but not unparalleled in other times. It would be hazardous to say that the absence of racial or religious solidarity was the prime cause of the collapse of their empire.

Our information indicates another potential source of weakness. The material resources of Khazaria were limited. Thus Muqaddasi says with reference to the steppes of the Volga in the vicinity of the capital that the country is bare and dry without cattle or fruits.[5] There is no doubt some exaggeration here. We know that the Khazars possessed camels.[6] They were perhaps of a particular breed, of small size, distinct from the "Bactrian" two-humped variety.[7] Muqaddasi himself in another place mentions the numerous sheep of the country.[8] The Khazars could mount many thousands of cavalry and must of course have had an abundant supply of horses. We read in fact

[4] Cf. Iṣṭakhri, quoted Chapter V.

[5] Ed. De Goeje, 361.

[6] As did the Bulgars apparently (abu-Ḥāmid al-Andalusi, ed. Ferrand, 238, quoting Qazwīni). The Burṭās possessed not only camels but cattle (*baqar*) as well (ibn-Rustah, 141).

[7] Zeki Validi, *Ibn-Faḍlān*, 15, n. 3, citing ibn-A'tham al-Kūfi (Sarai MS., II, 241b).

[8] Ed. De Goeje, 355.

that Marwān during the Arab invasion of Khazaria in 119/737 destroyed large studs in the course of his march up the Volga.[9] According to ibn-Sa'īd, the riding animals of the Khazars were unusually big[10]—presumably referring to the horses. The steppe was cultivated at least in places. Both the Hebrew Correspondence and Iṣṭakhri, as already noted, speak of the fields extending round the capital for a distance of 60 or 70 miles. Gardīzi also mentions the fields (*kishtzārha*) of the Khazars.[11] Crops of millet[12] and rice[13] were raised. Muqaddasi says that they used an inferior kind of bread called "*athīr*."[14] Fish formed part of the staple diet.[15]

As to other products of the country, Muqaddasi[16] and Gardīzi[17] both mention abundant honey, to which Gardīzi adds excellent wax. But Iṣṭakhri says more than once that the honey and wax which came from Khazaria were brought from elsewhere and reexported.[18] We hear also of Khazar fox-skins.[19] Iṣṭakhri makes clear that furs of different kinds, as well as the honey and wax, reached the Khazars from Russian and Bulgarian territory.[20] According to ibn-Rustah[21] and Gardīzi[22] there was much honey in the Burṭās country, upstream from Khazaria proper towards the Bulgars. As far as furs are concerned, though the sables of Bulghār were famous[23] and there was a special fox-skin of Burṭās,[24] where marten-skins were also

[9] Bal'ami, 540, cf. Zeki Validi, *Ibn-Faḍlān*, 304.

[10] Cf. Chapter I, n. 35. Ibn-Sa'īd accounts for the fact by the cold, wet climate.

[11] Ed. Barthold, 96.

[12] Cf. the story in Mīrkhwānd quoted D'Herbelot, art. Khozars.

[13] Cf. Iṣṭakhri, quoted Chapter V.

[14] Ed. De Goeje, 361, cf. 359.

[15] Iṣṭakhri, *ibid.*

[16] Ed. De Goeje, 355.

[17] Ed. Barthold, 96.

[18] *Ibid.*

[19] Abu-Ḥāmid al-Andalusi, 212.

[20] Iṣṭakhri (*ibid.*) mentions beaver-skins in two places. In one of these (Similarly the beaver-skins etc.) the Chester Beatty MS. (cf. Chapter V, n. 7) substitutes "otter-skins."

[21] Ed. De Goeje, 141.

[22] Ed. Barthold, 97.

[23] Abu-Ḥāmid al-Andalusi, *loc.cit.*

[24] The Chester Beatty MS. of Iṣṭakhri (n. 20) speaks of *julūd al-tha'ālib al-mansūbah ila Burṭās*. We learn from Mas'ūdi (*Tanbīh*, 63) that the black fox-skins of Burṭās were the best in the world. Mas'ūdi mentions other kinds, the red and the white, etc. The Caliph Mahdi, while living at Rayy before his accession, had tested different furs for

important,[25] a large quantity must have come from Russia, which of course unlike the first-named regions lay outside the Khazar empire. Ibn-Khurdādhbih[26] and following him ibn-al-Faqīh[27] speak of the beaver-skins and black fox-skins brought by the Russian merchants first to Constantinople, then by way of the Black Sea, the strait of Kertch and the Don to the Volga and the Khazar capital.[28] Here the Khaqan or his representative obliged the Russian merchants to pay a tenth of the value of their wares. These merchants continued their journey down the Volga to the sea, selling what they had brought, including sword-blades as well as furs, in Jurjān, on the opposite side of the Caspian. Ibn al-Faqīh also speaks of Khazar spears.[29] That the Russian merchants always traveled so far afield is unlikely. We find them in ibn-Faḍlān's time among the Volga Bulgars.[30] Undoubtedly they proceeded from there as far as Khazarān-Atil, as is explicitly stated by Iṣṭakhri[31] and ibn-Ḥawqal.[32] Mas'ūdi mentions them on one bank of the Khazar capital.[33] The traffic was probably lucrative, for there was a demand for these northern furs among the Muslim upper classes,[34] but it is doubtful if it can be reckoned a great Khazar asset, except in so far as consignments could be taxed.

Iṣṭakhri mentions other commodities reaching Khazaria. There was a trade in lead, also with the Russians, but this was perhaps obtained at Kiev by Khazar merchants.[35] More im-

---

heat, by the simple process of placing them in sealed bottles out of doors on a cold night, and satisfied himself by inspection that the black fox fur, which alone had not frozen in its container, was the warmest (!). The *qāḍi* of Aleppo Bahā'-al-Dīn ibn-Shaddād (d. 632/1234) as a very old man wore a mantle of Burṭās fur (ibn-Khallikān, II, 530).

25 Ibn-Rustah, 141.

26 Ed. De Goeje, 154. Cf. Chapter V, n. 44.

27 Ed. De Goeje, 270-271.

28 *Khamlīj madīnat al-Khazar*, according to ibn-Khurdādhbih. Ibn-al-Faqīh (*loc.cit.*) has "khalīj al-Khazar" "the gulf of the Khazars," which should be corrected.

29 Ed. De Goeje, 50 (cited Zeki Validi, *Ibn-Faḍlān*, 210).

30 Cf. Chapter VII, n. 195.

31 *Ibid.*

32 Ed. De Goeje, 281; ed. Kramers, 392.

33 Chapter VII.

34 Mas'ūdi, *Tanbīh*, 63; cf. n. 24 *supra*.

35 Iṣṭakhri, *ibid.*

portant was the brisk traffic in slaves down the Volga, which is mentioned by Iṣṭakhri and confirmed by ibn-Faḍlān.[36] The fact that the Russians brought slaves from the north is certain, and it is further implied that there was a slave-market in the Khazar capital,[37] whence they frequently passed to Muslim lands.[38] This need not surprise us, for in other parts of Europe at a much later date slavery survived.[39] Iṣṭakhri says that to sell their own children into slavery was repugnant to the Jews and Christians of Khazaria, as well as to the Muslims, and was only practiced by the heathen.[40] There was evidently no objection to the institution as such, nor did the Judaism of the rulers lead them to discountenance it. On the contrary, the existence of slaves was tolerated, and they were bought and sold openly like other marketable goods. A further stage of the slave-route from the north seems to have been at Darband (Bāb al-Abwāb).[41] Similarly in western Europe at the same period, in France and Spain, a traffic in slaves from north to south was kept up, and there is no reason to suppose that the part said to have been played by Jews is an invention of malicious enemies.[42]

If the Darband-Nāmah is to be trusted, the Khazars controlled silver and gold[43] (or copper)[44] mines in the Caucasus region, from the produce of which their troops on this frontier are said to have been paid. The province of Samandar, lying

[36] §§77, 83.

[37] Iṣṭakhri's words are "The slaves found among the Khazars are idolaters, who permit the sale of their children and the enslavement of one another," (quoted above, Chapter V). The sales evidently took place in Khazarān-Atil. Abū-al-Fidā' (217) says that Saray (see below) was a great slave-market.

[38] Iṣṭakhri, ed. De Goeje, 305, speaks of Ṣaqlab and Khazar slaves with those of other Turkish nations reaching Khwārizm, cf. Zeki Validi, *Ibn-Faḍlān*, 309. Cf. also ibn-Ḥawqal, ed. De Goeje, 281 (the Khwarizmians raid the lands of the Bulgars and Ṣaqālibah, plunder them and take them captive).

[39] In Scotland in A.D. 1178 and as late as A.D. 1258, see Cunningham's Church History of Scotland (1882), I, 110.

[40] *Ibid.*, following the remark quoted in n. 37, above.

[41] Cf. *Ḥudūd al-ʿĀlam*, §36. 40.

[42] *Maqqari*, I, 92.

[43] Ed. Kasem Beg, 477: "Near Qizilyār was a gold (?) mine, and at the source of the Terek a silver mine."

[44] Cf. Kasem Beg, 465.

on the northern side of the mountains, appears to have been rich and fertile. Iṣṭakhri and ibn-Ḥawqal refer to its gardens and vineyards, the latter numbering many thousands.[45] Elsewhere too in Khazar territory gardens were perhaps to be found, as mentioned by Gardīzi.[46] It is evidently not possible to give a systematic account of the material resources of the Khazars. The most important of these were doubtless livestock and the produce of their agriculture. There appears to have been no surplus of either. We have the striking statement of Iṣṭakhri that the only Khazar export, as distinct from what was brought into the country and reexported, was isinglass.[47]

Their activity as merchants seems none the less to have been considerable. Mas'ūdi's remark about the king of the Khazars possessing no ships (*marākib*) and his men being unaccustomed to their use[48] is misleading in this connection. Barthold has pointed out that it is inconsistent with what Ḥilāl al-Ṣābi' says about a sea-wall in the Caspian at Darband, the purpose of which was "to prevent the ships (*marākib*) of the Khazars from entering."[49] Further, Mas'ūdi's account of the Khazars shows some contradiction in saying explicitly elsewhere that the Khazars had vessels (*zawārīq*) in which people went upstream from the capital,[50] and that ships (*sufun*) passed back and forward between the Khazars and the Bulgars.[51] This is said also by Muqaddasi,[52] and ibn-Faḍlān mentions that when a ship (*safīnah*) put in on Bulgar territory, coming from Khazaria, the Bulgar chief (Yaltawar, Elteber) rode down in person and took a tenth of the cargo for himself.[53] It is not men-

[45] Iṣṭakhri's figure (quoted Chapter V) is 4,000, increased in the text of ibn-Ḥawqal to 40,000.

[46] Ed. Barthold, 96. [47] Iṣṭakhri, *ibid.* [48] Quoted, Chapter VII.

[49] Hilāl al-Ṣābi' ed. Amedroz, 217, cited *E.I.*, art. Khazar. This information apparently refers to the time of the celebrated vizier 'Ali ibn-al-Furāt (c. 288/900), for which Hilāl al-Ṣābi' (c. 390/999) cites contemporary authorities. But it could mean that the sea-wall was originally built against the Khazars by Anūshirwān (cf. Qudāmah, 261, speaking of al-ḥā'it fi-al-baḥr), in which case it may be legendary (cf. Chapter I). We do not in general hear of Khazar attacks by sea against the Caspian coast (but cf. below, Chapter IX).

[50] Quoted, Chapter VII. [51] *Ibid.* [52] Ed. De Goeje, 365. [53] §77.

tioned that the Bulgars possessed ships, and we can hardly suppose that the main traffic on the Volga was in Russian hands.[54] There was at all events a bridge of ships (*sufun*) across the river at the Khazar capital, according to Mas'ūdi's express statement.[55] The context of his remark first quoted is the Russian expedition down the Volga in 301/913, and possibly what he means is that the Khazar ruler had no navy to match the invaders. Alternatively, he has been misinformed. It is interesting to find that Mas'ūdi's opinion is still apparently current.[56]

The probable fact, however, is that Khazar ships sailed not only on the Volga but also on the Caspian, the so-called Sea of the Khazars, making use of the sea-routes indicated by Iṣṭakhri,[57] if not threatening Darband, as envisaged by the passage from Hilāl al-Ṣābi'. According to the short account of Khazaria in the Letter of Ḥasday, ships of the country appear to have come as far as Constantinople (circa 340/950), hardly from the capital on the Volga (using the Don-Volga passage), but rather from the Black Sea port of Tamatarkha (Phanagoria, Taman, Tmutorakan), where long before, as we have seen,[58] the Greek Emperor Justinian II found a vessel to take him back to his own country. It should be observed that the sea of Azov as well as the Caspian was sometimes called the Sea of the Khazars.[59]

Khazar trade was also carried on by land. The caravan route round the head of the Caspian must always have possessed considerable importance, though we can speak with some certainty only of the linking of Khazaria with Khwārizm.[60] In

[54] Mas'ūdi (*Tanbīh*, 62) says that large ships ply on the Volga (nahr al-Khazar) from Khwārizm and elsewhere with merchandise and all sorts of wares.

[55] See Chapter VII.

[56] Sava (cf. n. 1) mentions the remark of El-Musidi (*sic*) that the kings of the Khazars had no ships on the Caspian, for the Khazars were no sailors.

[57] Ed. De Goeje, 226-227.

[58] Chapter VII. [59] Mas'ūdi, *Tanbīh*, 138.

[60] It is implied by ibn-Faḍlān that there was regular traffic along the route his party took. Cf. n. 38.

ibn-Ḥawqal's story[61] a firm in the capital had its representative, as we should nowadays say, in Inner Bulghār, apparently Bulgaria on the Danube. According to the Jewish traveler Ibrahīm ibn-Ya'qūb (10th century) the Khazars spoke the language of the Ṣaqālibah.[62] If so, they hardly learned it except by travel in the country. We read in Mas'ūdi that there were Muslim merchants from Khazaria on the northern frontiers of Byzantium.[63] The 12th century traveler Benjamin of Tudela says that he met merchants of Khazaria in Constantinople and also in Alexandria.[64] Ya'qūbi remarks that among the profusion of merchandise which reached Baghdad were goods from Khazaria.[65] Russian merchants, as we have seen, made direct contact with the lands of the Caliphate, and the Jewish Rādhānīyah[66] visited the Khazar capital as well as Baghdad and other Muslim cities. Khazar merchants perhaps shared in the traffic. Ya'qūbi mentions a street or quarter in Sāmarra where the Khazars lived near the Turks and the natives of Farghānah.[67] It is not necessary to suppose that these were exclusively mercenary soldiers.

In regard to manufactures, isinglass has already been mentioned. This was evidently prepared from the catches of fishers along the Volga. We know at least that in the Khazar capital Muslim craftsmen were numerous.[68] It is remarkable, however, that according to Iṣṭakhri no clothing was produced in the country.[69] The long coats worn by the Khazars,[70] also their tunics, were imported from the Muslim lands or Byzantium. The Ghuzz (Oguz), who were politically dependent on the Khaqan, also bought clothing from the Muslims.[71] The absence

[61] See Chapter VII.

[62] Bekri, 39 (quoted Marquart, *Streifz.*, 192). Cf. T. Kowalski, *Relatio Ibrahīm ibn-Ja'ḳūb de itinere Slavico quae traditur apud al-Bakri* (*Monumenta Poloniae Historica*, *Nov. Ser.*, T.I., v, Cracow 1946).

[63] See Chapter VII.

[64] Ed. Adler, 12, 76. Asher's ed. omits the references.

[65] *K. al-Buldān*, 234. [66] Cf. Chapter VI, n. 69. [67] *Buldān*, 262.

[68] Mas'ūdi, quoted Chapter VII. [69] See Chapter V.

[70] Iṣṭakhri (*ibid.*) contrasts the long or full coats of the Khazars with the short coats of the Russians.

[71] Ibn-Faḍlān, §25.

of this important industry, though it can scarcely have been so complete as Iṣṭakhri says, suggests that Khazar manufacturing was at a low level of development,[72] and at the same time we have an indication of the cultural influence exerted on Khazaria by the Empire and the Caliphate.

The archaeologist T. J. Arne found that the Khazar civilization was strongly influenced by Persian models, and that, for certain, imitations of Sassanid craftsmanship were frequent in Khazaria.[73] Similarly he found that plates intended for the ornamentation of belts, discovered in western Russia and Sweden, bear characteristic Persian designs, and must have been manufactured within the limits of Khazar cultural influence, the type having reached the Khazars from Persia.[74] Again he speaks of clasps (fibules) of supposed Byzantine origin having been imitated in the countries dominated by Khazar culture after the 8th century.[75] But all this is less remarkable than the claim made by the well-known numismatist Zambaur that for the most part the imitations of Arab coinage, which are numerous in archaeological finds in Sweden and Russia, were systematically made in Khazar mints.[76] Arne objected to Zambaur (*a*) that such imitations have hardly been found in Khazar territory, and (*b*) that a mould of stone intended to counterfeit Samanid money has been found well beyond the Khazar sphere of influence at any time (Vitebsk). This stone mould from Vitebsk is mentioned by Barthold in connection with Russian minting.[77] It is of course striking that we have no native Khazar coinage[78] and almost impossible to

[72] Iṣṭakhri (213) mentions a regular trade between Astarābād and Khazaria, of which the silk produced in the neighborhood of Astarābād evidently formed an important part, no doubt already manufactured.

[73] *La Suède et l'Orient* (*Archives d'Études Orientales*, 8), Upsala 1914, 96-99.

[74] *Ibid.*, 157. [75] *Ibid.*, 143.

[76] E. von Zambaur, "Orientalische Münzen in Nord- und Ost-Europa" (Vortrag in der Wiener Numism. Gesellsch., 1902) and "Die Münzen der Chazaren" (*Monatsblatt der numism. Gesellschaft in Wien*, VIII, 1911), cited Arne, *ibid.*, 86.

[77] *Découverte*, 196, cited R. Hennig, "Die mittelalterische arabische Handelsverkehr in Ost-Europa," *Der Islam*, B. 22 (1935).

[78] Cf. Chapter VI, n. 18.

think that the commercial activity of Khazarān-Atil proceeded by primitive barter. But meantime no evidence seems to have accrued in favor of Zambaur's view.

The general impression which we gain from the facts given is that Atil was an important *entrepôt* for commerce, east and west, as well as north and south. The prosperity of Khazaria evidently depended less on the resources of the country than on its favorable position across important trade-routes. What we can learn of the fiscal system confirms this. Taxation seems to have fallen lightly on the natives, and perhaps the Khazars proper (White Khazars) had only the obligation of military service. According to Iṣṭakhri, whom we have so often quoted, the king had no right to the property of subjects.[79] This may refer to the Beg, for elsewhere it is said that the Khaqan enjoys payments and fixed subsidies which come to him from dues falling on the whole population.[80] In any case, the Beg was the chief executive power, and presumably his expenditure was the greatest single item on the Khazar budget. Iṣṭakhri's words are to the effect that the sources of the king's income were twofold, customs-dues and tithes on merchandise coming along the land and water routes of the country, and tribute levied in kind within the empire.[81]

As to the dues mentioned by Iṣṭakhri as the first source of revenue, we have already seen that the Russian merchants trading in furs and swords paid the Khazar Khaqan or his representative a tenth of the value of their cargoes. All the Russian trade appears to have been similarly taxed,[82] and we may perhaps infer that this tithing was general, i.e., incident also upon the Muslims who visited Khazaria. Possibly connected with the collection of such customs and the incidental legal cases was the function of two Khazar officials who appear to have occupied the same post, in ibn-Faḍlān's time a certain Khazz[83] and in Mas'ūdi's one Aḥmad ibn-Kūyah[84] (Gūyah). Both these

[79] See Chapter V, n. 17.
[80] Ibn-Ḥawqal, ed. Kramers, 396.
[81] See Chapter V, above.
[82] Ibn-Ḥawqal, ed. Kramers, 392.
[83] Chapter V, n. 99.
[84] Chapter VII, n. 199.

men certainly held an important office, which cannot have been that of Beg. They were Muslims, and the Beg was naturally a Jewish Khazar.[85] Nor apparently was either of them a regular Muslim judge. The Muslim judges, like those of the Jews and the Christians, were two in number,[86] but Khazz and later Aḥmad ibn-Kūyah were evidently independent in their own sphere, whatever it was.

The second of these two sources of revenue can be illustrated from the Russian Chronicle. We have already mentioned the Slav nations, Polians and others, who paid tribute to the Khazars in the 9th and 10th centuries.[87] Evidently the Khazars took as the unit of taxation of subject peoples the individual hearth or plough, and assessed payment at a sword or a sable-skin, or in other cases a piece of money per plough or per head.[88] The incidence of this was perhaps irregular, when a commodity was required, or as often as it was convenient to collect it. The Bulgar chief (Yaltawar, Elteber) similarly contributed a sable-skin for each household.[89]

Such then appears to have been a main part of the public revenue of the Khazars—customs and the tribute of subject peoples. The private wealth of the country, derived principally from commercial enterprises in the handling of imports, was no doubt considerable. But, as we have indicated, there were no large natural resources available for export, nor a steady supply of the products of home industry. The Khazar economy in these circumstances appears as highly artificial. Everything was dependent on political prestige and military strength. It is evident that heavy customs would be no more welcome to traders than the tribute in kind to the nations from whom it was taken. To secure both the one and the other force, or at least a display of force, was necessary. It appears from the

[85] Ibn-Rustah, Iṣṭakhri, see Chapter V. [86] Mas'ūdi, Chapter VII.

[87] See Chapter VII. [88] *Russian Chronicle*, cc. 12, 14, 15, 32.

[89] Ibn-Faḍlān, §77, cf. §56. Each household contributed a sable skin which the Yaltawar then transmitted to the Khazar authorities. Yāqūt (*Buldān*, art. Bulghār) quoting the same passage has for "sable-skin," "ox-hide," evidently in error.

Russian Chronicle that the Slav tribes were willing as soon as an opportunity offered to throw off their dependence on the Khazars.[90] We gather from ibn-Faḍlān that the central authority was no more popular in the east of the empire, among the Bulgars and Ghuzz.[91] As long, we may say, as the Khazars were able to hold their conquests as they had won them, by force of arms, such a system might work. But when once their military power had been broken, the whole economy was liable to collapse.

At some point this is undoubtedly what happened. Payments in kind and customs-dues must have in consequence ceased for the time being to flow into the treasury. Disaffected groups would seek their independence. A weakened central authority would be unable at once to send men to reoccupy strategic points formerly held, or to enforce the old contributions. The machinery of the state having been thus violently thrown out of gear, to set it in operation again was evidently found to be impossible. We may suppose that if the bases of their power in the area between the Volga and the Caucasus had been more richly endowed by nature, or if they had had a pronounced bent for the industrial arts, the Khazars might have been able to consolidate what remained to them, to win back by diplomacy or reconquer piecemeal the revolted peoples and gradually to reestablish their political and commercial system in their former territory. These conditions were, however, lacking.

Though the racial and religious differences within the Khazar empire no doubt contributed to its disintegration, the main cause of this is to be looked for in its character as an agglomeration of adjacent territories, without natural frontiers and far from self-sufficient, incapable in the long run of forming a permanently stable political and economic unit. For a time these territories had passed into the hands of a military aristocracy, the Judaized Khazars, who so long as their horsemen could control what lay between their garrisons and towns wielded a redoubtable power. In respect of geographical ex-

[90] C. 15. Cf. Platonov, *op.cit.*, 497, 498. [91] §§36, 48, 78.

tent and political importance Khazaria, as we have seen, for a period challenged comparison with the greatest nations of that age. This state of affairs did not last indefinitely. The military control was interrupted, and Khazaria fell, lacking a more permanent bond of unity. It is part of the paradox that some of the smaller groups which had been absorbed or threatened by the Khazar empire have survived till the present time. The Khazars themselves, once "incomparably more powerful"[92] than their neighbors are a barely remembered name.

For all this the parallel of national states in east and west is not particularly instructive. The history of France, for example, or Persia, is traceable continuously through periods of expansion and decline back to a remote antiquity. Ancient Gaul and Iran have still their living representatives in important communities of the present day. It is otherwise with the nomad empires which, rising with incredible rapidity to a leading place among the nations, have for a time seemed almost to dominate the stage of history and then as quickly passed away. Such were the empires of the Huns and the Mongols. We know in detail how the latter swept over much of the civilized world, engulfing great states in their vast territories. Yet the tide receded, and the Mongols came to be of far less importance than nations like Persia, which they had overthrown, or China, to which they gave a dynasty. The adventure of the Khazars was on a much smaller scale than that of the Mongols. The numbers of their fighting forces and the areas which they controlled were never even approximately as great, their rise to power nothing like so spectacular. Yet the eclipse of the Mongols, or of the Huns before them, permits us to understand the fate which overtook the Khazars, apparently in the 10th and 11th centuries of our era.[93]

[92] The words are Barthold's (*E.I.*, art. Bulghār) of the Khazars with reference to the Bulgars.

[93] The Russian archaeologists have already excavated a number of Khazar or kindred sites. Unfortunately detailed information is not easy to procure. A résumé of what had been done during a dozen years up to 1914, especially at Verkhni Saltov on the Donetz, was given by T. J.

Arne (*op.cit.*), with references to the Russian literature. Poliak (*Khazaria*, c. 5) discusses some of the finds. Other work which should be of importance has been done at Bulghār, cf. Smolin, *Po razval. drev. Bulgara*, Kazan 1926 (cited by Minorsky, *Ḥudūd*, 461, n. 2) and at Suwār. It is clear that at the latter site valuable results have already been obtained. Zeki Validi (*Ibn-Faḍlān*, 75 n.) cites A. P. Smirnov for the information that a two-storey palace of the 10th century was found and many coins. These should throw light on the question of Khazar reproduction of Arab coins raised above. There is a short notice in *Sovietskaya Archaeologiya*, IV (Moscow 1937). It may be added that there is now a good deal less than agreement that Verkhni Saltov is a Khazar site (Vernadsky, *Anc. Russ.*, 157, 241, cf. 269, citing N. Fettich, *Die Metallkunst der landnehmenden Ungarn*, *Archaeologia Hungarica*, 21 (1937) and A. Zakhanov and V. V. Arendt, *Studia Levedica*, same series, 16 (1935). Cf. also Chapter VI, n. 105.

CHAPTER IX

THE END OF THE KHAZAR STATE

HAVING in a previous chapter discussed where the weakness of Khazaria presumably lay, we have now to attempt to trace the course of events which led to its disintegration and final disappearance. In the middle of the 10th century, as we gather from the accounts of Iṣṭakhri (320/932) and Mas'ūdi (332/943), as well as from the Khazar Correspondence, the state was flourishing. If the Cambridge Document is to be relied on, the Khazars at this period had won notable military successes, especially against the Byzantines.[1] Yet evidently a serious threat to their empire had already developed in the consolidation of the Russian power. How early the Russian raids down the Volga began cannot be stated positively.[2]

At an early period the Russians seem to have been under Khazar influence, at least culturally.[3] The Russian Khaqan is mentioned in Arabic sources,[4] but also in the Latin account of a Byzantine embassy to the Emperor of the West in A.D. 839[5] (Chacanus). The title may have been borrowed from the Kha-

[1] See above, Chapter VI.

[2] The passage in Bal'ami (ed. Dorn, 500), according to which the Russians were dangerous in the Caucasus lands as early as 22/642-643, has been discussed in Chapter III. There is a parallel notice, as regards the date for the appearance of the Russians, in the well-known *Futūḥ al-Shām* (attributed to Wāqidi, *ob.* 207/823, but hardly written till the time of the Crusades), which mentions that Ṣaqālibah fought on the Greek side at the battle of the Yarmūk (15/636) under a Russian king Qanāṭīr (ed. of A.H. 1335, I, 97). This is pure phantasy. For the name, cf. Qanṭāl in Niẓāmī (Chapter I, n. 61).

[3] This matter has recently been discussed in Russia, in connection with the views of Artamonov, who favors Khazar influence on the Russians (see *The Times*, 12.1.1952).

[4] Ibn-Rustah, 145, etc. (cf. Marquart, *Streifz.*, 200).

[5] *Annales Bertiniani*, a. 839, *Mon. Germ. Scr.*, I, 434 (cited Marquart, *Str.*, 202).

zars, as Marquart thought.[6] Further, the Russian king in ibn-Faḍlān's time (A.D. 922) had like the Khazar Khaqan a lieutenant (*khalīfah*) who led the armies, waged war with enemies and represented him to his people.[7] Zeki Validi does not doubt that this office among the Russians was derived from the Khazar system.[8] It would seem that ibn-Faḍlān had heard about the Russian voevods.[9]

By the 9th century at all events the Russians were strong enough to occupy a part of the Khazar territory in the west, including the city of Kiev (?A.D. 878).[10] We begin to hear of specific Russian expeditions down the Volga. In the time of the Sayyid Ḥasan ibn-Zayd, ruler of Ṭabaristān between 251/864 and 270/884, the Russians reached the Caspian and made an unsuccessful attack on Ābaskūn on the eastern shore.[11] In 297/910 sixteen of their ships appeared at Ābaskūn, and this time they wasted and looted the settlement and the surrounding country, carrying off or killing a number of the Muslims.[12]

The presence of these ships on Caspian waters is probably to be explained by the commercial advantages accruing to Khazaria while the Volga route was kept open. As already noticed, Russian ships passing through the country were liable to a tax of a tenth on their cargoes. This is stated by ibn-Khurdādhbih, writing circa A.D. 840, but the traffic is vouched for long after the Khazars lost their western territory to the Russians.[13] We shall probably be right in assuming that the ships which raided Ābaskūn reached the Caspian with the goodwill of the Khazar government.

The situation, however, was changing. Shortly after the second of these recorded attacks on Ābaskūn, the Khazar authorities were requested to allow a Russian war-fleet to make use

[6] Zeki Validi ("Die Schwerter der Germanen," 32) thinks that the title Khaqan came to the Russians from their earlier association with the Huns (?).

[7] Ibn-Faḍlān, §93.

[8] *Ibn-Faḍlān*, 253.

[9] Cf. N. K. Chadwick, *Beginnings of Russian History*, 115.

[10] Cf. Vernadsky, *Ancient Russia*, 368.

[11] Ibn-Isfandiyār, 199.

[12] *Ibid.*

[13] Iṣṭakhri-ibn-Ḥawqal, cf. Chapters V and VIII, n. 82.

of the Volga water-way.[14] The Russians disclosed their intention of raiding the Caspian seaboard and offered the Khazars one half of the booty which they hoped to take, in return for this concession. Their application was granted.

Gibbon in one place remarks "In the history of the world I can only perceive two navies on the Caspian."[15] He is thinking of a Macedonian fleet under the admiral Patrocles, which is said to have descended the Oxus from central Asia,[16] and of the fleet and army conducted by Peter the Great from the neighborhood of Moscow to the Caspian coast. The Russian armament of which we now speak was also a war-fleet on an extensive scale. It contained 500 ships each manned by 100 men—clearly for those days a powerful striking force. We do not know why the Khazars allowed the Russians entry to the heart of their country, when they were strong enough to withhold it, as the sequel indicates. Perhaps their authorities, who had no special love for the Muslims, were well content by doing nothing to make a substantial gain at their expense, for of course the Russian expedition was directed at the Muslim provinces on the Caspian. In any case the decision of the Khazar leaders must seem to have set a highly dangerous precedent.

On this occasion (circa 913)[17] the Russians raided at a number of points along the Caspian shores, and even got as far as Ardabīl in Adharbayjān, three days' journey inland. An account of what happened in the sequel has already been given in Chapter VII from Mas'ūdi. Since then, to Mas'ūdi's knowledge, there had been no repetition of any such attempt on the part of the Russians. But in the year in which he was writing (332/943) they were again in the Caspian, with results only less disastrous, it would seem, to themselves and others. The expedition of 943 was indeed on a great scale. The Russians

[14] Mas'ūdi, see above.

[15] *Decline and Fall*, c. 46, n. 5.

[16] There is now doubt as to whether this expedition was ever made.

[17] The expedition perhaps took place in 301/913, soon after the accession of the Russian Igor (Minorsky, *E.I.*, art. Rūs). Mas'ūdi says "some time after 300," while ibn-Isfandiyār, *loc.cit.*, gives the date as A.H. 298.

captured Bardha'ah and held it for a year.[18] More than a generation afterwards their camp outside the city was still remembered.[19] They suffered on this occasion not at the hands of the Khazars—whose part in the affair can only be conjectured—but in consequence of a pestilence, which broke out among them, leaving them much weakened and unable to resist the Musāfirid, Marzabān ibn-Muḥammad, ruler of Adharbayjān, who drove those who survived to their ships. In what happened the pious Muslim saw a divine judgment for the miseries they had brought.[20]

Apparently another stage in the relations between the Khazars and the Russians is marked by the Reply of Joseph. The time came, it would seem, when the authorities in Khazarān-Atil denied a passage down the Volga to these foreign war-fleets. In the Short Version of the document Joseph says, as already quoted: "I live at the estuary of the river [Atil], and do not allow the Russians who come in ships to pass to [the Arabs] and likewise I do not allow any of their enemies who come by land to pass to their country. I fight a difficult war with them. If I allowed them, they would destroy all the country of the Arabs as far as Baghdad." This is somewhat expanded in the Long Version, as follows: "Know and understand that I live at the mouth of the river. By the help of the Almighty I guard the mouth of the river and do not allow the Russians who come in ships to come by sea to go against the Arabs, nor any enemy by land to come to [?Bāb al-Abwāb].[21] I fight with them. If I allowed them for one hour, they would destroy all the country of the Arabs as far as Baghdad and the

18 Ibn-al-Athīr, VIII, 134-135; ibn-Miskawayh, II, 62-67, who gives a valuable account, evidently from eyewitnesses, of the proceedings of the Russians when they reached Bardha'ah.

19 *Ḥudūd al-'Ālam*, 29, 144. Ibn-al-Faqīh mentions that a large number of villages, mostly ruinous, in the neighborhood of Bardha'ah were said to have been occupied by the Russians (Meshed MS., fol. 189a in Kahle's typescript translation, cf. *Z.D.M.G.*, B. 88 [1934], 43ff).

20 Yāqūt, *Buldān*, s.v. Rūs.

21 Lit. "to a gate" (*sha'ar*). Elsewhere in the Reply the expression Sha'ar Bāb al-Abwāb is used (Chapter VI, n. 111).

country of. . . ." Towards A.D. 960 we are to understand that the Khaqan regarded it as essential to keep the Russians from coming down the Volga to the Caspian.

Evidently these expeditions provided the Russians with stories to tell and defeats to avenge. More significantly, they must now have had a good idea of the nature and strength of the Khazar defences. The customary traffic apparently yet continued down the Volga.[22] The Khazars for their part may have decided to close the river to Russian war-fleets after the expedition of 332/943. The change of policy indicated had perhaps as a consequence the last and greatest of the Russian expeditions into Khazaria, which took place some twenty years later.

According to the *Russian Chronicle*, Sviatoslav, ruler of the Kievan Russians, in A.D. 965 defeated the Khazars under their Khan (Khaqan) and took their town of Biela Viezha. Then, having subdued the Yas and the Kasogs, he returned to Kiev.[23] Biela Viezha, "White Tower,"[24] is usually identified with Sarkil.[25] Marquart, however, contended that the Khazar capital, sometimes called in the earlier Arabic references al-Bayḍā', "the White," is here meant.[26] For an attack on the Khazar capital indeed it is more natural to think of a fleet than a land force. Nothing is said in the *Chronicle* about ships having been used by Sviatoslav in 965. Yet there is independent evidence that about this time Khazarān-Atil actually fell to the Russians.[27] We should of course expect some reference to such an important matter in the *Chronicle*. It is difficult to see why the capture of a Don fortress, assuming Sarkil to have been such, should be recorded and the other event omitted. Marquart's view therefore has considerable initial probability.

About the destruction of Khazarān-Atil there can be no doubt. Ibn-Ḥawqal, here supplementing Iṣṭakhri, states in more

[22] Cf. n. 13.

[23] *Chronicle*, c. 32.

[24] Or "White Tent," cf. Marquart, *Streifz.*, 3.

[25] The Greek equivalent of Sarkil "Aspron Hospition" has a similar meaning, cf. Chapter VII.

[26] *Streifz.*, 1-3; cf. Chapter III for al-Bayḍā'.

[27] See below.

than one place that it was destroyed by the Russians, giving the date 358/968-969. Speaking of the town of Bulghār on the Volga he says: "It was well known as a trading center for these countries [sc. the northern lands]. Then the Russians sacked it in A.H. 358, utterly destroying Khazarān, Samandar and Atil."[28] Again with reference to the fur trade he remarks: "So it was till the year 358, because the Russians [i.e., in this year] destroyed Bulghār and Khazarān."[29] A third passage of ibn-Ḥawqal indicates the source of his information about the Russian attack. "There were in Samandar many gardens, and it is said that it used to contain 40,000 vineyards.[30] I asked about it in Jurjān in the year 358 of a man who had recently been there. He said: There is not an alms for the poor in any vineyard or garden, if there remains a leaf on the bough. For the Russians descended upon it, and not a grape nor a raisin remained in the place. The Muslims used to live there, as well as other categories of people of different faiths, including idolaters, but they emigrated. Owing to the excellence of their land and the richness of growth three years will not pass till it becomes again what it was."[31] This passage suggested to Barthold that the date 358/968 properly refers not to Sviatoslav's raid, but to the visit of ibn-Ḥawqal to Jurjān.[32] Certainly, assuming ibn-Ḥawqal to have formed the impression that the devastation of Khazaria had taken place earlier in the same year, we should thus have an explanation for the discrepancy of the dates.

Zeki Validi attempts to find in the passage express confirmation that the Russian invasion was in 965, as the *Russian Chronicle* has it,[33] but this involves him in translating the words of ibn-Ḥawqal or his informant: "Owing to the excellence of their land . . . scarcely three years *have passed* till it has recovered." This is quite inadmissible,[34] and probably superfluous. Marquart has shown that the Yas and Kasogs mentioned in the *Russian Chronicle* as defeated by Sviatoslav after

28 Ed. Kramers, 15.
29 Ed. Kramers, 392.
30 Iṣṭakhri's figure is 4,000, see Chapter V.
31 Ed. Kramers, 393.
32 *E.I.*, art. Bulghār.
33 *Ibn-Faḍlān*, 319, n.
34 Text: *fa-lan tamḍiya thalāth sinīn.*

the capture of Biela Viezha are in all likelihood the Alans (As) of the Caucasus and the Kashaks, who also lived in or near the Caucasus and were perhaps subject to the Khazars.[35] We should thus take it that the *Chronicle* not only puts Sviatoslav's successful Khazar expedition in the right year, A.D. 965, but also indicates something like the full extent of his operations.[36] Incidentally it may be noted that the old theory which connects the Khazars with the Cossacks,[37] if it could be shown that Cossack=Kasog, would have a certain justification.

Marquart afterwards resiled to the view that Sviatoslav's raid mentioned in the *Chronicle* only extended to Sarkil. His later position was that the devastation of Khazaria spoken of by ibn-Ḥawqal actually happened in A.D. 968 but that those responsible for it were not Kievan Russians subject to Sviatoslav, and hence it is not mentioned in the *Russian Chronicle*.[38] As to this, it is of course possible that Sarkil might have been taken from the Khazars in 965 and their country devastated in 968 by other enemies, without any record of the major event being in the *Chronicle*. But on the whole the other solution commends itself. The notice in the *Chronicle* for A.D. 965, as Marquart's analysis itself showed, has a wider scope than the neighborhood of a Don fortress, and appears to record Russian victories in Khazar territory north of the Caucasus—exactly what we are to understand from ibn-Ḥawqal. There was not more than one wholesale devastation of Khazaria in these years. That the date which we have assigned to it (965) is correct, in spite of ibn-Ḥawqal, is further borne out by another passage in the Arabic sources.

[35] *Streifz.*, 2, 479. Marquart adduces Kashak and Kāsakīyah (*Tanbīh*, 184); *Kasakhia* (Con. Por., *De Admin. Imp.*, c. 42); Reply of Joseph, S. V. Bāṣa, correct in L. V. Kāṣa; etc. According to *Ḥudūd*, §48, Kāsak was in Alania. The form *Kasāk* also occurs; cf. Chapter IV, n. 104. See V. Minorsky, "Transcaucasica," *J.A.*, t. 217 (1930), 73-90.

[36] The assumption of Grätz (*Geschichte*, v, 307) that Sviatoslav raided Khazaria in 965 (Sarkil) and again in 968 (Atil and Samandar) does not depend on sources. Cf. *infra*.

[37] E.g., Fr. Bodenstedt's *Völker des Kaukasus*, Frankfurt-am-Main 1848, 238ff. Cf. most recently O. Pritsak, *Der Islam*, B. 30 (1952), 113, in a review of Grønbech, *Komanisches Wörterbuch*.

[38] *Streifz.*, 474.

Ibn-Miskawayh (d. 421/1030) records in his history that in 354/965 a body of Turks descended on Khazaria, whereupon the Khazars invoked the help of the people of Khwārizm. They were at first refused, he says, on the ground that they were Jews, being told that if they wanted help they must become Muslims. The Khazars agreed to this, and all adopted Islam in consequence, with the exception of their king.[39] The interpretation of "the people of Khwārizm" here has evoked differences of opinion. Marquart[40] suggested the Arsīyah of Khazaria, who were originally from Khwārizm,[41] while Zeki Validi thinks that the Khwarizmians proper may be meant.[42] There is, however, general agreement now that the "Turks" of this account are the Russians, and so cautious a writer as Barthold allows that the great expedition of Sviatoslav is here intended.[43] Ibn-Miskawayh's notice has been taken over by ibn-al-Athīr (d. 630/1234), who adds that the king of the Khazars later became a Muslim.[44] We may safely regard it as independent confirmation for 965 as the year in which the Russians invaded Khazaria.[45]

39 Ed. Amedroz, II, 209. According to Barthold (*E.I.*, art. Khazar) the notice comes from Thābit ibn-Sinān. The latter died 365/975 (Brockelmann, *G.A.L.*, I, 324).

40 *Streifz.*, 4.

41 Strictly according to Mas'ūdi "from the neighborhood of Khwārizm," see Chapter VII.

42 *Ibn-Faḍlān*, 320, cf. xvii.

43 *E.I.*, art. Khazar.

44 VIII, 196. The notice appears also (with the date A.H. 254 in error) in Dimashqi (d. 727/1327), ed. Mehren, 263.

45 Yet another construction has been put forward by Vasiliev (*Goths*, 120ff), which would save ibn-Ḥawqal's date 968 for the destruction of Khazarān-Atil, etc., while involving an alteration to 963 for Sviatoslav's raid on Biela Viezha (Sarkil). This is based on the Fragments of the Gothic Toparch (Chapter VI, n. 144), which afford astronomical evidence, as Vasiliev claims, following Westberg, fixing the date January, 963. According to the construction, the Khazars in 962 had attempted to restore their former predominance in the Crimea (which had come to an end owing to the growing power of the Pechenegs, and the support given them by the Byzantines at the beginning of the 10th century, Vasiliev, *ib.* 116), using a large number of horse and foot and devastating 10 cities and more than 500 villages in the Crimea (*ib.* 129). In the winter of 962 the Gothic toparch started out for Kiev to get help from Sviatoslav and his Russians, and the date already mentioned, January 963, found him on the return journey (*ib.* 130). (This alleged visit to Sviatoslav in Kiev is a particularly venturesome suggestion. It seems to

The statement of ibn-Miskawayh must be treated with caution, but Barthold does not appear to be justified in dismissing it as unhistorical. We have seen that a Khazar ruler under stress of circumstances appears to have made a temporary profession of Islam.[46] It is at least not impossible that something similar happened when Muslim help was necessary to repel the Russian invasion. There are persistent references to the Khazars as Muslims after this date. Muqaddasi, speaking of their town of "Khazar," evidently Khazarān,[47] says that at one point the inhabitants left it and went down to the coast, but that they have now returned (sc. circa 375/985, when Muqaddasi wrote) and are no longer Jews but Muslims. It should be observed that Muqaddasi has heard of the Russian invasion but apparently does not connect the evacuation of Khazarān with what then occurred. Though the claims made for him as "one of the greatest geographers of all time"[48] could hardly be substantiated by his remarks on Khazaria, in which he is perhaps not very happily inspired,[49] what Muqaddasi says about this evacuation and return is to be accepted. It is confirmed and to some extent amplified by ibn-Ḥawqal, who is quite unlikely to have been

---

be pure conjecture.) Sviatoslav marched in consequence against the Khazars in the following season (963), taking their town of Biela Viezha, as the *Chronicle* says, but *sub anno* 965, and proceeding against the Yas and Kasogs. Later in the 60's of the 10th century the Russians "crushed" the Khazar state (*ib.* 134).—If a Khazar attack on the Crimea actually took place in 962, this can hardly be the same event as is described in the Cambridge Document, which, if genuine, should have been written earlier.—L. Schmidt *Geschichte der deutschen Stämme bis zum Ausgang der Völkerwanderung*, Munich 1934, 400 (cited Vasiliev, *ib.*, 129 n.), thinks that the Khazars destroyed Doros in 962, after which the Toparch made Mankup his chief city.

[46] See above, Chapter IV, etc.

[47] Muqaddasi, 361; cf. De Goeje *in loco.*

[48] Barthold, *Turkestan* (*G.M.S.*), 11.

[49] He speaks of Bulghār "where the nights are short" (cf. Iṣṭakhri, quoted above, Chapter V) as nearer the Caspian than the Khazar capital. Zeki Validi attempts to defend this (*Ibn-Faḍlān*, 206) as referring to a new settlement of the Bulgars on the lower Volga after the destruction of their towns higher up. But Muqaddasi did not have a clear idea of Khazarān-Atil (cf. Marquart, *Streifz.*, 3), and is probably confused about the site of Bulghār.

his source. Ibn-Ḥawqal first tells us[50] that when the Khazars of Atil fled from the Russians, while some went to the island of Siyāh Kūh on the eastern shore of the Caspian, others withdrew southward to one of the islands off the "Naphtha Coast,"[51] where the Russians in 301/913 had maintained themselves very successfully against the Shirwān Shāh of the day.[52] After the Russian attack of 965, the surviving Khazar chiefs appear to have made contact with a later Shirwān Shāh and to have secured his assistance. For ibn-Ḥawqal goes on to say:[53] "At present [i.e., presumably towards 367/977] the Bulgars, Burṭās and Khazars have been left nothing by the Russians except a few ruins which they had already despoiled. They descended upon everything and attained in all their neighborhood more than they dreamed of. I have been informed that many of [the Khazars] have returned to Atil and Khazarān with the support of Muḥammad ibn-Aḥmad al-Azdi, the Shirwān Shāh, who helped them with his army and people. They [i.e., the Khazars] expect and hope to enter a pact with them [? the Russians][54] and be under their authority in a part of the continent which they will appoint for them." That the help of the Shirwān Shāh involved the acceptance of Islam is not impossible, if the affairs of the Khazars were as bad as they seem to have been.

Muqaddasi further reports that he has heard that Ma'mūn raided the Khazars from Gurgānj (Jurjānīyah) and having conquered them, summoned them to Islam[55]—yet another reference to the Khazars as Muslims with Khwārizm as the reputed source and possibly at about the same time. For Barthold, who indeed again denies that the notice is historical,[56] refers it not to the 9th century Caliph Ma'mūn, but to Ma'mūn ibn-Muḥammad, ruler first of Gurgānj (Jurjānīyah) and then of all

[50] Ed. De Goeje, 282.

[51] Called by ibn-Ḥawqal "the island of Bāb al-Abwāb," cf. Marquart, *Str.* 2, n. 1.

[52] Cf. above, Chapter VII.

[53] Ed. Kramers, 397.

[54] This is clearly understood by the other text (De Goeje, 286), i.e., the remark about the Shirwān Shāh is taken as parenthetic.

[55] Ed. De Goeje, 361.

[56] *E.I.*, art. Khazar.

Khwārizm after A.D. 995.[57] A connection of Khwārizm with Khazar history at this period is elsewhere attested by Muqaddasi, who remarks that the Khazar towns are frequently occupied by the ruler of Gurgānj.[58]

Though the Shirwān Shāh Muḥammad ibn-Aḥmad al-Azdi is an anomalous figure,[59] there is no reason to doubt ibn-Ḥawqal's circumstantial story that the Khazars were brought back by help from Shirwān. We shall see the Shirwān Shāh and the Khazars again in contact, and the erroneous characterization of the king of the Khazars in ibn-Isfandiyār as "Shirwān Shāh" is probably not fortuitous.[60] The connection with Khwārizm somewhat later as given by Muqaddasi is also to be retained, though we are at present uninformed about the circumstances. Khazar relations with these Muslim states after the Russian invasion must meantime remain a matter of speculation. It is, however, evident that after 965 we can no longer speak with confidence of an independent Jewish state on the Volga. The picture of Khazaria as represented in the pages of ibn-Rustah and ibn-Faḍlān, of Mas'ūdi, Iṣṭakhri and ibn-Ḥawqal, varies considerably, but the main traits—the double kingship, the seclusion of the titular head of the state, the profession of Judaism—confirmed by other sources, remain the same. Later we have no such descriptions by Muslim authors and no positive evidence from elsewhere that the characteristic institutions of Khazaria were maintained. The Khazar kingdom in its traditional form hardly survived the Russian invasion. On the other hand, it seems unlikely that the profession of Islam be-

[57] There is no indication elsewhere of any such exploit on the part of the Abbasid Caliph Ma'mūn. Marquart gets into great difficulty in trying to find a place for it in Ma'mūn's Caliphate (*Str.*, 3-4). On the other hand, it is surprising to find that Muqaddasi can refer to Ma'mūn ibn-Muḥammad in 375/985 simply as Ma'mūn, as though there was no possibility of confusion with anyone else, ten years before he attained the dignity of Khwārizm Shāh (cf. Minorsky, *Ḥudūd*, 174).

[58] Ed. De Goeje, 371 n.

[59] So Barthold, *E.I.*, art. Shīrwānshāh. Cf. Minorsky, *Ḥudūd*, 406. His title "Ṣāḥib Shirwān Shāh" (Ibn Ḥawqal, ed. De Goeje, 250, 254) is not necessarily *vitium ab auctore commissum* (De Goeje). Rather Shirwān Shāh here may be a place-name. Cf. Chapter VII, n. 253.

[60] *Loc.cit.*

came general among the Khazars who returned to their country, as our sources appear to say, though in their councils new influences were no doubt now preponderant. These were hardly Russian. Sviatoslav appears to have left the Khazar country after his victory there,[61] as Barthold says,[62] to join forces with the Byzantines against the Danube Bulgars.[63] Barthold regarded this fact as of great importance for Russian history. If the Russians had remained on the Volga, they would certainly, he thinks, have submitted to Muslim culture.

From ibn-Ḥawqal and Muqaddasi[64] it appears that an attempt was made to rebuild the Khazar capital, but this cannot have been permanently successful, in view of the indication that in the time of Bīrūni (d. 440/1048) Atil lay in ruins.[65] Presumably the town of Saqsīn took its place. The probability is that Saqsīn was identical with or at least at no great distance from Khazarān-Atil, and the name may be the older Sārighshin revived.[66] We cannot be certain that Saqsīn was in existence even in Bīrūni's time. He does not mention it.[67] Certainly it was flourishing in the 12th century, when abu-Ḥāmid al-Andalusi (circa 1150) speaks of it in connection with Khwārizm, having Bulghār 40 days above it, and it is mentioned by

[61] Ibn-Ḥawqal says expressly that the Russians left (ed. De Goeje, 14).

[62] In his work *The Discovery of Asia* (1925), in Russian (French transl. by B. Nikitine, Paris 1947, 195).

[63] According to Gibbon (c. 55) Sviatoslav on this campaign was accompanied by Khazars.

[64] Cited above.

[65] Cf. Zeki Validi, *Ibn-Faḍlān*, 206.

[66] So Minorsky, *Ḥudūd*, 453, n. 5, citing Westberg. Poliak ("Conversion," §2) attempts to show that Saqsīn was in the neighborhood of modern Stalingrad (Tsaritsyn), and supposes that it was an important city before A.D. 965 (*ib.* §1). Yet although it is in itself likely that there was a Khazar strong point controlling the Don-Volga portage (Khamlīj, according to Vernadsky, *Anc. Russia*, 215), there is nothing precise in our sources. Poliak's ground for thinking that Saqsīn existed before 965 is that it is mentioned in Josippon and the Book of Jashar, following Harkavy's identification of certain forms in these works with Saqsīn (in *Skazanya evreiskikh pisatelye o Khazarakh*, St. Petersburg 1874, 57, 73, 75), notably Meshech. But this is evidently very precarious. Meshech= Saqsīn, if a real identity seems to belong to a later period (cf. Chapter VII, n. 272).

[67] Zeki Validi, *Ibn-Faḍlān*, 206.

Qazwīni.[68] Aḥmad al-Ṭūsi speaks of Saqsīn as a large town on the Volga, surpassed by none in Turkestan.[69] It figures frequently in the history of the Mongol invasions,[70] and eventually was flooded out of existence,[71] perhaps by natural causes. Bātu, grandson of Chingiz Khān, built Sarāy, properly Sarāy-i Bātu, on its site.[72] Saqsīn may originally have been built and named by the Khazars. We cannot but regard it as significant that in none of the passages where it is mentioned (except in Qazwīni, who is secondary) is it said to be held by them, or to have had a Jewish population.[73]

It has frequently been stated that the Russian invasion entailed the destruction of the Khazar state. Thus abu-al-Fidā' (A.D. 1273-1331) speaks of "Khazaria and the Khazars, who were destroyed by the Russians,"[74] presumably with reference

[68] Ed. Ferrand, 87, 117. Cf. n. 73. A similar notice in Qazwīni, ed. Wüstenfeld, II, 402, who gives Saqsīn as a "great and populous town of the Khazars," occupied by "40 tribes of the Ghuzz."

[69] Zeki Validi, *Ibn-Faḍlān*, 205. Aḥmad Ṭūsi lived in the 12th century.

[70] Juwayni (I, 31) mentions that the fief of Chūchi, eldest son of Chingiz Khān, extended from Qayāligh (? near Lake Balkhash, cf. Minorsky, *Ḥudūd*, 277) and Khwārizm to the extremities of Saqsīn and Bulghār. Rashīd al-Dīn (ed. Blochet, 18) says that when Ogodāy succeeded Chingiz Khān, he sent 30,000 cavalry against the Khwārizm Shāh, and then despatched Kūkotāy and Sūbotāy Bahādur with a similar force against Qipchaq, Saqsīn, and Bulghār (cf. Juwayni, I, 150). Again, on the death of Ogodāy, Bātu Khān ibn-Chūchi refused to come to the Mongol assembly from his western fief of Saqsīn and Bulghār (Juwayni, I, 205). We may compare also Juwayni, I, 222; "When Qāan [i.e., Ogodāy] was established on his throne, he subdued all the territories near him, the remnant of Qipchaq, the Alans, Ās and Russians, as well as Bulghār, M-k-s and others. The Volga Bulgars had evidently survived to Mongol times, but scarcely so the Khazars. Minorsky has shown ("Caucasica, III," *B.S.O.A.S.*, 1952, xiv/2, 221ff) that M-k-s is for the Alan capital in the Caucasus.

[71] So Bakūwi (Brockelmann, II, 213), cited by Westberg (*Beiträge*, 290).

[72] So Waṣṣāf, cited Zeki Validi, *Ibn Faḍlān*, 204, n. 1, apparently from Juwayni (I, 222).

[73] According to abu-Ḥāmid al-Andalusi (Ferrand, 116) there were in Saqsīn in his time learned Muslims, mosques, markets, and palaces. Prisoners from Saqsīn were in the hands of the Turks (Qipchaqs or Ghuzz, cf. Qazwīnī, n. 68). The date should be circa 545/1150.

[74] Ed. Reinaud and De Slane, 203.

to the great disaster of 965. In modern times Kunik,[75] Howorth,[76] and Marquart,[77] to mention only a few names, have said the same thing.[78] The evidence which we have already cited, showing at most that the Khazars who survived returned to their country, does not conflict with what may be called the orthodox view that Khazaria ceased to have an independent existence in 10th century. On the other hand, at least since the time of Rasmussen,[79] some have held that the Khazar state finally disappeared only in the 13th century as a result of the Mongol invasions. More recently this has been argued vigorously, notably by Poliak.[80]

Before considering the further evidence, one general observation may be made. The ultimate source of all statements that the Russians destroyed Khazaria in the 10th century is no doubt ibn-Ḥawqal, whose words on the subject we have already given. Ibn-Ḥawqal, however, speaks as positively of the destruction of Bulghār on the middle Volga. It is quite certain that at the time of the Mongol attacks in the 13th century Bulghār was a flourishing community. Was the ruin of Khazaria also temporary?[81]

The *Russian Chronicle* mentions that in A.D. 986 Khazar Jews presented themselves before Vladimir, apparently at Kiev, and invited him to accept their faith. The long account given by the *Chronicle* represents Latins, Greeks and Muslims, as well as the Jews, arguing their respective creeds before the Russian ruler.[82] It is regarded by several critics as an interpola-

[75] Bakri, ed. Kunik and Rosen, St. Petersburg 1878, 73-74 (cited Westberg, *Ibrahīm ibn-Ya'qūb*, 79). Later Kunik adopted the view that Khazaria continued to exist (cf. Westberg, *Beiträge*, 292).

[76] "The Khazars, were they Ugrians or Turks?" *3rd Int. Congress of Orientalists* (1879), II, 138.

[77] *Streifz.*, 5, 27.

[78] Professor Minorsky has pointed out that the absence of any mention of the Khazars in connection with the migration of tribes from Mongolia in the 11th century can indicate that they had ceased to exist as an important state in the second half of the 10th century (*Marvazī*, 103).

[79] *J.A.*, I, v (1824), 306.

[80] "Conversion" and *Khazaria, passim.*

[81] Cf. Poliak, "Conversion," §1.

[82] *Chronicle*, c. 40.

tion.[83] Yet the presence of Khazar Jews in Kiev at this time is in itself unobjectionable, and the situation of Vladimir makes the fact of some kind of religious enquiry before his baptism at least a possibility. Grätz has argued that the story is authentic. He makes the Jewish missionaries come to the Russians from the Crimea, where, according to him, after the attack on Khazaria in 965 the survivors had been organized under a Khaqan with Bosporus (Kertch) as capital.[84]

For these statements Grätz relied on a document which he quotes, and which mentions the coming in A.M. 4746=A.D. 986 of "the envoys of the prince of the Russians and M-sh-k" from the city of Kiev to "our lord David, the Khazar prince," apparently resident in Tamatarkha (Taman), to make enquiry about religious matters, in the same year as, according to the *Russian Chronicle*, the Khazar Jews came before Vladimir. The correspondence of these dates is remarkable. It is difficult to avoid suspecting that this document, which passed through the hands of Firkovitch, and has, it may be said, quite a modern sound, was composed *ad hoc*.[85] Of the Khaqan David, as Grätz calls him, and an independent Khazar state in the Crimea there is no confirmation elsewhere. If, however, our suspicions are unwarranted, the man referred to as "our lord David" may have been the Khazar chief (hardly the Khaqan)[86] at Tamatarkha, which perhaps passed out of Khazar hands only in A.D. 988, when, according to the Russian Chronicle, Mstislav was installed there.[87]

Thereafter Khazaria and the Khazars continue to be mentioned. In A.D. 1016, according to the 11th century Cedrenus, a good authority, the Greek Emperor sent a force to Khazaria which in conjunction with the Russians rapidly subdued the country, having defeated its ruler, Georgius Tzul, in the first

[83] Cf. the remarks of Leger, *Chronique dite de Nestor*, 389.

[84] *Geschichte*, v, 341-342.

[85] Cf. *J.E.*, art. Jacob b. Reuben (Abraham ben-Simha of Kertch, the alleged author, is a personage invented by Firkovitch). On the other hand, Grätz says "Jedes Wort dieser Urkunde trägt den Stempel der Echtheit an sich" (*ib.* v, 476).

[86] Cf. n. 88 below.

[87] *Chronicle*, c. 43; cf. c. 52.

encounter.[88] It is not surprising to read of a Khazar with the Christian name Georgius. In earlier times (8th century) there was a *ṭarkhān* George,[89] and Christianity among the Khazars, as we have seen, is widely attested. The name Tzul is possibly to be connected with Tzur or Ṣūl, as the pass of Darband was sometimes called.

The question of where this expedition was directed is of some importance. According to Grätz, it operated against the Khazar state in the Crimea whose existence he finds vouched for in his document already quoted, and destroyed the last vestige of the Khaqan's rule.[90] According to others, the combined attack of Greeks and Russians in 1016 was made against the coasts of the sea of Azov.[91] Kutschera did not doubt that the Caucasus region is indicated. This is perhaps borne out by the statement of Cedrenus that after the defeat of Georgius Tzul, the ruler of "upper Media" was obliged to offer his submission. Kutschera supposes that the latter, "Sennacherib" according to our text,[92] was a Khazar ruling somewhere in the Caucasus. For a Jew at all events a less likely name is difficult to imagine.[93] Perhaps on the whole we are justified in thinking that the expedition of the Greeks and Russians against Khazaria had the Caucasus as its main objective. In Tamatarkha from A.D. 988, when Mstislav was settled there, the situation is obscure.[94]

The Khazars are mentioned in the *Russian Chronicle* for A.D. 1023 when Mstislav is said to have marched against his brother Jaroslav, accompanied by the Khazars[95] and Kasogs.[96] The Khazars of Tamatarkha may possibly be intended.

88 Ed. Bonn, II, 464. Grousset (*L'empire des steppes*, 237) speaks of Georgios Tzoulos as Khan of Taman.

89 Biography of Stephen, Bishop of Sudak, cited Poliak, "Conversion," §2.

90 *Geschichte*, v, 342.

91 Cf. Poliak, "Conversion," §1; *Khazaria*, 210.

92 Cf. Sanḥārīb ibn-Sawādah al-Ṣanārī (Chapter VII, n. 126), a Christian prince ruling in the Caucasus in the 10th century (V. Minorsky, "Caucasica IV," *B.S.O.A.S.*, 1953, xv/3, 519, 522, 526).

93 For the Talmudic opinion of Sennacherib, cf. *Sanhedrin*, 94b.

94 Cf. Vasiliev, *Goths*, 134. 95 Cf. n. 63, above. 96 *Chronicle*, c. 52.

We have also a reference in ibn-al-Athīr under 421/1030 to what he calls "the raid of Faḍlūn the Kurd against the Khazars."[97] Barthold identified this personage with Faḍl ibn-Muḥammad of the Shaddādid dynasty, who ruled at Ganjah,[98] now Elizavetpol in Transcaucasia. According to ibn-al-Athīr, after an attack on the Khazars he was returning to his own country, when they fell upon him unexpectedly and killed more than 10,000 of his troops. It is added that they recovered the booty which Faḍlūn had taken from them and captured the equipment of the Muslims. This last remark may have importance, as Poliak notes,[99] for it appears to indicate that the Khazars were unbelievers, quite as in their hey-day. Though Marquart accepted the notice as it stands, making it the last appearance of the Khazars in history,[100] Barthold, doubting the reading, suggested that not the Khazars but Georgians or Abkhazians are meant. The fact of large numbers being apparently involved might itself exclude the Khazars of the new dispensation, after A.D. 965.

Later still, Oleg, grandson of Jaroslav, was in Tamatarkha in A.D. 1078, according to the *Russian Chronicle*. Next year he is said to have been captured by the Khazars and taken by sea to Constantinople—as if the Greeks were playing off against each other the two contestants for power—Russians and Khazars—in Tamatarkha. About the same time his brother Roman was killed by the Polovtsi. In 1083 Oleg, having arrived from Greece, took vengeance for his brother on "the Khazars, who had advised his death and declared against him."[101] It is possible that the Khazars are here to be understood as directing the actions of the Polovtsi, as they had controlled so many foreign groups in earlier times. The two at all events are not identical. In 1106 a raid of Polovtsi was driven off by certain Russian chiefs acting with "Ivan the Khazar."[102]

97 IX, 142.

98 *E.I.*, art. Khazar. Cf. for Ganjah, infra.

99 "Conversion," §1 (cf. *Khazaria*, 218).

100 Cited Barthold, *ibid.*

101 *Chronicle*, cc. 70-71.

102 *Russian Chronicle*, *s. anno*, cited N. K. Chadwick, *Beginnings*, 128. Mrs. Chadwick is surely right in remarking that the combination is significant. Cf. below, n. 151.

Thus Khazaria and the Khazars are mentioned long after the disaster which befell them in 965. Barthold, who canvasses the evidence, finds that the Russian texts "refer to the Khazars as subject to the Russians," adding that the subjection can apply only to a part of the Crimean peninsula and the peninsula opposite it.[103] In principle this is similar to Klaproth's view, who a long time ago supposed that the Khazars lost the Crimea in the first years of the 11th century and were thereafter confined to the Caspian and lower Volga.[104] Are we to understand, then, that where there is no specific mention of Russian predominance, notably in the central provinces of the old Khazar empire, they retained their independence? The fact is that between the Volga and the Caucasus we hear nothing for certain about them after the Russian attack of 965, except that the survivors returned.[105] It is evidently hazardous to argue that since there is no suggestion that the lower Volga was in Russian hands, the Khazar state did not disappear but continued, weakened indeed and reduced in extent, with Saqsīn as capital till finally overthrown by the Mongols.[106] All positive statements to this effect in the sources are—we do not say conspicuously—lacking.

On the other hand, the continued existence of the Khazars as late as the 12th century is attested by the evidence of various sources. Two distinct groups may here be mentioned. The first of these consists of Hebrew documents from the Cairo Genizah, which are of exceptional interest as pointing to developments in Khazar Judaism going considerably beyond anything recorded during the period before A.D. 965, when politically Khazaria was flourishing. The documents are two in number, of which the more important was published by Mann[107] and in-

[103] Barthold, *loc.cit.*

[104] *J.A.*, I, iii (1823), 155.

[105] The Jewish traveler Ibrāhīm ibn-Ya'qūb speaks indeed as if the Khazars were still flourishing in his time (probably 973) as noted by Kunik (Bakri, ed. Kunik and Rosen, 74, cited Westberg, *Ibrahīm ibn-Ya'qūb*, 79).

[106] So Westberg, *Beiträge*, 288-292.

[107] *R.E.J.*, 71 (1920), 89-93. I have not seen Mann's article in *Ha-Tequphah*, Vol. xxiv, cited by Poliak, *Khazaria*, 339.

cludes the following passage: "In the days of the ruler whose name was al-Afḍal, the sons of the oppressors of the people of Israel arose and set themselves to establish prophecy, and they stumbled in their words. In the mountains which are in the land of Khazaria there arose a Jew whose name was Solomon ben-Dugi. The name of his son was Menahem, and with them was an eloquent man whose name was Ephraim ben-Azariah of Jerusalem, known as ben-Sahaḷon [?Sahlūn].[108] They wrote letters to all the Jews, near and far, in all the lands round about them. . . . They all said that the time had come in which God would gather His people Israel from all lands to Jerusalem, the holy city, and that Solomon ben-Dugi was Elijah and his son the Messiah." Poliak[109] observes that Mann identified Menahem ben-Solomon ben-Dūgī with Menahem ben-Solomon al-Rūhi or David El-Roi, the pseudo-Messiah, hero of one of Disraeli's novels, who is usually said to have been born at 'Amādīyah in Kurdistan and to have perished in an insurrection there about 1160. The name David was explained by Mann as appropriate to one who claimed to be king of Israel, and El-Roi and al-Rūḥi are according to the same authority blunders for al-Dūgi. The Genizah document says that the beginning of this Messianic movement was in Khazaria, and Poliak thinks that David El-Roi was undoubtedly a Khazar Jew, who with his supporters came to 'Amādīyah en route for Jerusalem. The only available dating for the document is offered by mention of a Muslim ruler al-Afḍal, in whose days the Messianic movement is said to have begun. Al-Afḍal here was taken by Mann to be the well-known Fatimid vizier of that name who ruled Egypt 1094-1121. The comparatively early date presents some difficulty, but undoubtedly Poliak's suggestion tends to clear the obscurity surrounding the trouble at 'Amādīyah preceding David El-Roi's death, by affording light on its possible origin and significance.

The other Genizah document also refers to a Messianic movement in Khazaria apparently in 1096. The text, first published

108 Poliak's suggestion, see following n.
109 *Khazaria,* 232ff, cf. 15.

by Neubauer, is so obscure as to permit of no certain conclusions. It includes the following: "And all the congregations were agitated and returned to the Lord with fastings and alms. And so from the region of Khazaria there went, as they said, seventeen congregations to the 'wilderness of the nations,' and we know not if they met with the tribes or not."[110] Here also a march to Jerusalem seems to be envisaged. As Poliak notes, the "wilderness of the nations" is a Biblical phrase,[111] describing the place where God will make a new covenant with His people, before bringing them back to the land of Israel. Since according to this second document adherents of the movement brought news of it to Byzantium, a connection between Khazar and Byzantine Judaism is implied. A yet wider range of influence, affecting directly the Jewries in central Europe, is indicated for Khazar Judaism if Poliak's theory of the "shield of David" as a new popular Jewish symbol called forth by the Messianic movement is tenable.[112]

Poliak is undoubtedly right in calling attention to the evidence for a Messianic movement in Khazaria during the late 11th and 12th centuries.[113] In attempting to account for it (assuming that it was on a considerable scale) we must think of new troubles descending on the Khazars, and notably, in the same 11th century, of the appearance of the savage Qipchaks (Polovtsi).[114]

In the second place, evidence for the continued existence of the Khazars is offered by poems written in Persian in the 12th century. Reference has already been made to the epic of Niẓāmi (circa 1141-1203) on Alexander the Great, into which he strangely introduces the Russians and Khazars.[115] His older contemporary Khāqāni (circa 1106-1190), on the other hand, mentions the Russians and Khazars in panegyrics of Akhsatān,

[110] *J.Q.R.*, IX (1896-1897), 27.
[111] *Ezek.* 20. 35; cf. *Khazaria*, 232.
[112] *Khazaria*, 233-234.
[113] Landau's strictures on this head in his review of Poliak's *Khazaria* (*Qiryath Sēpher*, XXI [1944], 19ff) seem unduly severe.
[114] For the dating, cf. Minorsky, *Ḥudūd*, 316 (A.D. 1054).
[115] See Chapter I, n. 61.

a Shirwān Shāh of the 12th century, who had defeated them.[116] Both poets were familiar with local circumstances in the Caucasus region, having spent much of their lives in the service of the rulers of Ganjah (Elizavetpol) near Baku. Khanykov, who discussed the poems of Khāqāni, found that the Russians took part in an invasion of Shirwān as allies of the Khazars. He was unable to date this more definitely than some time between 1135 and 1193.[117] Barthold, putting the reference to the Khazars in Khāqāni circa 1175, suspected that the Ghuzz or Qipchaq are meant.[118] Yet Khāqāni mentions the Qipchaqs distinctly elsewhere.[119] There can be no doubt that Niẓāmi, whose epic on Alexander (Sikandar-Nāmah) is generally regarded as his last work, completed shortly before his death circa 1203, is thinking of the same circumstances when he there wrote of Khazars and Russians, and is in effect another contemporary witness of the existence of the Khazar name at this period. From Khāqāni's remarks we have probably to think of the invaders of Shirwān advancing by land through the Caucasus passes[120] with the Russian fleet—72 ships are mentioned[121]—in support. It is significant for this that in one passage he names the Alans with the Khazars.[122] That in later days the local rulers south of the Caucasus had to deal with invaders from the north which formerly were the concern of the Caliph's governors is

[116] Cf. V. Minorsky, "Khāqānī and Andronicus Comnenus," *B.S.O.A.S.*, 1945, xi/3, 550-578.

[117] "Lettre de M. Khanykov a M. Dorn, 8/20 May, 1857," in *Mélanges Asiatiques*, III, 120-121.

[118] *E.I.*, art. Derbend; cf. *ibid.*, art. Khazar.

[119] Khanykov, *ibid.*, 117, 121.

[120] Or from Darband. Cf. Minorsky, "Khāqānī etc.," 557, who follows the suggestion of Pakhomov that the invasion of Shirwān by the Russians and Khazars was initiated by the independent emir of Darband Bek-Bars ibn-Muẓaffar.

[121] Khanykov, *ibid.*, 125.

[122] *Ibid.*, 127. Another reference is (*ibid.*, 132) "The Russians and the Khazars flee, for they are mingled in confusion on the sea of the Khazars thanks to the benefits of that [the victor's] hand." Cf. Minorsky, *B.S.O.A.S.* (1930), 905. In the sequel (*ibid.*, 133) "Baku through his existence exacts tribute from the Khazars, Rayy and Zirihgirān." The last-named is probably Zirīgarān (Minorsky, *Ḥudūd*, 450), in the E. Caucasus.

natural in itself. The situation is illustrated by the reported death of an earlier Shirwān Shāh, 'Ali ibn-al-Haytham, and the incident involving Faḍlūn the Kurd,[123] as well as the invasion of Shirwān alluded to by Khāqāni. It is remarkable that in these similar cases, all after 965, the Khazars are mentioned by name.

But for the history of the Volga-Caucasus region in the period before the Mongol conquest the great fact—almost the only event indeed which we can speak of as certain—is the appearance of the Qipchaqs or Cumans (identified with the Polovtsi of the *Russian Chronicle*). When they established themselves in somewhat differently estimated,[124] but their mastery of the steppes came to be complete.[125] They, not the Khazars, were the principal enemy with whom the Mongols had to deal in this region, as the stories of Sinjār of Khwārizm[126] and Bachmān[127] show. Whatever may have happened before their arrival,[128] when the obscurity which in general surrounds the history of the Khazars is at its darkest and meanwhile at least remains impenetrable, it is hardly to be thought of that any existing Khazar state survived thereafter for long.

The connection of the rise of the Seljuks with the declining state of Khazaria, first suggested by Kutschera,[129] yields interesting possibilities and may yet become more apparent. Zeki Validi[130] has drawn attention to a passage from the *Kitāb*

123 For both of these see above.

124 According to Marquart (*Ost.-türk. Dialektstudien*, 102, cited Barthold, *E.I.*, art. Ḳipčaḳ) in the 12th century, cf. Pelliot, "À propos des Comans," *J.A.*, xi, xv (1920), 148-150. This is probably too late, cf. n. 114 *supra*.

125 Consonantly with this, in the sources for the Mongol period Dasht-i Qipchāq, "desert of the Qipchaqs" appears regularly as equivalent for the older Dasht-i Khazar, "desert of the Khazars."

126 *History of Jalāl al-Dīn*, ed. Houdas, text 48, transl. 81.

127 *Rashīd al-Dīn*, ed. Blochet, 44-45, cf. Juwayni, ii, 9-11. There is now an English translation in V. Minorsky, "Caucasica iii," *B.S.O.A.S.* (1952), xiv/2, 225.

128 To take Qazwīni rigorously (cf. n. 68), Saqsīn passed at some time into the hands of the Ghuzz, but no doubt the Qipchaqs were later in control there as elsewhere.

129 *Chasaren*, 104.

130 *Ibn-Faḍlān*, xxvii n.

Tafḍīl al-Atrāk (On the Preeminence of the Turks) by abu-al-'Alā' ibn-Ḥassūl,[131] where Sarjuq or Seljuk, the eponym of the Seljuk Turks, is reported to have assaulted the king of the Khazars in person. This, as Zeki Validi notes, clearly opens the possibility that there was fighting at one time between the Khazars and the Ghuzz, to whom as is generally admitted the Seljuks originally belonged. Ibn-Ḥassūl was a prominent Ghaznawid official in Rayy at the beginning of the Seljuk supremacy.[132] His book was submitted to Ṭughrul Beg by the vizier 'Amīd-al-Mulk,[133] probably not long after 437/1045. The author is therefore unlikely to have taken liberties with accepted facts about the new dynasty. The passage cited by Zeki Validi runs in full: "As to the lineage of the Sultan [i.e., Ṭughrul Beg]—may God make him greatly victorious—it is a sufficient proof of his nobility that it ends not like the lineage of others in some unknown and obscure slave. Among his ancestors was Sarjuq [Seljuk], who struck the king of the Khazars with his sword and beat him with a mace which he had in his hand, till his horse foundered and he fell on his face. Such a deed is not done save by a free soul and a spirit that aspires above the star Capella. From him [i.e., Seljuk, or perhaps "from it," the deed just mentioned] began the [Seljuk] empire and their claim arose."[134]

The oblique reference here to the Ghaznawids, descended from the slave Sabuktigīn, is appropriate, but ibn-Ḥassūl may have transferred to Seljuk an exploit of his father's. We read in ibn-al-Athīr of a similar scene,[135] involving Tuqāq, the father of Seljuq and the "king of the Turks who is called Payghu." This last should be not the Khazar Khaqan, but the Yabghu of the Ghuzz (Payghu⟨Yabghu), a title mentioned by ibn-Faḍlān.[136] Further, Bar Hebraeus gives an account from the

[131] The Arabic text as edited by 'Abbās al-'Azzāwi and the latter's introduction—in Arabic—were reproduced by the late Professor Ş. Yaltkaya, who added a Turkish translation, in *Belleten*, No. 14-15 (Istanbul 1940). Professor Yaltkaya was kind enough to send me a copy.

[132] *Tafḍīl*, 10. [133] *Ibid.*, 45. [134] *Ibid.*, 49-50.

[135] IX, 162, *s. anno* 432. [136] §33.

Malik Nāmah,[137] according to which Tuqāq was one of the commanders of the Khazar Khaqan, and when he died, his infant son Seljuk was taken and reared at the Khaqan's court. Later the Khatun took offence at his free behavior towards her husband and it became necessary for Seljuk to leave.[138] Again, there is a statement in ibn-al-ʿAdīm's *History of Aleppo* that "the emir Seljuk ibn-Duqāq [Tuqāq] was one of the chiefs of the Khazar Turks."[139] It may well be that the "unknown reason" mentioned by Barthold[140] for the emigration of the Ghuzz under Seljuk, first to the lower course of the Sayḥūn (Sir Darya) and then to the region of Bukhara, was Seljuk's final rupture with the Khazars.[141]

The sons of Seljuk were called Mīkā'īl, Yūnus, Mūsa, and Isrā'īl, while Dā'ūd appeared in the next generation (brother of Ṭughrul Beg). It has been thought that the Biblical names of the early Seljuks indicate that the family was originally Christian.[142] This does not seem very likely. As far as the names are concerned, Mīkā'īl and Isrā'īl or their equivalents are attested Jewish names in the Middle Ages,[143] and when found among the Muslims, point presumably to an alien origin.[144] But Isrā'īl

137 Called by him Mulk Nāmah, which I have elsewhere adopted ("Zeki Validi's *Ibn-Faḍlān*," *Die Welt des Orients*, 1949, 310; "Aspects of the Khazar Problem," *Transactions of the Glasgow University Oriental Society*, XIII [1951], 42). Claude Cahen ("Le Malik-nâmeh et l'histoire des origines seljukides," *Oriens*, II (1949, 32-33, nn.) compares the Shāh Nāmah and suggests that the work may have been dedicated to Alp Arslān, for whom as Cahen shows it was composed, when he held the title of Malik, before becoming Sultan on the death of Ṭughrul Beg in 455/1063.

138 *Syriac Chronicle* ed. Budge, text fol. 69, col. 1=transl. 195.

139 Zeki Validi, *Ibn-Faḍlān*, 143, also XXVI. Cf. *al-Fakhrī*, ed. Derenbourg, 392.

140 *Turkestan* (*G.M.S.*), 256.

141 In the articles mentioned in n. 137, I have assumed that the Khazar king took hostages from the Ghuzz (cf. Zeki Validi, *Ibn-Faḍlān*, 143). It is clearly not possible to say that Seljuk in ibn-Faḍlān's time was one of these.

142 Cf. *E.I.*, art. Seldjuḳs.

143 Zunz, "Namen der Juden," *Gesammelte Schriften*, Berlin 1875, B. 2, 21, 25.

144 Cahen (*op.cit.*, 42) discusses these Seljuk names and (57) mentions a Turkoman chief called al-Ḥājj Isrā'īl. This name is probably to be connected with Isrā'īl ibn-Seljuk, or has a similar origin.

at all events is not a Christian name. In view of what has already been said, the suggestion is that these names are due to the religious influence among the leading families of the Ghuzz of the dominant Khazars. The "house of worship" among the Ghuzz mentioned by Qazwīnī[145] might well have been a synagogue.

While there is thus ground for connecting the Seljuks with the Khazars in the 10th century, it is on the other hand almost certainly an error to suppose that the Seljuks did what the Russians in 965 seem to have failed to do and were the real conquerors of the Khazar state. The main Seljuk thrust was first east into Transoxiana and Persia, and only later westward. If great victories had been gained against the Khazars, they would presumably have been followed up, and the development of Seljuk power would have had another setting, west of the Caspian. That the Seljuks did not move in this direction is no doubt due to the fact of there being on the Volga a power strong enough to contain them—surely another indication that towards the end of the 10th century the Khazar state still existed. We can thus merely affirm again that the Khazars survived the Russian invasion, but are still in the dark as to the course of events which brought about their final downfall. This, as already said, appears to have been complete before the Mongol invasions of the 13th century.

It only remains now to consider the theory that the modern Jews of eastern Europe, or more particularly those in Poland, are the descendants of the mediaeval Khazars.[146] This can be dealt with very shortly, because there is little evidence which bears directly upon it, and it unavoidably retains the character of a mere assumption. It is of course plain that the frequency with which a blonde, fair-skinned, often blue-eyed type appears among the east European Jews calls to be accounted for, and

[145] Ed. Wüstenfeld, II, 395.

[146] Kutschera, *Chasaren*, 13-17, citing the anthropologist K. Vogt. The question has deeply interested Poliak. See his *Khazaria*, Introduction and especially 255-270. Reference has already been made to Zajączkowski's view of the Karaites of Poland and the Crimea as representatives of the ancient Khazars.

the most natural explanation (widespread intermarriage with non-Jewish elements of the population) can only doubtfully be accepted. The suggestion has seriously been made that the Jewries of eastern Europe were, if not established, at least recruited in substantial numbers from Jews from farther east.[147] On the linguistic side, investigations have tended to establish the absence of western influences in Yiddish,[148] though on the other hand affinities with German dialects of the east and south-east have been indicated.[149] Historically, apart from the Khazars who went to Hungary (where for a time the Magyars are credibly said to have been bilingual, speaking the Khazar language as well as their own)[150] other important transfers of population from the former Khazar lands appear to have occurred,[151] especially at the time of the Mongol invasions.[152] In estimating the probability of the theory we should take into account the description from more than one source of the Khazars as themselves fair,[153] and, whether these indications are accurate or not, the undoubted fact that the Khazar empire included men of various races and physical types, among whom

147 W. E. D. Allen, *History of the Georgian People* (London 1932), 323, citing Ripley, *Races of Europe.*

148 Mieses, *Historical Grammar of Yiddish* (1924), cited by Professor H. Smith in *Transactions of the Glasgow University Oriental Society*, v, 67.

149 H. Smith, *ibid.*

150 See Chapter VII.

151 In the 10th century the Hungarian duke Taksony is said to have invited the Khazars to settle in his domains (Vasiliev, *Goths*, 100). Khazars came to Vladimir Monomach for refuge from the Cumans (Qipchaq, Polovtsi) and built a town which they called Biela Viezha near Chernigov (Kutschera, Chasaren, 175). (If this is right, these Khazars had previously lived at Biela Viezha [Sarkil] and were now [A.D. 1117] settled at Chernigov. So Brutzkus, *Encycl. Jud.*, art. Chasaren.) Earlier than this, Jews possibly Khazars (cf. N. K. Chadwick, *Beginnings* 129) had been introduced by Svyatopolk into Kiev.

152 On the approach of the Mongol Bātu, the Cumans proposed to Bela, king of Hungary, that they should be allowed to enter his country, on condition of becoming Christians, and were permitted to do so, it is said, to the number of 40,000, with their slaves. If these people later joined the Mongols against the Magyars (Raverty, *Ṭabaqāt-i Nāṣiri*, 1167 n.), it remains none the less likely that the Jews of eastern Europe were at this time considerably reinforced by their coreligionists.

153 Cf. Chapter I, nn. 34 and 35.

no doubt the religion of the rulers made headway. But to speak of the Jews of eastern Europe as descendants of the Khazars seems to involve the Ashkenazim in general,[154] i.e., by far the greater part of the Jewish people in the world today, and would be to go much beyond what our imperfect records allow.

[154] N. Slouschz (*Mélanges H. Derenbourg*, 75) thinks rather of the sabbatic sects as descendants of the Khazars.

BIBLIOGRAPHY AND ABBREVIATIONS

a.—anno.

Abu-al-Fidā'—*Geography*, ed. Reinaud and De Slane, Paris 1840.

Abu-Ḥāmid al-Andalusi—*Tuḥfat al-Albāb*, ed. Ferrand, *Journal Asiatique*, tome 207 (1925).

Ad fin.—*ad finem*, at the end.

A.H.—Anno Hegirae.

Ad init.—*ad initium*, at the beginning.

A.K.M.—*Abhandlungen für die Kunde des Morgenlandes.*

A.M.—Anno Mundi.

Arne—*La Suède et l'Orient, Archives d'Études Orientales*, Upsala 1914.

art.—article.

Assemani—*Bibliotheca Orientalis*, Rome 1719-1728.

Balādhuri—*Futūḥ al-Buldān*, ed. De Goeje, Leiden 1866.

Bal'ami—*Chronicle*, ed. Dorn, *Nachrichten über die Ghazaren, Memoirs of the Russian Academy*, 1844.

Bar Hebraeus—*Syriac Chronicle*, ed. and translated Sir E. A. Wallis Budge as *Chronography*, Oxford 1932.

Barthold—*Découverte de l'Asie*, French transl. by B. Nikitine (Paris 1947) of Barthold's *Istoriya Izucheniya Vostoka*, 1925.

Bashmakov—"Une solution nouvelle du problème des Khazares," *Mercure de France*, July 1931.

Baumstark—*Geschichte der syrischen Literatur*, Bonn 1922.

B.—Band.

B.G.A. / *Bibl. Geog. Arab.*—*Bibliotheca Geographorum Arabicorum*, ed. De Goeje.

Bibl. Ind.—*Bibliotheca Indica.*

B.R.A.—*Bulletin of the Russian Academy.*

Bretschneider, *Researches*—*Mediaeval Researches from East Asiatic Sources*, 1910.

Brockelmann—*Geschichte der arabischen Litteratur*, Weimar 1898-1902, Leiden 1937, etc.

Browne—*Literary History of Persia*, London and Cambridge 1902-1930.

B.S.O.A.S.–*Bulletin of the School of Oriental and African Studies*, London.

Bury, *L.R.E.*–J. B. Bury, *A History of the Later Roman Empire from Arcadius to Irene*, London 1889.

Bury, *E.R.E.*–J. B. Bury, *A History of the Eastern Roman Empire from the Fall of Irene to the Accession of Basil I*, London 1912.

Bury, *Gibbon*–*Gibbon's Decline and Fall of the Roman Empire*, edited by J. B. Bury.

Bury, *Theodosius*–*History of the Later Roman Empire from the Death of Theodosius I to the Death of Justinian*, London 1923.

Buxtorf–*Cosri* (*Kuzari*), ed. Buxtorf, Basle 1660.

c.–chapter, or *circa*.

Carmoly–*Des Khozars*, in *Itinéraires de la Terre Sainte*, Brussels 1847.

Carra de Vaux–*Le livre de l'avertissement et de la revision*, Paris 1896.

Chabot–*Chronique de Michel le Grand*, ed. and transl. J. B. Chabot, Paris 1899, etc.

Chadwick, *Beginnings*–Mrs. N. K. Chadwick, *Beginnings of Russian History*, Cambridge 1946.

Chavannes, *Documents*–E. Chavannes, *Documents sur les T'ou-Kiue occidentaux*, St. Petersburg 1903.

Chronicle–*Russian Chronicle*, transl. Leger, *Publications de l'École des Langues Orientales, II série*, xiii (1884).

col.–column.

Constantine Por.–Constantine Porphyrogenitus.

Darband Nāmah–Kasem Beg's edition in *Memoirs of the Russian Academy, Divers Savants*, 1851.

Découverte–see Barthold.

Dorn / Dorn, *Bal'ami* –*Nachrichten über die Chasaren, Memoirs of the Russian Academy*, 1844.

Dubnov, *Geschichte*–*Weltgeschichte des jüdischen Volkes*, Berlin n.d.

ed.–edited by, edition of.

ed. Bonn–*Corpus Scriptorum Historiae Byzantinae*, Bonn.

edd.–editors.

E.I.–*Encyclopaedia of Islam*.

Enc. Jud.—*Encyclopaedia Judaica.*

Eranshahr—see Marquart, *Eranshahr.*

E.R.E.—see Bury, *E.R.E.*

Ferrand—see abu Ḥāmid al-Andalusi.

flor.—*florvint*

fol.—folio.

Fragmente—Westberg, *Die Fragmente des Toparca Goticus, Memoirs of the Russian Academy,* 1902.

Frähn, *Khazars*—*Veteres Memoriae Chasarorum, Memoirs of the Russian Academy,* 1822.

G.A.L.—see Brockelmann.

Gardīzi—ed. Barthold in *Memoirs of the Russian Academy,* 1897.

Gibb, *Arab Conquests*—H. A. R. Gibb, *The Arab Conquests in Central Asia,* Royal Asiatic Society, 1923.

G.M.S.—*Gibb Memorial Series.*

Grégoire—H. Grégoire, "Le nom et l'origine des Hongrois," *Z.D.M.G.,* B.91 (1937).

Grätz—*Geschichte der Juden,* ed. 3.

Harkavy, *Denkmäler*—*Altjüdische Denkmäler aus der Krim, Memoirs of the Russian Academy,* 1876.

Historische Glossen—see Marquart, *Historische Glossen.*

Ḥudūd—see Minorsky, *Ḥudūd.*

ib. / *ibid.*—*ibidem.*

Ibn-Aʿtham al-Kūfi—*Kitāb al-Futūḥ,* Seray MS. 2956, cited by Zeki Validi, *Ibn-Faḍlān,* etc.

Ibn-al-Athīr—ed. Cairo, A.H. 1303.

Ibn-Faḍlān—ibn-Faḍlān's *Riḥlah,* ed. Zeki Validi, whom see. § means section of this text.

Ibn-al-Faqīh—ed. De Goeje, *Bibl. Geog. Arab.,* v.

Ibn-Ḥajar, *Iṣābah*—*al-Iṣābah fi Tamyīz al-Ṣahābah, Bibl. Ind.,* 1856-1873.

Ibn-Ḥawqal—1 ed. De Goeje, *Bibl. Geog. Arab.,* II; 2 ed. Kramers, 1939.

Ibn-Isfandiyār—*History of Ṭabaristān,* transl. E. G. Browne, *Gibb Memorial Series.*

Ibn-Khaldūn—ed. Būlāq, A.H. 1284.

Ibn-Khurdādhbih—ed. De Goeje, *Bibl. Geog. Arab.,* VI.

Ibn-Qutaybah, *Ma'ārif—Kitāb al-Ma'ārif* ed. Wüstenfeld, Göttingen 1850.

Ibn-Rustah—ed. De Goeje, *Bibl. Geog. Arab.*, VII.

Ibn-Sa'd—*Ṭabaqāt*, ed. E. Sachau, Leiden 1904-1917.

id.—idem.

Iṣṭakhri—ed. De Goeje, *Bibl. Geog. Arab.*, I.

J.A.—Journal Asiatique.

J.A.O.S.—Journal of the American Oriental Society.

J.E.—Jewish Encyclopedia.

J.Q.R.—Jewish Quarterly Review.

J.R.A.S.—Journal of the Royal Asiatic Society.

Juwayni—*Ta'rīkh-i Jihān-gushāy*, ed. Mirza Muḥammad in *Gibb Memorial Series.*

K—Professor Paul Kahle's collation of the Chester Beatty MS. of Iṣṭakhri.

Kasem Beg—*Darband Nāmah* (ed.), *Memoirs of the Russian Academy*, 1851.

Kmosko, "Araber"—"Araber und Chasaren," *Kőrösi Csoma-Archivum*, 1924-1925.

Kmosko, "Quellen"—"Die Quellen Iṣṭachri's in seinem Berichte über die Chasaren," *Kőrösi Csoma-Archivum*, 1921.

Kokovtsov—*Evreisko-khazarskaya perepiska v X veke*, Leningrad 1932.

Kutschera—*Die Chasaren*, ed. 2, Vienna 1910.

l.—*lege.*

Landau, *Beiträge—Beiträge zum Chazarenproblem*, Breslau 1938.

Landau, "Present Position"—"The present position of the Khazar problem," *Zion*, 1942—in Hebrew.

Lat.—Latin.

Leger—see *Chronicle.*

L.V.—Long Version of the Reply of Joseph.

Mann, *Texts and Studies—Texts and Studies in Jewish History and Literature*, Vol. I, Cincinnati 1931; Vol. II, Philadelphia 1935.

Marquart, *Eranshahr—Ērānšahr nach der Geographie des Ps. Moses Xorenac'i, Abhandlungen der königlichen Gesellschaft der Wissenschaften zu Göttingen, Neue Folge*, III, 2, Berlin 1901.

Marquart, *Historische Glossen*—"Historische Glossen zu den alttürkischen Inschriften," *Vienna Oriental Journal* (*Wiener Zeitschrift für die Kunde des Morgenlandes*), XII, 1898.

Marquart, *Streifzüge*
Marquart, *Streifz.*
Marquart, *Str.* —*Osteuropäische und ostasiatische Streifzüge*, Leipzig 1903.

Mas'ūdi
Mas'ūdi, *Murūj* —*Murūj al-Dhahab*, ed. Barbier de Meynard and Pavet de Courteille, Paris 1861-1878.

Mas'ūdi, *Tanbīh*—ed. De Goeje, *Bibl. Geog. Arab.*, VIII.

Minorsky, *Ḥudūd*—*Ḥudūd al-'Ālam, Gibb Memorial Series.*

Minorsky, *Marvazi*—*Sharaf al-Zamān Ṭāhir Marvazi on China, the Turks and India*, Royal Asiatic Society, 1942.

Minorsky, "Tamīm"—"Tamīm ibn-Baḥr's Journey to the Uyghurs," *Bulletin of the School of Oriental and African Studies*, 1948, xii/2, 275-305.

Mon. Germ. Scr.—*Monumenta Germaniae Historica: Scriptores.*

M.R.A.—*Memoirs of the Russian Academy.*

MS.—manuscript.

MSS.—manuscripts.

M.T.—Massoretic Text.

Muqaddasi—ed. De Goeje, *Bibl. Geog. Arab.*, III.

n.—note.

n.d.—no date.

Neubauer—"Where are the Ten Tribes?" *Jewish Quarterly Review*, I (1889).

Nicephorus—ed. Bonn.

Nöldeke, *Beiträge*—*Beiträge zur Geschichte des Alexanderromans, Denkschriften der Wien. Akad.*, XXXVIII, 5.

ob.—*obiit.*

Pelliot, *Noms turcs*—Paul Pelliot, "Quelques noms turcs d'hommes et de peuples finissant en 'ar,'" *Oeuvres posthumes de Paul Pelliot*, II, Paris 1950.

Platonov, *Russie Chrétienne*—S. F. Platonov, *La Russie Chrétienne* in Avaignac, *Histoire du Monde*, t. vii (Paris 1931).

Poliak, "Conversion"—"The Khazar Conversion to Judaism," *Zion* 1941—in Hebrew.

Poliak, *Khazaria*—*Khazaria*, Tel Aviv 1944—in Hebrew.

Qāmūs—*al-Qāmūs al-Muḥīṭ* of al-Fīrūzābādi, 4 vols., Cairo 1353/1935.

Qazwīni—*Cosmography*, 2 vols., ed. Wüstenfeld, Göttingen 1848.

Qudāmah—ed. De Goeje, *Bibl. Geog. Arab.*, vi.

Rashīd al-Dīn—ed. Blochet, *Gibb Memorial Series.*

R.E.J.—Revue des Études Juives.

Schultze—*Das Martyrium des heiligen Abo von Tiflis, Texte und Untersuchungen zur Geschichte der altchristlichen Literatur, Neue Folge,* xiii (1905).

s.—sub.

ser.—series.

Strack—*Firkovitch und seine Entdeckungen*, Leipzig 1876.

Streifzüge, Streifz.—see Marquart, *Streifzüge.*

S.V.—Short Version of the Reply of Joseph.

s.v.—*sub voce*

t.—tome.

Ṭabari—ed. De Goeje and others, Leiden, 1879-1901.

Tafḍīl-Kitāb Tafḍīl al-Atrāk, ed. 'Azzāwi, reproduced by Ş. Yaltkaya, *Belleten*, No. 14-15, Istanbul 1940.

Theophanes—ed. Bonn.

Theophanes Con.—Theophanes Continuatus, ed. Bonn.

Vasiliev / Vasiliev, *Goths*—*The Goths in the Crimea*, Cambridge, Mass., 1936.

ver.—verso.

Vernadsky / Vernadsky, *Anc. Russ.*—*Ancient Russia*, Yale 1943.

vol.—volume.

Westberg, *Beiträge—Stadt und Volk Saksin, Beiträge zur Klärung orientalischer Quellen über Osteuropa, Bulletin of the Russian Academy*, 1899.

Westberg, *Ibrāhīm ibn-Ya'qūb—Ibrâhîm's-ibn-Ja'ḳûb's Reisebericht über die Slawenlande aus dem Jahre 965, Memoirs of the Russian Academy*, 1898.

Westberg, *Gothic Toparch*—see *Fragmente.*

W.Z.K.M.—Wiener Zeitschrift für die Kunde des Morgenlandes.

Ya'qūbi / Ya'qūbi, *Historiae*—*Historiae*, ed. Houtsma, Leiden 1883.

Ya'qūbi, *Buldān*—ed. De Goeje, *Bibl. Geog. Arab.*, vii.

Yāqūt, *Buldān—Mu'jam al-Buldān*, ed. Wüstenfeld, Leipzig 1866-1870.

Zajączkowski, "Culture"—"O kulturze chazarskiej i jej spadkobiercach" (The Khazar Culture and its Heirs), Myśl Karaimska, Breslau 1946.

Zajączkowski, "Problem"—"Problem językowy Chazarów" (The Problem of the Language of the Khazars), Proceedings of the Breslau Society of Sciences, 1946.

Zajączkowski, *Studies—Ze studiów nad zagadnieniem chazarskim* (Studies on the Khazar Problem), Polish Academy, Cracow 1947.

Zambaur—*Manuel de Généalogie et de Chronologie*, Hanover 1927.

Z.D.M.G.—Zeitschrift der Deutschen Morgenländischen Gesellschaft.

Zeki Validi
Zeki Validi, *Ibn-Faḍlān* } —*Ibn Faḍlān's Reisebericht, Abhandlungen für die Kunde des Morgenlandes*, XXIV (1939).

Zeki Validi, "Völkerschaften"—"Völkerschaften des Chazarenreiches im neunten Jahrhundert," *Kőrösi Csoma-Archivum*, 1940.

Zeki Validi, "Die Schwerter der Germanen"—in *Z.D.M.G.*, B. 90 (1936), 19-37.

Zeuss, *Die Deutschen—Die Deutschen und die Nachbarstämme*, Munich 1837.

Zh.M.N.P.—see *Z.M.N.P.*

Zichy—"Le voyage de Sallâm l'interprète," *Kőrösi Csoma-Archivum*, 1921.

Z.M.N.P.—Zhurnal Ministerstva Narodnogo Prosveschenia.

Zotenberg—*Chronique de Tabari*, Paris 1867-1874.

INDEX

The page references in italics are the main or special reference

p 89ff conversion

111ff Ibn Fadlan